Straight to Jesus

Straight to Jesus

Sexual and Christian Conversions
in the Ex-Gay Movement

Tanya Erzen

UNIVERSITY OF CALIFORNIA PRESS
Berkeley • *Los Angeles* • *London*

University of California Press, one of the most distinguished university presses in the United States, enriches
lives around the world by advancing scholarship in the
humanities, social sciences, and natural sciences. Its activities are supported by the UC Press Foundation and
by philanthropic contributions from individuals and institutions. For more information, visit www.ucpress.edu.

Grateful acknowledgment is made for permission to
reuse material from the author's essays "We Shall Over-
come: Changing Politics and Changing Sexuality in the
Ex-Gay Movement," in *Local Actions: Cultural Ac-
tivism, Power, and Public Life in America,* edited by
Melissa Checker and Maggie Fishman, © 2004 by
Columbia University Press and used by permission of
Columbia University Press; and "Sexual Healing: Self-
Help and Therapeutic Christianity in the Ex-Gay Move-
ment," in *Religion and Healing in America,* edited by
Linda L. Barnes and Susan S. Sered, © 2004 by Oxford
University Press and used by permission of Oxford
University Press.

University of California Press
Berkeley and Los Angeles, California

University of California Press, Ltd.
London, England

© 2006 by The Regents of the University of California

Library of Congress Cataloging-in-Publication Data

Erzen, Tanya.
    Straight to Jesus : sexual and Christian conversions in
the ex-gay movement / Tanya Erzen.
        p.   cm.
    Includes bibliographical references (p.   ) and index.
    ISBN-13 978-0-520-24581-5 (cloth : alk. paper),
    ISBN-10 0-520-24581-4 (cloth : alk. paper) —
    ISBN-13 978-0-520-24582-2 (pbk. : alk. paper),
    ISBN-10 0-520-24582-2 (pbk. : alk. paper)
        1. Church work with gays—California—San
Rafael—Case studies. 2. Ex-gay movement—
California—San Rafael—Case studies. 3. New Hope
Ministries—Case studies. I. Title.

    BV4437.5.E79   2006
    306.6'6183576—dc22   2005023504

Manufactured in the United States of America

15 14 13 12 11 10 09 08 07 06
10 9 8 7 6 5 4 3 2 1

This book is printed on New Leaf EcoBook 60, contain-
ing 60% post-consumer waste, processed chlorine free;
30% de-inked recycled fiber, elemental chlorine free;
and 10% FSC-certified virgin fiber, totally chlorine free.
EcoBook 60 is acid-free and meets the minimum requirements of ANSI/ASTM d5634–01 (Permanence of Paper).

For WJQ

Contents

Abbreviations

AA	Alcoholics Anonymous
AFA	American Family Association
APA	American Psychiatric Association
CC	Christian Crusade
CRA	Center for Reclaiming America
CWA	Concerned Women for America
DOB	Daughters of Bilitis
DSM-II	*Diagnostic and Statistical Manual of Psychiatric Disorders,* second edition
EC	Evangelicals Concerned
ERA	Equal Rights Amendment
EXIT	Ex-Gay Intervention Team
JONAH	Jews Offering New Alternatives to Homosexuality
LGBT	Lesbian, Gay, Bisexual, Transgendered
LIA	Love in Action
MCC	Metropolitan Community Church

NARTH	National Association for the Research and Treatment of Homosexuality
SCA	Sexual Compulsives Anonymous
SLAA	Sex and Love Addicts Anonymous
TVC	Traditional Values Coalition

Introduction

In a run-down community center in San Rafael, California, a middle-aged man spoke haltingly in front of fifty people sitting on rickety folding chairs. As he testified to the power of Jesus in changing his life, there were murmurs of assent. He told the assembly, "I will never be the same again. I have closed the door." What would be a fairly normal evangelical church experience was transformed as he recounted his pornography addiction and his anonymous sexual encounters with other men. Rather than expressing shock or outrage, the members of the audience raised their arms and called out, "Praise him" and "Praise the Lord." Hank was one of a dozen men who had come to New Hope Ministry to rid themselves of homosexuality.[1] At this annual Friends and Family conference, his testimony provided assurance to the gathering that after three years, he was a living example of the possibility for change.

Listening raptly in the audience was a new member of the program. Curtis, twenty-one years old, with streaks of blond in his hair and numerous facial piercings, had arrived from Canada a month before. Raised in a nondenominational conservative Christian family of missionaries, Curtis believed that having same-sex desire was antithetical to living a Christian life. At age sixteen, he had come out to his family as "someone with gay feelings who wants to change." Instead of attending college, he had been involved in Christian youth groups since he was eighteen. Aside from a clandestine sexual relationship in high school, he had never allowed himself to date men. Eventually, with the encouragement of his parents and youth pastor, he decided that in order to conquer his same-sex attractions, he needed to devote himself to an ex-gay program. His ultimate goal was to overcome what he called his "homosexual problem" and eventually get married. "I don't want to be fifty years old, sitting in a gay bar because I just got dumped and have no kids, no family—and be lonelier than heck," he reasoned. Unable to secure a green card, Curtis was working in the New Hope ex-gay ministry administrative offices for the year. Whether filing or copying, he moved around the office tethered to a five-foot Walkman cable, listening to Christian techno music and reminiscing about his nights in the clubs of his hometown.

During the course of his year in the program, Curtis would experience moments of elation, severe depression, crushes on other men, homesickness, and boredom. He eventually would return home with the expectation that he would apply everything he had learned at New Hope to his old life in Canada. Instead, during the next several years he experienced only more uncertainty regarding his sexual struggles. He began occasionally dating men at the same time that he volunteered at a local ex-gay ministry. Later, he embarked upon a chaste relationship with a woman he hoped to marry, but he broke it off when he realized he could never be attracted to her sexually. Finally, he resumed his career as a hairdresser and moved from his rural hometown to Montreal, the first city he had ever lived in.   'UNSUCCESSFUL'

Curtis's story represents a familiar pattern for many ex-gay men and women who come to New Hope with the objective of healing their homosexuality, controlling sexual compulsions, becoming heterosexual, or even marrying someone of the opposite sex. Curtis arrived with the idea that, after a year, his homosexual struggle would subside. He left feeling stronger in his Christian identity, but not necessarily with diminished homosexual urges. It was through religious growth that he believed he would eventually conquer his attractions to men. Struggling with these attractions his entire life was acceptable to him. He reasoned that his faith in God would sustain him and provide him with hope that change was possible.

The controversy around the ex-gay movement has tended to fixate on whether people can change their sexuality. In their testimonies, Hank and Curtis both swore they were altered people, but their assertions encompass a range of possibilities for change that do not necessarily include sexual orientation, behaviors, or desires. When they spoke of personal transformation, they were more likely to refer to their religious identities and sense of masculinity. Christian Right groups claim that

CHANGE IN DESIRES, BEHAVIORS, AND IDENTITIES

men and women can become heterosexuals, and they present men like Hank as confirmation. Opponents of the ex-gay movement argue, based on their evidence of the men and women who have left ex-gay ministries to live as gay- or lesbian-identified, that ex-gay men and women are simply controlling their behavior and repressing their desires. Both sides neglect the centrality of the religious belief system and personal experiences that impel men and women to spend years in ex-gay ministries. Rather than definitive change, ex-gays undergo a conversion process that has no endpoint, and they acknowledge that change encompasses desires, behavior, and identities that do not always align neatly or remain fixed. Even the label "ex-gay" represents their sense of being in flux between identities.

While many conservative Christian churches and organizations condemn homosexuality, New Hope Ministry represents a unique form of nondenominational Christian practice focused specifically on sexuality. New Hope combines psychological, therapeutic, and biblical approaches in an effort to change and convert gay men and lesbians to nonhomosexual Christian lives. Unlike previous Christian movements in the United States, the ex-gay movement, of which New Hope Ministry is a part, explicitly connects sexual and religious conversion, placing sexuality at the core of religious identity. By becoming a born-again Christian and maintaining a personal relationship with Jesus, ex-gay men and women are born again religiously, and as part of that process they consider themselves reconstituted sexually. They grapple with a seemingly irreconcilable conflict between their conservative Christian beliefs and their own same-sex desires. In their worldview, an ex-gay ministry becomes a place where these dual identities are rendered temporarily compatible. Their literal belief that the Bible condemns homosexual practices and identity leads them to measure their success in negotiating their new identities through submission and surrender to Jesus in all things. Even if desires and attractions remain after they have attended an ex-gay ministry like New Hope, their relationship with God and Jesus continues intact. That relationship supersedes any sexual changes, minimizing their frustration and disillusionment when the longed for sexual changes do not occur. In the words of Curtis, "Heterosexuality isn't the goal; giving our hearts and being obedient to God is the goal."

New Hope Ministry is the oldest of five residential ex-gay programs in the United States. Frank Worthen formed New Hope in 1973 after a revelation in which God exhorted him to abandon homosexuality.[2]

With the help of a board of directors and house leaders who have successfully completed the program, Frank, a spry man in his mid-seventies who still jets around in a cherry-red convertible, oversees New Hope, teaches classes to the men in the program, and serves as an assistant pastor in an ex-gay-affiliated church called Church of the Open Door. His wife of over twenty years, Anita, spearheads a ministry for parents of gay children from the same office. She is not an ex-gay but the mother of a gay son. Frank and Anita live a few minutes away from the residential program in a tiny but immaculate studio apartment. After two decades of marriage, they are paragons for other Christian men and women who pray that they will also get married. New Hope is now one of hundreds of evangelical Christian ministries in the United States and abroad where men and women attend therapy sessions, Bible studies, twelve-step-style meetings, and regular church services as part of their "journey out of homosexuality."

In 2000 and 2001, fifteen men participated in the New Hope program. A similar program for women existed throughout the 1980s, but New Hope eliminated it in the early 1990s because of a lack of space. Instead, New Hope sponsors Grace, a weekly ex-gay women's support group led by Suzanne, an energetic woman in her late thirties, now with three children, who spent years in the New Hope program and eventually married a man from Open Door. Participants in Grace and New Hope attended the events at Friends and Family Weekend in 2000, listening as Hank gave his testimony. During the conference, ex-gays and their families enthusiastically participated in small encounter-group discussions for women struggling with lesbianism, parents and spouses of ex-gays, pastors, and church leaders.

After the activities for the Friends and Family Weekend conference concluded, men and women returned to the New Hope residence, Emmanuel House, a two-story stucco apartment complex on a suburban cul-de-sac. Unlike Curtis, most of the men in New Hope's program tended to be in their late thirties and forties. They were predominantly white, from working-class and middle-class families, and raised primarily in rural areas or small towns of the United States. There also were a few men from Europe who, like Curtis, had obtained religious worker visas, which enabled them to be employees of New Hope. They worked in the New Hope offices, located directly across the street from the ex-gay residential apartments. The number of international participants was low, since many now have the option of joining ministries in their home countries as the ex-gay movement expands throughout Europe, Asia, Australia, and South America. Most of the men in the New Hope program grew up with conservative Christian backgrounds and fervently believed not only that homosexual attraction and behavior are sins according to the Bible but also that life as a gay person means being separated from Jesus. This had created a wrenching conflict, causing estrangement from their families and churches. In some cases, it had led to drug and alcohol abuse, isolation, obsessive-compulsive tendencies, and depression.

Although there were a few men from mainline Protestant denominations and one Catholic in the program, at some point most had become involved in an evangelical form of Christianity and undergone a born-again experience. All of the New Hope participants maintained a personal relationship with Jesus and believed to differing degrees in the infallibility and literal truth of biblical scripture. With few exceptions, the informal, experiential religious style of New Hope and Church of the Open Door was familiar to them. All those in attendance believed that through Christian faith, religious conversion, and a daily accountable relationship with one another and with God they could heal their homosexuality. Desires or attractions might linger for years, but they would emerge with new religious identities and the promise that faith and their relationships with one another and God would eventually transform them.

A week before the Friends and Family conference, I ventured up to New Hope for an initial meeting with the intention of making it my fieldwork site. I had interviewed Frank, the New Hope director, on the phone a year before about the early history of the movement, but we had never met. As I approached, it was hard to distinguish the ministry from other nondescript buildings lining the placid, tree-lined street. However, when I peered closely, I could discern signs for Alanon, psychotherapy practices, and various drug rehabilitation centers scattered among the two-story houses. There was nothing to mark the ministry office except a profusion of bright flowers, a few bristling cacti, and vines trailing down from the first-floor landing, which I later learned were assiduously tended by two men in the program. Upon arriving, I was ushered into a small room by Anita, who made it clear that in order to talk to Frank, I would have to pass muster with her. Anita was in her early fifties, with short brown hair and a no-nonsense manner that some considered brash, but I found refreshing. Slightly heavyset but not overweight, she struggled with dieting, I later learned, even as she bustled around the office with ease. We sat in a small prayer room with a plaque on the wall that read:

> Some Facts from God to You:
> You need to be saved
> You can't save yourself
> Jesus has already provided for your salvation
> Jesus will enable you to overcome temptation
> Your part: Repent

After I explained that I hoped to comprehend the perspectives of men and women in an ex-gay ministry through prolonged fieldwork and interviews at New Hope, Anita informed me that "we are in a battle," and the battle is between "us versus them." I was unsure what she meant, and she clarified that "them" meant Satan, and she was convinced that many people were in his service. Her next question, "Who do you serve?" was calculated to establish where my allegiances lay.

I had never been faced with the choice of God or Satan, but I replied that since I was at the ministry to understand their viewpoint rather than simply to dismiss or ridicule them, I supposed I was on the side of "us." Somehow, I passed the test, and my answer enabled Anita to assimilate me into her religious universe. From my own patchwork religious background of first-generation immigrant Catholic grandparents and brief childhood forays into a New England United Church of Christ congregation, Anita read me as a Christian, albeit an unsaved one. She remained undecided about my research, but the New Hope leadership team would "pray on it" and get back to me. After a few weeks of group prayer and consultation, Anita and the other leaders determined that it was part of God's wider plan for me to come to New Hope. They incorporated my research agenda into their own worldview through the idea that it was part of a divine scheme, and they had faith that God was directing the course of my research. Implicit within my acceptance by the New Hope leadership team was their belief that I, too, had the potential for conversion to a Christian life. However, no one ever directly proselytized to me or insisted that I pray or give a testimony in church. Instead, Anita and the men I met imparted their stories of healing as reminders of what God could effect in my own life if, in their words, I allowed my heart to be open.

Ethnographic research has a tradition of investigating groups with whom the ethnographer shares a political, cultural, or social affinity. Only within the past decade have ethnographers begun to document their experiences with groups they may disagree with politically. These ethnographers have illustrated how they grapple with conflicting emotions and expectations when the social and religious conservatism of the people or groups they study—which have ranged from anti-abortion activists, to Jerry Falwell, to the women's Ku Klux Klan, to the Christian Right—reflect moral and political ideals that are distinct from their own.[3] Their studies also highlight crucial questions about what it means to have a fieldwork agenda when one's research subjects are conservative Christians with their own conversionary agendas for the researcher. There are inherent tensions in this situation, especially when writing about a proselytizing community means committing to understanding the community's belief instead of viewing it as "false belief." For instance, in her book on Jerry Falwell, Susan Harding raises complicated questions about how to comprehend the experience of faith, asking whether academic understanding necessitates conversion to her subject's religious belief system.[4] As one researcher bluntly put it, we go to coffee with them for data, and they want to save our souls.[5] From my first meeting with Anita, in which she pressed me to choose between God and Satan, it was evident that there would always be inherent frictions and incongruities between the biblically based language of evangelism and the language of ethnography. Knowing I was entering a community that placed a premium on the ability to evangelize, I accepted with some trepidation Anita's invitation to attend Friends and Family Weekend a month later.

However, I later learned that despite New Hope's religious interpretation of my research agenda, Anita's motives were not merely godly. Around the time we met, the ministry had been praying for someone to update their Web site, which was functioning but required editing and reorganization. In what I considered a fortuitous coincidence and Anita considered "God's work," I had done freelance Web programming throughout graduate school and discovered that helping New Hope with its Web site and other computer woes would provide a basis to spend time in the office. I thus became an unofficial volunteer as well as a researcher. Performing concrete tasks like reviewing New Hope's booklets and testimonies and spending hours on the phone with Pacific Bell because no one in the office could connect to the Internet eased my entry into the world of New Hope. Being in the office also led to my first meetings with Brian, a thirty-two-year-old who had originally designed the New Hope Web site and now worked full time as a computer engineer, and his close friend, Drew, New Hope's affable Danish office manager, also in his thirties, both of whom had completed the program several years earlier.

Although gradually everyone at New Hope became aware that I was there to conduct interviews and research, to them, the idea that a single woman would move across the country to spend time at New Hope was more inconceivable and bizarre than their decision to spend a year in an ex-gay residential program. The desk that I used faced the wall behind Drew's desk, so I found myself sitting back to back with him in the office every day I was there. Our unavoidable proximity made informal conversation necessary, and his wry humor made it comfortable. Because the office was the focal point for the ministry and people dropped by after work and throughout the day, I gradually became a familiar presence to the men in the program. Drew oversaw the office and the application process for the program, while Curtis, the newest arrival, bore the brunt of less exalted work like copying and collating hundreds of pages to make the workbooks for the classes men attended. He worked in another room, across the hall, at a crowded desk pushed against an oversize window. From there he could monitor who came and went from the ministry apartments across the street. As in any office, the dynamic between these two colleagues ranged from camaraderie to outright annoyance. Drew seemed perpetually bemused by Curtis's antics, especially his bold fashion choices and tendency to alternate between Christian techno music and Ukrainian polkas on the stereo.

The offices were sparse aside from computers and a literature table. The main decoration was a colorized photograph of a lighthouse, New Hope's official symbol, on the wall. Frank and Anita had separate offices that sandwiched the room where Curtis worked, jammed with file cabinets and poster boards covered with photographs of men who had completed the program. At the end of the first month, I noticed that my bag with my laptop computer in it had mysteriously disappeared when I returned from talking to Anita in her office. As I began to panic, I heard Brian laughing outside. I had become the latest victim of his infamous pranks. His antics were so frequent that when his bike was stolen, it took days for the other men to convince him that it wasn't in revenge for his practical jokes. Unlike most of the men, who had been amiable toward me, Brian had been suspicious from the beginning, and this fake theft represented a thawing in his attitude. At our first encounter, he had plopped down next to me without introducing himself and asked confrontationally, "Why are you here, and what are you going to write about us?" He had been living out of a storage room in the office until he could move into his own apartment and was therefore around all the time. By our second meeting, he had put my name into the Google search engine, and he quizzed me relentlessly about conferences I had attended and places I had worked. "So, you're basically a liberal who thinks we're crazy, right?" It took many conversations over several months before we began inching toward friendship and a wary trust.

Once Curtis, Drew, and Brian had accepted my presence and incessant questions, it was easier to interact with others in the program. Men sauntered into the office after work to chat with Drew and, gradually, with me by extension. Many seemed flattered that I deemed their lives important enough for an interview, and they were curious about what I had found in my research. Some assumed that I had objective or even expert knowledge of the movement, even though in the ex-gay world, expertise is not based on credentials but entirely on personal experiences of sexual addictions and familial dysfunction—none of which I possessed. As the only young woman they interacted with on a daily basis, I was an anomaly and an outsider. After a while, I unexpectedly came to be a safe repository for advice, confidences, and complaints about life in the ministry for some men. When the day-to-day became familiar, I had to continually remind myself to take note of what would have seemed extraordinary only months earlier. It was never simple to gauge when it was appropriate to record fragments of casual conversations and occurrences into my notebook. As one anthropologist explained, "They told their subjects carefully who they were, but then did their best research when their subjects forgot."[6]

During my eighteen months at New Hope, I conducted two-to-three-hour interviews with forty-seven men and women, with nineteen follow-up interviews. I often talked and interacted informally with these same people in other contexts, like dinners, church, and the office. I formally interviewed Curtis, Brian, Hank, and Drew two or three times over the span of a year and a half. I chose New Hope as my research site because of Frank's position as the founder of the ex-gay movement and because, at the time, it was the oldest and most established residential program. Aside from men enrolled in the program, I interviewed ministry leaders and men and women living in the surrounding area who had completed the program. Four of these people were married but remained affiliated with New Hope in some way. One had married but sought out a church where he did not have to reveal his sexual struggles and history. I also interviewed seven men who had left the program to live as gay-identified. Later, I interviewed members and leaders of Jewish and Catholic ex-gay

groups in New York City and at the annual Exodus conference. This
broad focus was especially important given that a coalition of Jewish,
Catholic, Mormon, Christian, African American, and therapeutic
groups formed an organization called Positive Alternatives to Homosexuality in 2003 as a way to reach out to members of more religious
denominations on a national and global scale.

My research received a huge boost when Drew mailed a letter I
drafted to sixty ex-gay people in the immediate vicinity, asking them to
complete interviews, and it was through these early contacts that I met
others. After a few months, Frank granted me permission to peruse his
carefully cataloged archive of articles, letters, and pictures related to
homosexuality and the ex-gay movement from the early 1970s, and I
spent part of my days reading and copying these files. Other times, I
taught men how to use and edit the Web site, fixed computer problems,
and engaged in long conversations with Anita, Frank, Drew, Curtis, and
the various men who wandered through the offices during the day.
Sometimes Brian and I would meet for dinner outside of the ministry
since he was no longer in the program or working at New Hope. At
night, before I drove back to San Francisco, I would often eat with the
entire house of men and listen to their praise and worship sessions, and
I met others through church on Sundays and group outings on weekends. In the course of the research, I volunteered in the ministry's offices;
attended classes, dinners, conferences, and parties; and maintained over
a span of several years relationships with men and women affiliated
with the ex-gay movement, three of whom I am still in contact with. I
viewed ethnography as an extended and sometimes never-ending conversation, and inevitably that conversation changed me just as my presence at New Hope changed the fabric of everyday life there. I never
converted to Christianity, which was the change perhaps Anita and
others desired, but my relationships with the people at New Hope radically altered how I understood their faith and their desire to change
their sexualities.

Doing extended participant observation and interviews provided me
with access to a perspective on the ex-gay movement and the Christian
Right that journalists' undercover exposés of ministries or ex-gay testimonial accounts of change have tended to ignore. Similarly, although
political science and sociological scholarship on the Christian Right and
conservative political movements is rich and varied, it has tended to
focus on leadership and political rhetoric rather than ground-level participation. This work often discounts the worldviews of participants in

Christian Right organizations, issues of gender and sexuality, and, in some cases, religion.[7] The majority of these studies have been concerned with measuring the Christian Right's success, in "re-Christianizing America," in making legislative inroads, or in growing its numbers,[8] and they draw upon social movement theory approaches to understand conservative social and cultural movements.[9] Although I consider the ex-gay movement a political, cultural, and social movement, I did not situate New Hope within this body of theory, choosing instead to analyze daily life and interactions. Many of the studies of conservative groups have generally involved national surveys and interviews conducted by field researchers rather than prolonged fieldwork.[10] Participants' observations and interviews revealed how religious and sexual conversion occur as a complicated process over time. They also demonstrated that the ex-gay movement is far from politically cohesive and that there is a wide gulf between leadership and laity.

Although my sample was not necessarily representative of the entire ex-gay movement, my focus on a concentrated group of individuals revealed why people joined, what they did while they were there, and what became of them after they left. I compiled basic statistics about age, race, class, gender, and religious background, but I was less interested in quantifiable conclusions proving or disproving change than in the worldviews of men and women. These worldviews became a window onto the larger ex-gay movement and the way Christian political organizations have appropriated ex-gay narratives of change. However, to understand the connection between the local experiences of ex-gay men and women and the wider political implications of the movement, I situate the ex-gay movement within the wider historical currents of twentieth-century evangelical religion; self-help culture; psychiatric and psychological theories on sexuality, gay and lesbian liberation, and feminism; and the history of the Christian Right.

Gaining information from men and women was greatly facilitated by the manner in which ex-gays are encouraged to confess and testify as part of their process of sexual transformation. With the exception of Brian, they were much more interested in talking about themselves than in questioning me. The testimony, with a sin and redemption narrative, has long been a hallmark of evangelical Christianity. Testifying for men and women at New Hope was central to their process of sexual and religious conversion, illustrating their stories before and after dedicating their lives to Jesus, from sinner to saved. The testimony is the narrative form into which all ex-gays eventually fit their lives before and after becoming Christians. It attests to their religious transformation and their hope that sexual transformation will follow. Ex-gays are accustomed to continually sharing testimony about the most private and harrowing aspects of their lives in public, group settings. Continuous testimony in small groups and at church is the centerpiece of the ex-gay residential program, and reluctance or refusal to give testimony is a liability.

Unlike many mainline Protestant denominations where personal problems are not aired publicly, the evangelical religious style of New Hope encourages and rewards public confessions of intimacy. Repentant narratives about homosexuality, drug abuse, sexual abuse, abortions, and promiscuity provide former sinners with unimpeachable authority in the ex-gay culture because expertise is predicated on experience. The emphasis on personal testimony is also emblematic of the therapeutic dimension of the ex-gay process of conversion. The ministries assert that sexual healing occurs through these public confessions, or "offering problems up to Jesus." Talking in interviews was a natural extension of the wider public discourse of testimony and public emotionalism for most men and women. Hank, for example, would often break into tears as he spoke to me, and I found that in the course of conversations, ex-gay men and women would casually slip in intimate details about abuse or addiction as if they were everyday topics.

A person's testimonial narrative of conversion becomes more structured and even rigid the longer he or she has been involved in an ex-gay ministry. Although the religious and sexual testimony generates a life history, I found that it was crucial to talk to men and women before they placed their experiences within the frame of what they learned at the ministry, read in the ex-gay literature, and heard from others. These testimonial life stories were messier but more revealing than that of someone like Hank, who had spoken and written widely about his life for years. A common theme in ethnographies of conservative Christians has been a focus on the narrative strategies expressed through life stories.[11] In her book on pro-choice and pro-life women, Faye Ginsburg uses the term "procreation stories" to analyze the formal strategies these activists employ to give meaning to their own activism around abortion and to challenge the expected outcomes of their lives. Ex-gay men and women also express their life stories through the form of the testimony, even if their actual experiences do not fit neatly into the testimonial structure. As they hear other testimonies through day-to-day interactions in the program, they learn to strategically position and locate their own lives into a similar framework of sinner and saved. Testimonies circulate in published materials as pamphlets and cassettes sent throughout the world, and men and women perform them in front of churches and large audiences.

There is also a social and collective aspect to testimony, and giving one becomes a rite of initiation into the religious world of a ministry. These stories of trauma and healing are central to the culture of therapy that predominates at New Hope and other ex-gay ministries. Testifying as therapy keeps the focus on the individual's experience of pain and trauma but permits each person to relive it within the safety net of a wider religious narrative and community. Religious transformation is deeply connected to a therapeutic process that allows men and women to renarrate their pasts as part of being born again. Through subsequent retellings, the trauma lessens and a person heals. The object of testifying is forgiveness and redemption from other Christians and from God, and the personal relationship a person has with Jesus is an extension of this focus on healing the self. As a narrative strategy, these confessions are proof of religious and sexual conversion and grant the testifier power as a witness to non-Christians or those living in sin. Testimonies become a form of evangelism that is necessary to self-healing and to the wider dissemination of the ex-gay movement. The testimonies of hundreds of conservative Christian men and women who have felt compelled to participate in ex-gay ministries function as evidence that change is possible through a relationship with Jesus. Everything in a person's preconversion life becomes a story that illustrates how a relationship with Jesus transforms people. The mission statement on the ex-gay movement's Web site claims to offer "Freedom from homosexuality through the power of Jesus Christ." The testimonial narratives attest that freedom and redemption can only be obtained by dedicating one's life and sexuality to Jesus.

In the ex-gay movement, change is a complex process that incorporates developmental theories of sexual identity, religious proscriptions against homosexuality, biblical prayer, therapeutic group activities, counseling, and self-help steps. The idea of change is the financial, political, religious, and personal basis of the ex-gay movement, and it continues to be the fulcrum on which the debate over the fixity or fluidity of sexual identity turns. Change is a conversion process that incorporates religious and sexual identity, desire, and behavior. Sexual identity is malleable and changeable because it is completely entwined with religious conversion. A person becomes ex-gay as he accepts Jesus into his life and commits to him. Much has been written about the widely

publicized sexual scandals of prominent ex-gays, but in the ex-gay
movement, it is far more scandalous to abandon Jesus than to yield to
same-sex desire. It is commonly accepted that a person will continue to
experience desire and even occasionally lapse into same-sex behavior as
part of the overall conversion process. Recovery and relapse are built
into the creation of an ex-gay identity, and sexual falls are expected.
Rather than becoming heterosexual, men and women become part of a
new identity group in which it is the norm to submit to temptation and
return to ex-gay ministry over and over again. As long as the offender
publicly repents and reaffirms her commitment to Jesus, all is forgiven.

I call this process of religious and sexual conversion, sexual falls, and
public redemption through testimony "queer conversion." The word
"queer" literally means "odd," "peculiar," or "out of the ordinary," but
I use "queer" in the context of the academic discipline of queer theory
and its indebtedness to queer activism, which has reappropriated the
word "queer" from its history as a negative or derogatory term. In queer
theory and activism, "queer" means to challenge the very concept of the
normal, and it can encompass a range of sexual acts and identities historically considered deviant that the words "gay" and "lesbian" sometimes exclude. Queer theorists refute the idea that sexuality is an
essentialist category determined by biology or judged by eternal standards of morality and truth.[12] Instead, queer theory argues for the idea
that identities are culturally and historically determined rather than
fixed; sexual practices and desires change over time and do not consistently line up with masculine or feminine gender expectations. The idea
of queerness accounts for the possibility that a person's sexual orientation, behaviors, and desires can fluctuate, moving between different
identities, political affiliations, and sexual arrangements.

Although the political goals of the ex-gay movement and queer
activists are radically distinct, by accepting that a person's behavior and
desire will not necessarily correspond with their new ex-gay identity or
religious identity, ex-gay men and women enact a queer concept of sexuality when they undergo queer conversions. Although men and women
in ex-gay ministries do not and cannot envision homosexuality as a positive way to be, their lives also exemplify the instability of the religious
and sexual conversion process. Their narratives of testimonial sexuality
are performances that, while sincere, point to the instability and change-
ability of their own identities rather than serve as a testament to heterosexuality. The ex-gay notion of sexuality as a religious process of
transformation may be fraught with sexual falls, indiscretions, and

moments of doubt, and ex-gays' notions of change are fluid even if their eventual goal is heterosexuality or celibacy. In its insistence on the influence of cultural, familial, and religious factors on sexuality, the ex-gay mode of religious and sexual conversion unwittingly presents a challenge to a conservative Christian construction that a person can and must move from homosexuality to heterosexuality.

The ex-gay position complicates debates between those queer activists who, on the one hand, argue for a politics of civil rights for gays and lesbians based on biology, and those who, on the other, envision sexual practices, desires, identities, and affiliations as variable over a lifetime. Proponents of queer theory are wary of the strategy of predicating civil rights on anatomy or genetics because of the history of eugenics, the pseudoscience of improving the human race by selective breeding. They fear that this strategy could easily be used against marginalized people to justify sexual, racial, and gender inequalities as it was in the past. The well-documented history of medical interventions imposed on lesbians and gay men also makes them cautious of theories of a gay gene. The ex-gay movement shares the queer mistrust of biological explanations for a different reason: the immutability of sexuality would signify that conversion is irrelevant or impossible. However, the ex-gay position goes beyond this to argue that even if science were to prove that homosexuality was biological, Jesus can effect miracles, and it is ultimately with Jesus that ex-gays place their faith in change. Members of the ex-gay movement believe that heterosexuality is God's intent, regardless of behavior; queer theorists and activists posit that heterosexuality itself is neither natural nor stable. Further, the ex-gay movement is wedded to the idea of a binary system of gender roles in which heterosexuality connotes masculinity for men and femininity for women.

The liberal rights position, the foundation of organizations like the National Gay and Lesbian Task Force and the Human Rights Campaign, both of which vehemently oppose the ex-gay movement, is another important voice in the debate over sexuality and change. Politically, these organizations are invested in the idea that sexual identity is fixed, unchangeable, and possibly even biological. Many other gay activists and writers espouse the view that sexual orientation is innate, or that people are born that way.[13] Studies such as those of Simon LeVay and Dean Hamer, which argue that a gay brain or gay genes exist, are revered as the basis for a minority identity and entrance into U.S. civil rights discourse.[14] The Human Rights Campaign and the National Gay and Lesbian Task Force position considers a biological rationale for homosexuality as strategically advantageous in the political realm, despite the problems associated with providing biological explanations for social inequalities. This position contends that if sexuality has the same immutable status as race, the law must grant gay men and lesbians the rights of full citizenship. Their stance is in opposition to the way ex-gay literature differentiates between being "gay" and being "homosexual," describing the former as a misguided choice or false lifestyle in order to repudiate gay identity and any accompanying political rights. In the wake of the 2004 presidential elections, when eleven states passed anti-gay-marriage referenda, some conservative Christian organizations are using the idea that homosexuality is changeable to continue to dismantle gay and lesbian civil rights protections. In these public debates, the queer position is often absent.

Despite the ex-gay movement's antipathy to biological approaches, it conceives of homosexuality in multiple ways: as religious sin, sexual addiction, gender deficit, and psychological disorder. On the one hand, the movement utilizes developmental models and the diagnosis of gender identity disorders to explain the origins of homosexuality. These theories argue that men and women become homosexuals because of a gender deficit in masculinity or femininity as children, an overbearing mother, an absent father, or familial dysfunction. They also argue that a person may develop attractions to someone of the same sex because of trauma. For instance, the same literature often describes lesbianism as a result of sexual or physical abuse. To help recover lost masculinity and femininity, or repair "gender deficits," the leaders of the ex-gay movement organize workshops and teachings where women learn to apply makeup to be feminine and men learn to play sports to be masculine. These performances also point to the idea that masculinity and femininity are constructed in the social world, not ingrained in the body. Other ex-gay literature discusses homosexuality as an addiction, and some ex-gay ministries model themselves on twelve-step recovery groups. The developmental and addiction explanations provide alternatives to the model that homosexuality is sin. These overlapping accounts about how a person's sexuality develops enable the movement to explain huge variations in the life stories and experiences of people who come to a ministry, oftentimes conflating morality, disease, and addiction.

The basis for the live-in program at New Hope stems directly from the developmental and addiction models of the ex-gay movement. At New Hope, men are urged to form same-sex friendships, which will rebuild their sense of masculinity and, by extension, their heterosexuality.

The nonsexual relationships they forge through group living are the answer to reclaiming lost masculine potential. The structure of the program is also designed as a form of bodily discipline, monitoring the behavior and actions of participants so they are less likely to have a sexual fall or revert back to their prior addictions. The structure and constant surveillance require the men to be accountable for others' behavior and to report any deviations from the rules in weekly house meetings. Although they complain about the isolation and rigorous structure, for many it is the day-to-day interactions with roommates, God, and other people that make the program appealing. At New Hope, the men and women engage in forms of religious practice that occur in both secular spaces, such as playing sports, living communally, and cooking together, and religious spaces, such as attending church, bible studies, and praise and worship sessions.[15] Through the practices and the rituals of everyday life in an ex-gay ministry, ex-gays are supposed to learn to reconcile their sexual and religious identities.

New Hope accepts what the ex-gay movement calls "broken" individuals as long as they are invested in the process of religious and sexual conversion. I argue that by combining biblical, developmental, and twelve-step principles, New Hope also creates new familial and kinship arrangements and networks of ex-gays. The ministry's close-knit, highly regulated programs foster a sense of religious belonging based on same-sex bonds rather than the conservative Christian ideal of heterosexual marriage. The ministries also function as unlikely havens for those banned from conservative churches and alienated from family members and even from gay organizations or social networks. Individuals remain affiliated with ex-gay ministries for years because they offer religious belonging, acceptance, and accountability. Ex-gay ministries flourish because the men and women grappling with same-sex behavior and attraction desperately want to locate themselves in a supportive cultural world. Places like New Hope provide the material conditions for community in addition to a more diffuse sense of religious and sexual belonging and kinship. In conversations, the men and women at New Hope invoked a utopian aspect to their chosen families; some men even referred to finding a sense of belonging at New Hope as a coming-out process. In many ways, the community and religious aspects of the program became more important than any sexual changes they experienced.

While individuals at New Hope understand the transformation of their sexual identities as a choice and a right, organizations of the Christian Right have utilized their testimonies as living proof that homosexuality

is merely a choice, a developmental disorder, or a lifestyle, promoting a
wider anti-gay agenda cloaked in the rhetoric of choice, change, and
compassion. Organizations of the Christian Right exploit the example of
ex-gay conversion to counter legislative proposals that would grant
workplace protection, partner benefits, adoption rights, and health care
to gay men and lesbians. Rather than explicit anti-gay rhetoric, groups
like Focus on the Family and the American Family Association frame the
debate over change in terms of "hope for healing," despite that fact that
ex-gays' testimonies and queer conversions often contradict these politics. The ex-gay movement has internal fissures and disagreements, even
as the national leadership attempts to maintain the pretense of unity.
Concentrating on individual testimonies illuminated the disparities
between ground-level participants, ministry leaders, and Christian Right
organizations. It also exposed why some men and women become disillusioned with ministries. This cynicism was borne out in the ways ex-gay
men and women I talked to disassociated themselves from the politics of
the Christian Right and even the leadership of the ex-gay movement.
Some men and women in ex-gay ministries resent that the wider ex-gay
movement showcases and distorts their stories to promote an anti-gay
political agenda. Many ex-gays admit that although some changes in
behavior and identity take place, it is more probable that they will continue as "strugglers" their entire lives.

In chapter 1, I provide historical background for the emergence of
New Hope, the ex-gay movement, and the Church of the Open Door in
the 1970s. I focus on the differences among the evangelical, Jewish, and
Catholic ex-gay ministry approaches to sexual conversion, and how
these ideas translated to New Hope's sister ministry in Manila, Philippines, run by evangelicals under the auspices of the Catholic Church.
The globalization of ex-gay ministries in the last decade provides the
opportunity to trace how U.S. Christian notions of sexual identity shift
in different national contexts. The context for the process of religious
and sexual conversion is the subject of chapter 2, in which I examine the
everyday understanding of theology and religious practice of the men
and women at New Hope. Both their conservative religious beliefs,
based on early experiences within their churches and families, and their
theological interpretations of the Bible shape how they conceive of
homosexuality as a sin and a moral issue. They speak of their lives in
terms of conversions and turning points, like becoming born again, recognizing their sin, and having a personal relationship with Jesus. While
their evangelical belief system condemns homosexuality, it also provides

a way to bridge the divide between their sexual and religious identities, creating a theology of conversion that links religious and sexual identity formation.

Chapter 3 explores the concept of religious belonging through a close examination of the New Hope program structure. Despite the emphasis on marriage in the ex-gay movement, ex-gays create new forms of belonging in which same-sex friendship with other men and women becomes more important than eventual marriage or procreation. New Hope and other ex-gay ministries counter the model of the privatization of sexuality into nuclear family units through the creation of public communities of ex-gay men and women. While ex-gay men and women critique the gay community as an invalid identity group and the "lifestyle" as harmful and dangerous, New Hope has simultaneously created its own identity group. Fearful that men and women will permanently embrace the label "ex-gay" as their identity and concerned that men and women are not creating relationships outside ex-gay networks, the movement leaders warn members of ex-gay ministries not to get stuck in what they call an "ex-gay ghetto."

Chapters 4 and 5 examine how the developmental, self-help, and recovery models conceptualize sexual identity, homosexual development, and same-sex attraction as gender deficits and addictions. The ex-gay movement has reconfigured psychological and psychiatric models and theories about the origins of homosexuality and lesbianism in the postwar period through its own medical institution, the National Association for the Research and Treatment of Homosexuality (NARTH). NARTH trains therapists, psychiatrists, and medical professionals to counsel ex-gay men and women and to speak out on policy issues. Chapter 5 looks at how the rise of the self-help movement and addiction rhetoric of the 1970s intersected with the emergence of the ex-gay movement. The ex-gay appropriation of twelve-step recovery incorporates the idea that men and women will experience relapses or sexual falls as part of their healing. Rather than becoming heterosexual, ex-gay counselees and leaders become part of a new identity group in which it is part of the regulatory behavior and norms of their identity to fall (succumb to same-sex desire) and be saved (return to ex-gay counseling).

Ex-gay movement members, like other conservative Christians, view themselves as part of a positive transformation of American culture and religious life, often describing themselves as embattled or besieged by secular culture or the gay rights movement. They present a cultural critique of conservative Christianity, which often ignores homosexuality, of a secular culture that denies them the right to attempt sexual conversion, and of the possibilities for living as gay men and women. While Christian Right organizations lobby against gay marriage and same-sex partner benefits by drawing on the ex-gay movement's testimonies as proof that sexuality is a choice, the ex-gay movement also envisions itself as a pocket of resistance and tolerance in contrast to conservative Christian homophobia. Chapter 6 traces how the politics of Christian Right groups have shifted as a result of the growing visibility of ex-gay testimonial narratives.

The ex-gay movement has fused a culture of self-help, with its emphasis on personal transformation and self-betterment, to evangelical Christianity, with its precepts of conversion and personal testimony, to build a global para-church movement. Yet it is the stories of men and women that illuminate the ways that individuals grapple with the conflict between sexuality and religious belief, forge community and kinship, envision their own conversions, and conceive of politics. Just as the stories of ex-gay men and women have been appropriated in wider political debates, these men and women speak back. And just as some ex-gay men and women held the ex-gay movement accountable for the representation of their testimonies, they also held me accountable for my representation of them. In the spirit of reciprocity but with much apprehension, I sent the ministry a copy of my book while it was still a dissertation, where it circulated among the men and women.

After he had read it and offered criticism and suggestions, Hank told me frankly that he felt I had downplayed why it was people wanted to change. He was adamant that I did not underscore what it is like for the men at New Hope to have their deepest moral beliefs clash with their sexuality. "The misery and pain . . . that motivated me to want to change," Hank sighed wearily on the phone. "I worry that people will come away from reading this asking, 'Why would people want to do that?' They don't realize the conflict we deal with." I told him that many of the people who had read the book expressed feeling unexpectedly moved by the individual stories of pain and misery, despite their hostility toward the idea of changing one's sexuality. If anything, when I presented this work at conferences, I received some criticism that the project was too sympathetic to the plight of men and women at New Hope.

This question of empathy has continued to pursue me whenever I discuss the ex-gay movement at conferences, where I am inevitably asked by someone in the audience if I am a Christian or born again or sympathetic to right-wing politics.[16] As Faye Ginsburg writes of the pro-choice and pro-life women she studied in North Dakota, "I found that when I began to present my work and explain the way the world looked from the point of view of these 'natives,' I was frequently asked if I had, indeed, become one of them."[17] Hank's comments highlighted how ethnography is an act of translation and negotiation between different worlds and constituencies, in which things are always lost and misunderstood. My conversations with Frank and others who read the early manuscript forced me to think carefully about Robert Orsi's warning to ethnographers, "What can you give them once you've translated what you understand of their experience into other academic idioms so that they will no longer be able to recognize it as their experience?"[18] Hank's critique of the project as not sympathetic enough to his pain and misery is as valid as the critique that blames the ex-gay movement for adding to the pain and misery of gay men and women who have struggled to build lives despite homophobia, persecution, and discrimination. Somewhere in between those two places, I have sought to find a space for both the everyday lives of men like Hank and Curtis and the political implications of the ex-gay movement as a whole.

CHAPTER I

Steps Out of Homosexuality

In 1973 Frank Worthen heard from God for the first time in years. Frank, then a forty-four-year-old gay man, had spent twenty-five years living in the San Francisco Bay Area as a businessman and participating peripherally in early gay liberation struggles. According to Frank's recollections, on May 24 he locked his office door and headed for the back entrance of his import store, planning to check out a new gay bathhouse in San Francisco. Unbeknownst to Frank, one of his employees, a young Christian named Matt, had been secretly praying for him for months. Frank recalled: "I was leaving my office and the Lord just spoke to me and said, 'I want you back.' I generally don't share that with a lot of people because they don't understand that God can talk to you." He laughed, "They think there's something wrong with you if God can talk to you. But he did. It scared the life out of me."[1] Frank immediately contacted Matt, who met him at a chapel where he led Frank in the sinner's prayer, a prayer that many conservative evangelical Christians generally understand signifies the initiation of conversion or the promise that you will give your life to Jesus Christ. Frank prayed, "Lord Jesus, I need you. Thank you for dying on the cross for my sins. I open the door of my life and receive you as my Savior and Lord. Thank you for forgiving my sins and giving me eternal life. Take control of the throne of my life. Make me the kind of person you want me to be."[2]

Frank confessed the sins he had accumulated over many years, and as he did, he sensed a growing release from what he characterizes as twenty-five years of rebellion. He had been a devoted member of a Disciples of Christ Church in San Jose, California, as a child, where he had excelled at the organ. However, he was molested by a minister at the church and had avoided any religious affiliation since he had come out in the 1940s. In the intervening years, Frank had built a thriving import business and tentatively embraced a gay identity. He had recently been involved with a much younger man who was married but dependent on Frank for financial assistance. Right before his conversion experience, the relationship had turned sour and ended for good. May 1973 signified the closure of his old life and the beginning of his new one. Despite subsequent years of setbacks and doubts, he never returned to what he calls "the gay lifestyle."

With Matt's urging, Frank began attending his charismatic Agape church in Marin County several times a week.[3] Matt revealed that the church had been praying for "Matt's gay boss" and his deliverance from homosexuality for over a year. As Frank rededicated himself to God, the church sent other men struggling with same-sex feelings to talk to him, and he suddenly found himself counseling other gay men looking for a "way out" of homosexuality. After a short time, the minister at the Agape church challenged him to "reach back to his own people." Six months later, Frank recorded his testimony about leaving behind homosexuality on a cassette tape and advertised it in the *Berkeley Barb,* a now-defunct underground newspaper. The ad read, "FIND Homosexuality & Christianity incompatible? Send $8.00 for a new Christ-centered tape: Steps Out of Homosexuality." Initially, sixty people sent for the tape, and the "Brother Frank Tape Ministry" was born. The deluge of letters and responses Frank received provided the impetus for him to close his business and eventually form one of the first ex-gay ministries in the United States, New Hope Ministry—at the time called Love in Action.

JESUS, THE REVOLUTIONARY

When Frank first decided he could no longer live as a gay man, he turned for support to the pastors at the Agape church. The Agape church competed for members with another church called Open Door, led by Pastor Kent Philpott and Associate Pastor Mike Riley. Frank recalls that "One night the Lord woke me up and said, 'I want you to talk to Kent at Open Door.' I thought, 'No way, my pastor would have a fit if I went and talked to him.' God didn't let up. Finally I told God I'd do it." Kent Philpott considered Frank the answer to his prayers because three gay people had come to his office that week seeking help. Kent urged Frank to join Open Door and help him counsel homosexuals. Frank resisted out of loyalty to Agape, but when Agape closed in 1977, he joined Open Door permanently. In 1979 Church of the Open Door ordained Frank as a pastor. Founded in 1972 by a pastor who had a vision that his mission was to start a church in Marin County, Open Door had opened new branches in Mexico City, Phoenix, Los Angeles, and London by 1976. Pastor Mike Riley, known as "Pastor Mike," a lanky man in his mid-fifties with a boyish grin, still leads Church of the Open Door in downtown San Rafael, a charismatic nondenominational church and the only one of the four Open Door churches with a congregation primarily composed of ex-gays. New Hope is a "para-church ministry," meaning that it exists outside an official religious denomination. Even though New Hope offers Bible studies, group prayer, and worship sessions, it is not a church itself and instead affiliates itself with Open Door. Open Door is perhaps the only church in the United States for men and women who are dealing with sexual addiction and homosexuality. While New Hope considers itself a ministry for men struggling with sexual issues, Open Door provides an institutional church structure where ex-gays can worship with other people as part of a wider religious community.

Open Door's roots lie in the era of beach baptisms and mass conversions known as the Jesus movement, a movement initiated in the early 1970s, when hippies and other members of the counterculture joined charismatic and spirit-filled churches en masse.[4] Reacting to what many conservative Christians viewed as the excesses of feminism and the gay rights and countercultural movements of the 1960s and 1970s, evangelicals began actively seeking to convert members of the counterculture. Jorstad Erling writes that conservative pastors viewed young men and women in the countercultural movements of that period as potential converts who would expand their churches and contribute to their evangelizing mission. Rather than condemn hippies or drug users, evangelical pastors opened their churches to the younger generation and even recruited hippie liaisons to their ministerial staff.

One of the leaders of this religious revival, Chuck Smith, was a charismatic preacher in Southern California who became disillusioned with institutional Christianity. Abandoning his larger church, he started ministering to a small congregation called Calvary Chapel in Costa Mesa, California. Despite initial disdain and even revulsion for the hippies and surfers he noticed hanging around Venice Beach, near Los Angeles, he gradually began proselytizing to them. At first, Smith and his wife allowed early Christian converts to live in their home. When the initial group doubled from twenty-five people to fifty in six months, they could no longer accommodate everyone, and Smith rented a house where the young people could make a transition from drugs to Jesus. As the movement expanded, the number of Jesus houses increased, and the conversions skyrocketed. Mass baptismal services in the ocean, exuberant prayer meetings, long-haired evangelists, and Christian rock musicians contributed to the growth of the Jesus movement in other cities. Calvary Chapel relocated to larger and larger spaces until Smith began training the zealous young converts to plant their own Calvary Chapels in their local communities.

Today, Calvary Chapel has a reported membership of approximately fifteen thousand, with "church plants" of six hundred Calvary Chapels in the United States and a hundred in other parts of the globe. The first Vineyard Fellowship started in 1974 as a result of the Jesus movement, and it now has hundreds of churches in the United States and abroad.[5] These nondenominational Christian churches emerged at a period when attendance in mainline Protestant churches was declining and fewer people under thirty were attending church services. Liberal Protestant denominations lost much of their membership as church movements like Calvary and Vineyard tapped into the inchoate energy of the youth movement, reinventing their services and using contemporary music to appeal to a generation seeking spiritual guidance. The Jesus movement reflected a significant shift in American Protestantism toward nondenominationalism, part of a wider shift in religious organization in which liberal and conservative Protestants, even within the same denomination, split into their own churches. Many churches with similar social agendas around issues like abortion, the family, and homosexuality began connecting across denominations, leading to the rise of parachurch organizations like that of the ex-gay movement. The churches like Open Door that emerged from the Jesus movement succeeded because they created associational networks and small groups geared toward all facets of a member's life.[6] A member of a Calvary Chapel or Vineyard Fellowship church could and still can attend services every day of the week, multiple services on Sunday, Bible studies, and groups for men, women, singles, teens, addicts, or single parents. Most churches have ministries or outreach programs, which are both global and local. They might run a shelter for the homeless, a drug rehabilitation program, or a missionary program. Church members also gain the civic capital of learning communication and organizational skills through volunteering in one of the many church groups or ministries, which they can apply to their job or other aspects of their lives. Unlike many mainline churches, the laity or congregation of these churches drives the programs, and there are multiple venues for personal involvement beyond attending services.

New Hope and Open Door are part of the wider proliferation of independent churches in the United States, what some scholars have termed a postdenominational era or nondenominational movement in Christianity.[7] In many parts of the country, the adjective "nondenominational" usually refers to a nonaffiliated community church of conservative evangelicals, depending on the background of the pastors and congregants. These churches may or may not be affiliated with an umbrella denomination such as the Southern Baptists, Presbyterians, or Assemblies of God. They call themselves nondenominational because they are not under the oversight of a denominational board and because the members of these churches often come from various Christian traditions and do not subscribe to a single creed. According to Don Miller, the United States is witnessing a second reformation in which new paradigm churches like Open Door are thriving.[8] These new local congregations and churches began to set the agendas of larger denominations rather than be constrained by the institutional framework and theological dogma of their parent organization.

Miller writes that the characteristics of new paradigm churches like Open Door include the fact that most were started after the 1960s, seminary training of clergy is optional, worship is contemporary, and lay leadership is highly valued. Although Mike Riley is the pastor, Open Door has ordained other members of the church, like Frank Worthen, who don't have the educational or professional credentials to be considered a pastor or minister elsewhere. Members of the congregation are encouraged to participate in sermons and exercise their feelings at almost any time by giving testimony, shouting, participating in call and response, or raising their arms in the air. The ministry rejects the formalism and liturgy of traditional churches and urges people to act on their feelings. In churches like Open Door, personal experience validates religious belief and commitment, and experience and testimony supersede doctrine and scripture. Open Door and New Hope eschew many of the symbols of organized religion, and the emphasis in worship is on creating a church community that is loving and caring but also influenced by pop psychology, self-help principles, biblical counseling, and the importance of moral choices in one's everyday life.

Pastor Mike was caught up in the fervor of the Jesus youth movement, and Open Door was modeled on Vineyard and Calvary, even if it never achieved the same level of national prominence. "It was a time of revolution in our country—the late 1960s," he recalled with a bit of nostalgia. "It was another revolution. In those days it went over well to go preach on the streets." As a college student at Chico State University in California, Pastor Mike Riley wore blue work shirts with patches on the breast pocket and arm that read, "Jesus, the revolutionary." It was in college that he began a ministry to reach hippies; later he joined Church of the Open Door. He oversaw twelve Christian houses full of drug addicts by the early 1970s. For Pastor Mike and others in the Jesus movement, even the most marginalized elements of society were potential Christian converts. Whereas other mainstream denominations may have been squeamish about ministering to drug addicts, homeless people, and hippies, Church of the Open Door embraced them. The idea that anyone could be a Christian enabled Open Door to promote the possibility of converting homosexuals.

LOVE IN ACTION

After Frank's arrival at Open Door, Kent Philpott and Pastor Mike, who was only an associate pastor at the time, decided that a ministry for homosexuals would correspond with Open Door's wider calling. Frank started meeting on a weekly basis for counseling and discussion at Open Door with six people, who contacted him because of the personal testimony he advertised in local newspapers. A woman in the group suggested the name Love in Action (LIA), and Philpott and Frank agreed. As we discussed the early history of New Hope and Open Door, Frank jokingly referred to LIA as "Lots of Action," a reference to the unintended and unsanctioned dating that went on at the weekly support group. Although he appeared reserved and soft-spoken, Frank frequently surprised me with one of these trademark sardonic comments. He was not afraid to occasionally poke fun at the ministry or the ex-gay movement.

In the late 1970s, Kent Philpott became the director of Love in Action, with Frank acting as assistant director. With Frank's input, Philpott authored two books, *The Third Sex?* in 1975 and *The Gay Theology* in 1979, that presented the personal testimonies of the men and women who attended the support groups at LIA. *The Third Sex?* contained dialogues between Philpott and ex-gay men and women: Jim,

Susan, Bob, Polly, Ted, and Eve. The stories of how these six individuals became homosexuals provided a model for how New Hope and the ex-gay movement would structure their testimonies of conversion for decades. The books also generated publicity and enabled Philpott and Frank to continue counseling. Philpott called the first book *The Third Sex?* to argue against the idea of the legitimacy of homosexuality as an identity: "There is no third sex! For many reasons—some known, some unknown—men and women have exchanged the truth about God for a lie and have become homosexual. Homosexuality is a choice, a choice to be and do what was not intended. . . . The simple conclusion is that there is no such thing as a bisexual or homosexual according to God's established order. Both distortions of original sexuality exist for the same reason man hid from God in paradise—rebellion."[9] Philpott also established the religious basis for the LIA program: homosexuals could change not through counseling alone but through a relationship with God. It was the failure to achieve this relationship that triggered sexual falls. Philpott wrote about how at one of the first LIA meetings, a brazen man who had lived as a homosexual for six years claimed he had been converted. This man denied ever having temptations and argued that he had erased all traces of his former life. An enthusiastic Christian organization had already sponsored him, and he was counseling at prisons and rehabilitation centers. Philpott writes that less than a month after the LIA meeting, this man had "fled with a young boy from a rehabilitation house and had returned to homosexuality. The problem? This man simply wasn't honest. . . . God wants us to be honest with him, others and ourselves. It saves us from drastic mistakes."[10]

Love in Action began with a regular group of ten to twelve people meeting at Open Door on alternate Thursday evenings. The men came from a wide range of church affiliations, but they quickly established a routine of sharing their stories and devotions, praying, and listening to Kent Philpott speak. Later, when too many men and women arrived unannounced at the door with suitcases, it became necessary to find a long-term solution. In 1979 Love in Action was inaugurated as the first residential ex-gay program, and it soon had ten to twenty men and women living in its houses. Many had already read *The Third Sex?* and they arrived with hopeful and somewhat unrealistic misconceptions about the process of change. Frank recalled, "We took people off the street. No screening, no nothing. They stole everything. It was really bad, but again, we didn't know what we were doing. So after a year or two we began to screen people." Frank and Mike Riley integrated these "strugglers" into the church community houses despite ridicule from the heterosexual Christian men already living there and reluctance on the part of the church elders. Their idea was to foster interaction between "straight" men and LIA men to promote healing. Eventually, the number of LIA-affiliated people eclipsed the other Christians in the houses.

One of the men whose story Philpott chronicled in *The Third Sex?* joined LIA permanently and began writing a monthly newsletter for the ministry. Bob, a former schoolteacher, dedicated the first LIA newsletter in December 1975 by sharing the philosophy behind the group: "In making a positive commitment to Christ, we hold firm the belief that He will lead us through this valley, give us victory over homosexual desires and give us a new life and a new walk that is within His will. He will do this if it means our remaining single and celibate. This is a costly price for people so highly oriented towards sex, but worth it, if we are to hold our faith up in truth."[11] LIA also created the "Brother Bob Tape Ministry," with Bob's personal testimony on it to supplement that of "Brother Frank." The newsletter advertised more tapes for purchase on topics such as sex and the Bible, biblical demonology, the normal Christian family, and the second coming. The local Christian general store, where Anita took me on one of my first visits to New Hope in 2000, agreed to sell these booklets and more cassette tapes with titles like *Pitfalls, How to Counsel a Homosexual,* and *Examination of Gay Theology.*

Many of the ministry's ideas about sin, forgiveness, and healing homosexuality emerged from these early meetings and newsletters. At one meeting, Philpott writes, Frank, Philpott, and the men were discussing forgiveness. One of the recent arrivals was fretting about his past sins and wondering if God could forgive him. They all encouraged him, reminding him of God's mercy, and Frank said, "If God can forget, so can I." Frank rarely discusses his life before he began LIA, and Anita still knows very little about his first forty years. She told me that sometimes Frank would mention something about his past life during a speech or testimony that she had never heard before, but that she preferred it that way. Even from the beginning, LIA held to the idea of each participant becoming a "new creation" in which his or her previous life no longer mattered as long as he or she had a relationship with God. In the LIA newsletter, Bob stressed that homosexuality was forgiven by God through the process of being born again. "If we are truly a 'born again' Christian and it is in fact a *real* experience, then we are called to claim our new lives and step out and be the new creatures that we are declared to be. God sees us as new creatures, not new *homosexual* creatures, however." Bob wrote prolifically and earnestly about the idea of conversion as a God-induced process.

> This very weekend one of our brothers said to me, how can I last through even one more year of this? I said in response, how can I last one more week? But I will last and so will he. We have each other, and the sharing and fellowship and caring are God's ingredients to healing, long-lasting healing that will impart strength as God does it in *His* time and not in ours. So we continue to hold together supporting one another in every way possible, bearing the hardships as Christ bore them. We stumble along, making mistake after mistake and He forgives and forgets and we pick ourselves up and start back up the mountain.[12]

He also coined the term "ex-gay" as a way to describe the conversion process. "But I am a homosexual, really, even though I lay claim to my new life. The old *hasn't* passed away. That's *man's* thinking, not God's. God sees us as *ex-gay,* but He also sees us as struggling and dealing with the old nature with its spiritual warfare."[13]

The LIA residential program had its first house of women in the summer of 1986. Jeanette Howard, an Australian, wrote her book *Out of Egypt: Leaving Lesbianism Behind* during her time as the house leader. It was the first ex-gay book to focus on women's experiences, and it set the precedent for the ex-gay movement's ideas about lesbianism. Jeanette Howard revealed her own sexual abuse by a relative and the lack of attention she received from her father as the root causes of her homosexuality. The book was eventually distributed widely in the United States and translated into Spanish. There were four other women involved with the program who still remain affiliated with New Hope or live in the area, but the women's ministry ended in the early 1990s after no one proved willing to be the house leader. However, some members of the women's program are still active in the ex-gay movement, such as Anne Paulk, who has become a minor celebrity since marrying fellow LIA graduate John Paulk. Frank has never devoted much energy to ministry for women, and New Hope and other residential programs still continue to be geared toward men. Despite Jeanette's book and the years of a woman's program, Frank has always been the driving force behind the ministry, and his ideas about the root causes of homosexuality are central. He admits that he is less informed about women's issues around sexuality. This has contributed to inequity in the movement as a whole, which tends to be male dominated and focused on male homosexuality, a problem I discuss in chapter 4.

In 1981, after a major scandal that involved accusations of Kent Philpott's sexual impropriety with his own adopted daughter, the congregation and board ousted Philpott from Open Door, and Mike Riley became the head pastor. After a great deal of wrangling, Philpott reluctantly relinquished directorship of LIA to Frank a few months later. By 1989, with the combined men's and women's programs, Love in Action had three full houses running with over fifty people receiving ministry. In terms of numbers, the program was a success. However, LIA never established any consistent way to measure what happened to men and women after they left the program. It lost track of many people and relied on self-reporting from those who stayed in touch.

FREE ALL GAYS

Throughout the 1970s, Frank had searched eagerly for other people who were involved in ex-gay ministry, even though he believed that LIA was unique. Frank had been ministering at Love in Action for three years when he received a phone call in 1975 from a distraught woman named Barbara Johnson, whose son had recently revealed that he was gay and fled her house. Johnson contacted Frank after listening to *The Third Sex?* cassette that summer at her church. She explained that she had sought help from Melodyland Hotline, a program of Melodyland Christian Center, a large evangelical church based in Anaheim, California. The hotline was designed to deal with homosexuality, but the counselors there did not work with grieving parents of gay children like Barbara, and she was begging Frank for help. Astounded and thrilled that there were other ex-gay counselors in California, Frank flew to Anaheim the next morning to meet at Melodyland with EXIT (Ex-Gay Intervention Team), a group directed by two men in their early twenties, Michael Bussee and Jim Kaspar. Their meeting became the basis for Exodus, a national organization to address how men and women could become heterosexuals after living as gay men and lesbians.

Melodyland emerged out of the Pentecostal movement, which emphasized speaking in tongues and healing, but the church was less concerned with doctrine or formality than with validating personal experiences and emotionalism. Formed by Ralph Wilkerson, Melodyland became the center of the concept of charismatic renewal during the 1970s.[14] Wilkerson was a former Assemblies of God preacher who had departed to found an independent congregation that would be receptive to a more charismatic form of worship. An independent and interdenominational

Christian Center, Melodyland outgrew its suburban church in Orange County and bought the Melodyland Theater from Disney in 1969, from which it derived its name. Spurred on by the Jesus movement, Melodyland initiated a telephone hotline to counsel drug addicts and "alienated youth" that eventually grew into EXIT.

Michael Bussee and Jim Kaspar, the heads of EXIT, had become fervent Christians in 1971 after feeling troubled by their own homosexual feelings. They started working for the center's hotline service because they sensed the current volunteers were not properly trained or knowledgeable enough to handle homosexual issues. According to Bussee, "I grew worried when I heard operators of the center's hotline tell gay and lesbian callers that they were possessed by demons. I told them [the church members] I was a Christian homosexual, and they replied that 'there's no such thing. If you trust God, all your homosexual desires will be replaced by heterosexual ones.'"[15] Both men began counseling people who called the center with concerns about their homosexuality, claiming they received up to two hundred and fifty calls and letters per month.[16] Through their hotline, they located twelve other ministries counseling homosexuals in the following year. With a staff of eight, an office, and the support of the church, Kaspar and Bussee also participated in speaking engagements and worked on publications that would frame the problem of homosexuality within a psychological or psychoanalytic framework, an approach which differed from Frank's spiritual methods. Frank recollects that his work was "all spiritual because I didn't have any background in psychology so we were miles apart." When he arrived in Anaheim, Frank was impressed by EXIT's efficiency and organization. The ministry had color-coded handouts on every aspect of homosexuality, and Frank immediately borrowed these materials, which he used exclusively for the next five years.

Frank, Barbara Johnson, Michael Bussee, and Jim Kaspar decided to organize a weekend seminar for anyone involved in "helping homosexuals find freedom," which became the first annual ex-gay conference. LIA sent out requests for donations in its newsletter, and eventually it gathered the funds to hold a conference over the weekend of September 10–12, 1976, at Melodyland. In addition to the LIA and EXIT staff, the organizers flew in Dr. Walter Martin, author of *Kingdom of Cults*, and Greg Reid, who was leading an ex-gay ministry called EAGLE (Ex-Active-Gay-Liberated-Eternally). It was at this first conference that the organizers, emboldened by the presence of sixty other men and five women, officially founded Exodus International. Roberta Laurila, a participant and former lesbian, coined the name Exodus because "homosexuals finding freedom reminds me of the children of Israel leaving the bondage of Egypt and moving towards the Promised Land."[17] (The original name, Free All Gays, was quickly scrapped after the organizers realized the potential contradictions of its acronym.) The delegates adopted a statement of intent, which remained in place until 2001, when a new president took over Exodus: "EXODUS is an international Christian effort to reach homosexuals and lesbians. EXODUS upholds God's standard of righteousness and holiness, which declares that homosexuality is sin and affirms HIS love and redemptive power to recreate the individual. It is the goal of EXODUS International to communicate this message to the Church, to the gay community, and to society."[18] Frank recalls having a sense that the movement would eventually become something much grander. "That Sunday we knew that it was bigger than we had planned. We all felt that God was laying the foundation for something far bigger than we expected. You might say we felt a sense of destiny." The delegates elected Bussee and Kaspar the first presidents of the organization, and the participants agreed to meet again the following year. "We were high on God," Frank remembers. "We truly believed that God could do anything. He could change homosexuals to heterosexuals." Despite the heady atmosphere of the conference, Exodus operated on a principle of blind faith in the efficacy of being born again as Christians to heal homosexuality. They had no structure for determining what constituted a ministry and no clear explanation of what change entailed. Frank refers to their situation at the time as the "stray condition." "We had left the gay lifestyle, we had hope for full change to heterosexuality, but at that point, we were neither gay nor straight. We were merely hopeful."

By the next conference in 1977, at a church called Shiloh Temple in Oakland, California, there were pastors in attendance, but there were also gay protesters. One newspaper reported, "The tone of the conference was paranoia, the delegates did not want to be photographed and acted for the most part, like a bunch of closet cases. Many of the people present were pathetic messes."[19] Gay activists picketed Frank's weekly drop-in group for months afterward. The lack of a clear idea about the meaning of change became a liability during the third Exodus conference, held in Saint Paul, Minnesota, in 1978. One guest speaker contradicted the Exodus founding statement, telling the attendees that change was not possible for most gay people, but God gave people the power to remain celibate. He informed participants that there wasn't a next level of change and that they should make the best of their situation. To Frank and other leaders' dismay, the beleaguered men and women at the conference found this message depressingly accurate. Frank recalls that "they were on the ex-gay plateau," a state of not being homosexually identified but not feeling heterosexual either. They did not accept that celibate homosexuality could lead to heterosexuality. Despite this, Frank and the other leaders clung to their belief that people could become heterosexual even though they had yet to see it happen in practice. It was simply a matter of faith. However, none of the members had heterosexual relationships, and many were repulsed by the idea. Toward the end of the conference, Frank grabbed the microphone and presented the official Exodus viewpoint that "God will not take a person half-way and then abandon them. God would do a complete work." Yet the controversy that began in 1978 continued to fester.

The divisions and contradictions within Exodus were exacerbated as the ex-gay movement experienced upheaval and scandal in the early 1980s. Some leaders, like Greg Reid, defected from Exodus when they realized they could not handle the sacrifices required to live as an ex-gay. The most infamous Exodus scandal occurred in 1979 and has become legendary within the ex-gay movement and its opposition. On a plane en route to speak at a church in Virginia, Michael Bussee and Gary Cooper, a volunteer with Exodus, realized that after years of working together, they were in love. They rewrote their speech, arguing that the church should come to an understanding and acceptance of gay people. Not surprisingly, this proclamation shocked the members of the staid congregation, who were expecting reformed homosexual men. Later that night, Bussee and Cooper checked into their hotel. Bussee recalls in the documentary *One Nation under God* that they interpreted the fact that they were booked in a room with only a single bed as a sign from God.[20]

Bussee had been married for several years and was a founding member of Exodus, so his defection was hard on other members like Frank. The extremely public disclosure of the failure of ex-gay identity, and Bussee's subsequent avowals to the media that rampant sex between men transpired at ex-gay conferences, instigated mayhem within the leadership of Exodus. Neither Bussee nor Cooper ever returned to the movement or repented. They exchanged rings in 1982 through a Metropolitan Community Church (MCC) and continued to criticize the ex-gay movement until Cooper's death from AIDS-related illnesses in 1991, calling Exodus "homophobia with a happy face."[21] In an MCC publication, Bussee wrote, "After dealing with hundreds of gay people, I never met one who went from gay to straight. Even if you manage to alter someone's sexual behavior, you cannot change his or her true sexual orientation. If you got them away from the Christian limelight and asked them, 'Honestly now, are you saying that you are no longer homosexual and you are now heterosexually oriented?' Not one person said, 'Yes, I am actually now heterosexual.'"[22] Frank was vague and uncomfortable talking about this period in Exodus's history. "We had a terrible time the first few years. One of the reasons I wanted Exodus to become an organization was because I wanted to set a standard of ethics for that kind of ministry. Most of the people were in it for their own needs. They were lonely, they felt guilty and stayed on the fence and started ministries that should never have been started. We had a terrible time—a terrible time, initially."

The problem of Exodus in the seventies was that many ex-gay leaders had been Christians only for several months, and having a testimony was the only qualification for ministry work. Contrary to Frank's hopes and experience, a testimony was not insurance against temptation. Another contentious issue was the clash between various religious belief systems and approaches, as members came from Baptist, Pentecostal, nondenominational, and other churches. Some delegates believed in demonic deliverance rather than therapy for homosexuals, and others advocated treatments for instant change rather than long-term healing and participation in ministries. Most of the early ex-gay ministries had no ties to a denomination or an advisory board to provide oversight. It was perhaps predictable that many "flamed out," in Frank's words. When Frank became president in 1979, the organization was in chaos from within and without. There were protests by gay-liberation groups and internal defections and rivalries. The sexual scandals in particular were salacious fodder for newspaper reports and ex-gay critics, and they highlighted the lack of any regulatory mechanism for the organization. The scandals also raised the recurrent question of how the movement would distinguish between behavior and identity when it came to sexuality. Frank and other ex-gay leaders began to assert that change was a long and difficult process, emphasizing the parallel to the exodus out of Egypt. "There is a desert to be crossed between our old homosexual lifestyle and our new life in Christ. Many have perished in that desert. The world sees the bodies in the desert. It doesn't see those who have successfully made it across."

Although Frank briefly considered abandoning Exodus to focus on Love in Action, he felt compelled by an almost messianic impulse to build a global movement. Scandals still occurred, but by 1982 Exodus had established guidelines for people forming a ministry, which included some oversight by a national board of ministry leaders. Exodus belatedly admitted that many people attending conferences should not have been involved in an ex-gay ministry, and a purge of leaders ensued. The main spokespeople of the movement emerged in the 1980s: Bob Davies, the original "Brother Bob," who acted as Exodus's president until 2001; Joe Dallas, a Christian counselor and ex-gay speaker; Andy Comiskey, director of Desert Stream Ministries in Southern California; Alan Medinger, head of Regeneration in Maryland; and of course Frank Worthen, who continued to lead LIA. These men became the real founding fathers of Exodus. There were still few visible female ex-gay leaders in the organization, and again, by virtue of their own experiences and biases, these men helped further determine that the organization would primarily characterize homosexuality as a male problem through its ministries, theories, and materials. At the Exodus 2000 conference in San Diego, there was a table with pictures from the early conferences in the 1980s. The photographs revealed Frank and Alan, now in their seventies, looking young, hopeful, and spry. One of the pictures was of Sy Rogers, a former transvestite who appeared on numerous talk shows, moved to Singapore to start an ex-gay ministry, and is now a highly respected Exodus speaker. Rogers is legendary within the ex-gay movement for his response to a viewer on the *Donahue* show in 1983. When the person said Rogers did not look heterosexual, Rogers proclaimed, "I may not be Burt Reynolds, but I'm light years from pantyhose." In the photograph from the early 1980s, a man is presenting Rogers with a T-shirt that reads, "Welcome to the Hetero World." Frank said, "What we saw only in faith in the seventies, we saw in reality in the 1980s."[23]

Even by the 1980s, the infrastructure of the residential programs was underdeveloped, and the organization relied on an ad hoc method of counseling people, based loosely on the structure of recovery groups like Alcoholics Anonymous (AA). Although Exodus incorporates elements of the "one step at a time" approach to this day, ex-gays who disagreed with psychological explanations and wanted to focus entirely on the twelve-step method established Homosexuals Anonymous, which declared itself a separate organization from Exodus. (Colin Cook, one of the founders of the Quest Learning Center/Homosexuals Anonymous and a visible ex-gay ministry leader, resigned in the mid-eighties because of accusations that he was having sex with male counselees.) For the time being, Exodus ministries used an amalgam of biblical passages and twelve-step rhetoric in their materials and classes, combining what Frank characterized as "the best of the religious and psychological." Michael Bussee criticized the changes in Exodus models this way: "At first they said prayer would lead you to change, then they changed it and said only a long struggle would lead to change, and then therapy and residential programs became the only way to change."[24] Today, New Hope utilizes a model of residential living and relationships with God and other ex-gay men to promote healing from homosexuality. Other ex-gay ministries base their programs on an AA model and extensive psychological testing and counseling with trained therapists and psychologists.

NEW HOPE IN MANILA

Frank continued to oversee Love in Action throughout the 1980s, as he completed and refined the "Steps Out Residential Program" four-part workbook and his guide for pastors and counselors, "Helping People Step Out of Homosexuality." Sometime in the late eighties, Frank explained that he sensed a calling from God to begin ex-gay missionary work abroad. At first he ignored these calls, but God's voice was insistent, and he became sure that the place he needed to go was Manila, Philippines. "Sometime around 1984, God gave me the word that Anita and I would be ministering in the Philippines. At the time, it wasn't exactly a welcomed word. I pondered this for about two years, then in talking with Sy Rogers I found that God had told him that he and his family would be going to Singapore, too. It was at this time that I shared this word with Anita."[25] The calling coincided with efforts by Exodus to expand the organization internationally through ministry church plants in countries without an ex-gay presence. "Planting" ex-gay ministries abroad was necessary for the creation of an international network that would counteract the emergence of pro-gay movements in parts of Asia and Europe. Despite some foot-dragging and a lack of initial enthusiasm from Anita, the Worthens moved to the Philippines to initiate an ex-gay ministry called Bagong Pag-Asa that would be the sister ministry to Love in Action. Anita and Frank went to Manila as Exodus North American missionaries, and Exodus gave them an official send-off at the annual conference in San Antonio in 1990. They had made a three-year commitment.

Manila was disconcertingly unfamiliar and a far cry from the suburban streets of San Rafael. Frank, who was then in his sixties, suffered

various illnesses during the first year, including a bout of Bell's palsy, a
nerve condition that paralyzes one side of the face. Although their
"calling" was ex-gay ministry, Frank and Anita tried to integrate into
the local community through service projects, and one of their first was
to set up a feeding program for infants. Through a Catholic church in the
area that provided space and referrals, and with the help of an interpreter,
Frank began a weekly meeting for men dealing with homosexuality.
Unlike the LIA men, most Filipino men who came to Bagong Pag-Asa
were married but engaging in homosexual behavior. In these sessions,
Frank said he became aware that homosexuality was linked to deep
cultural feelings of shame. He contended that the issues for men in
Manila were similar to the men at LIA, but then conceded, "Certainly
there's this different twist. The shame is greater. They don't even have
words to talk about homosexuality. They have only dirty words, street
words, because they don't talk about this." The unremitting fear of
divine retribution for participating in same-sex behavior rather than
any hope for complete heterosexuality brought men to Frank's fledgling
ministry. Frank also found that his ideas about the "gay lifestyle" were
inapplicable in the context of Manila, where the men he encountered
did not identify as gay. For many men who had never called themselves
"gay" or attached an identity to their sexual behavior, Bagong Pag-Asa
created an identity for them, giving the name "ex-gay" to what had
only been a series of sexual practices.

At the end of the three years, Anita returned to California because
her son's partner was dying of AIDS-related illnesses, and she wanted to
help care for him. Although she was working to establish an ex-gay
ministry abroad, this did not create an obstacle for her in terms of supporting her son, Randy, through the last years of his lover's life. Frank
had planned to come home, but Exodus sent one of its board members
over to request that he remain in Manila another two years because the
board felt Bagong Pag-Asa could not yet stand on its own feet. He reluctantly reached a compromise with them and stayed an additional year.
When Frank finally left Manila, the residential part of Bagong Pag-Asa
ended due to a lack of funding, but the ministry still exists under the
leadership of Rene Gomez, a Filipino man who now attends Exodus's
annual conference and events in the United States. In 2001 Frank and
Anita returned for a ten-year reunion to see whether the ministry they
planted had been able to endure (see below).

Before leaving for Manila, Frank had officially turned Love in Action
over to a former program member and house leader named John Smid.

Smid, who bears an uncanny resemblance to the actor Jeff Goldblum, albeit with blond hair, had an air of severity, but LIA continued to thrive under his leadership. Frank had hoped to return to California for a year's sabbatical to rest and recuperate: "At that time I had had twenty-two years of ministry without a break and I was longing for some time off." Then Frank planned to proceed to Hong Kong, where he had made some initial contacts through occasional visits to the Hong Kong branch of his Manila church. He was contemplating the establishment of another ministry there. His plans were foiled, however, when in mid-1994 an Open Door pastor phoned him with the news that John Smid had decided to relocate LIA to Memphis, Tennessee, where he had received a lucrative offer from a church to house the program. "At first I thought he was joking, so he had Mike Riley phone me to tell me it was really happening. It was quite a jolt." Even though John Smid had the right to move the ministry because Frank had ceded control to him, Frank asked him to delay for one year so that the transition would be gradual and Frank could enjoy a year of sabbatical, but Smid felt he could not wait that long.

The LIA residential program operated out of Frank's two apartment complex properties, and Frank lived on that source of revenue. When LIA moved, Frank lost his income from the program, making a sabbatical and work in Hong Kong impossible. Frank recalled, "It was a very traumatic time for me." He described himself as "depleted, emotionally, physically and especially financially." Frank returned to California in time to see about thirty people affiliated with LIA and Open Door Church pack up and move to Memphis. He defined this period as one of the lowest points in his life because the ministry was stripped bare of people and resources. Smid had taken everything, including cabinets from the walls. Joined by several carpenters from Church of the Open Door who worked without compensation, Anita and Frank were able to rebuild the properties that had been modified for group living and rent them over a period of several months. Frank said that because he had always been very responsible financially, it pained him to run up his credit cards and his equity loan. Hank arrived at New Hope during this transition period and quickly became Frank and Anita's right-hand man. Some of the people who had followed Smid to Memphis returned, and Frank officially renamed the ministry New Hope on January 1, 1995. After several false starts, Frank and Smid achieved a rapprochement, and Frank participated in the twenty-fifth anniversary of LIA in Memphis in 1998, even though most of the twenty-five years occurred under Frank's leadership in California. However, their relationship appeared strained, judging from my encounters with both of them. At the annual Exodus conference in 2000, LIA and New Hope held separate information sessions for men and women interested in a residential program. At the LIA session, Smid was defensive when someone asked how his ministry differed from New Hope. "We're a professional therapeutic program with staff and clients," he replied. The only time I ever saw Frank evince stress and frustration in the entire time I knew him was when he mentioned this period of LIA/New Hope's history. Still, Frank invited John to fly out and join New Hope in their thirty years of ministry celebration in May 2003.

Despite LIA's awkward move to Memphis, Open Door and New Hope have maintained a symbiotic relationship since the early 1970s due to Frank's long history with Pastor Mike. New Hope meant a steady stream of new congregants at Open Door, and the church provided spiritual support and refuge for the ex-gay men and women in the program. Beyond Open Door, New Hope's relationship with other churches has been tentative, and a central preoccupation of Frank's has always been the relationship of the ex-gay movement to conservative churches in general. After LIA moved to Memphis, Frank wanted to find another church to sponsor and build up the program, but he had difficulty locating one willing. Frank organized events in other churches, and he often brought in the men from the New Hope program to sing as a way to familiarize others with the ex-gay program. New Hope consistently had talented singers and musicians in the program—a former gospel singer, a concert violinist, a man who could play keyboards, drums, violin, and guitar, for example—and they were quite impressive as a musical group. However, some of the men privately griped about being on display at the church excursions. Curtis once commented after a church visit, "Hello. It's us, the ex-gay freaks, here for your entertainment."

Initially, conservative churches rather than gay organizations opposed the establishment of an ex-gay movement. Frank and Pastor Mike contacted church leaders during the 1970s, and none of them would have anything to do with Love in Action or Open Door. Frank remembers, "Initially, all our opposition came from the Christian community, rather than the gay community. . . . It will take the church about one hundred years to really understand what we're doing. I think we've made some inroads. But the gay community has made a lot more progress—in the past twenty years, they have almost captured the church." Frank conveys a sense of feeling embattled, and he frequently complains about conservative churches' refusal to address homosexuality or sexual addiction. Frank worries that the "Open and Affirming" movement in liberal Protestant churches will make mainline churches gradually more sympathetic to gay and lesbian concerns. In the June 1976 LIA newsletter, Bob wrote about how the Santa Clara County council of churches was "institutionalizing sin" when it voted to admit the MCC of San Jose to membership. Frank and others at LIA feared that the culture at large would gradually accept MCCs, while the ex-gay movement would dwindle without institutional church support.

Today, Church of the Open Door is dependent on New Hope for a large percentage of its membership. However, it sponsors other ministries, like a Christian village in Tanzania, a pregnancy resource center with a pro-life agenda, an alcohol and drug recovery program, and Gilead House, a home for single mothers. Mike Riley is now middle aged, and his offices are cluttered and slightly run down. The church lacks its own building and meets weekly in a community center near the main supermarket downtown. Pastor Mike acknowledges that a church so closely linked to an ex-gay ministry is a difficult calling, but he maintains that this is what God meant for him to do. "We would ask God, 'Can we do something else?' We'd see other churches that were prospering more and think that this isn't fair. But God always said, If you want to do something different, go ahead; I won't be there with you." He continued, "I'm not sure we'd exist without the ex-gay part. It's part of our destiny. Sometimes I ask myself, Why do we exist? We're a small church; we could just disband and send people to all the other churches. But we're one of the few churches in the world to do this." Even though ex-gay ministry has been his primary focus for over thirty years, Riley expressed some disillusionment. "It's a hard ministry. Everything about it is hard. People come in and see the church and get frustrated with the ex-gay guys and leave because they never want to get married. The gay guys can be somewhat fickle. The gay lifestyle is very self-focused, and they can take and take and take and let you down and leave. But some of our greatest leaders have come through the program. They are the backbone of the church, and God has given us tremendous men and women." Part of the Church of the Open Door's statement of faith includes the idea that the church is the body of Christ on earth and that the church must welcome "all who place their hope of salvation and forgiveness of sins in Jesus Christ. We seek to identify with all believers in Christ." Although Pastor Mike and members of Open Door have more contact with men and women struggling with homosexuality than most conservative Christians, they accept ex-gays on the basis of their willingness to change. Pastor Mike believes that being gay forecloses any relationship with Jesus.

THE EX-GAY MOVEMENT

There are now over two hundred evangelical ministries in the United States, Europe, South America, Canada, Australia, the Philippines, Singapore, Japan, China, and Mexico under the umbrella of Exodus International.[26] Ministries affiliated with Exodus such as Desert Stream, Breaking Free, and Whosoever Will are locally run but under the administrative control of Exodus. Exodus sponsors a national conference every year and an international conference once every two years. It has a board of directors with revolving membership as well as regional representatives who oversee ministries in fourteen regions within the United States. The board of directors includes Alan Chambers, the new president of Exodus, John Smid of Love in Action in Memphis, Tom Cole, the director of Bridges across the Divide, and Mike Haley, a graduate of the New Hope program who now works in the public policy division of Focus on the Family. Many of the regional directors are ministry leaders as well. For instance, Anita was coordinator for the Northern and Southern California regions, but there are coordinators for the northwest Pacific, middle Pacific, north-central tier, central Rockies, mid-central, south-central, western Great Lakes basin, eastern Great Lakes basin, southern Gulf, north Atlantic, mid-Atlantic, and south Atlantic. These coordinators are responsible for making sure the local ministries are run by trained staff and ministry leaders who have applied to Exodus to become accredited.

Bob Davies, the original newsletter author, was president of Exodus for over seventeen years. Bob was married, and with his bushy beard and spectacles, he imparted a serious and studied leadership to the organization. He decided to step down from the post to pursue a music career at his Presbyterian church in 2001. Alan Chambers, an ex-gay man who had worked with a ministry in Florida, took over and moved the central offices from a shabby strip mall outside Seattle to a modern executive suite in Orlando, Florida. The new Exodus is sleeker, media savvy, and more explicitly political. Chambers, who is bright and irrepressibly sunny, like Orlando, has revamped the Web site, logo, and publications and changed the organization's mission statement to "Proclaiming to, educating and impacting the world with the Biblical truth that freedom from homosexuality is possible when Jesus is Lord of one's life." The logo on many of the materials reads, "Change Is Possible. Discover How." Chambers has hired a media and ministry relations manager, Randy Thomas, who sends out regular Exodus Media Spotlights emails with news updates on social and political issues related to homosexuality. The emails have news information on youth, Christian matters, marriage, civil unions and partner benefits, activism, and legislation. The Web site includes a speaker bureau to provide organizations with an Exodus representative to discuss issues like same-sex marriage, one issue where it has become increasingly vocal. Exodus has links to the Florida Coalition to Protect Marriage and information about initiatives in other states. Under Chambers, the original Exodus newsletter has been updated from a basic black-and-white format, which featured a testimony on the front and local news inside, to a more professional color format with shiny paper, graphics, and photographs. New promotional materials feature on the cover a group of men and women of all races and nationalities wearing white shirts.

In addition to ministries geared toward women, the deaf, and multicultural outreach, Exodus has devoted considerable energy to promoting its youth ministry, Exodus Youth, an outreach to teens and other youth struggling with homosexual issues. It has developed a separate Exodus Youth Web site with music, CD-ROMs, and teaching materials as well as a program called Refuge, an outpatient program for teenagers between the ages of thirteen and eighteen who are struggling with "broken" behaviors like pornography, drugs and alcohol, sexual promiscuity, and homosexuality. The idea behind the Exodus Youth campaign, as I discuss in chapter 6, is to provide an alternative to chat rooms and online resources for gay youth, instead telling them that if they feel same-sex desire, they should attempt to transform themselves rather than take on a gay identity. The Exodus Web site was designed by Westar media group in Colorado Springs, Colorado, which has a mission "to glorify God through excellence by providing innovative radio products, creative marketing services, and unsurpassed client representation." Westar, according to its Web site, serves as a liaison between Christian ministries and radio stations in order to enable those ministries to reach their audience with the message of Jesus Christ.

The ex-gay movement has been slow to include racial justice as part of its platform, but the Exodus leaders stress the idea of multiculturalism in speeches. The organization is primarily white, and each year there are very few African American, Latino, or Asian American men and women who apply to its programs. As Andrea Smith has argued in her work on the Christian Right and racial reconciliation, Exodus, like many conservative evangelical groups, views racism as an individual problem of prejudice that can be solved through evangelism and personal healing rather than attention to the structural or institutional practices that maintain racism.[27] The Exodus strategy of racial reconciliation is only applied to groups who are deemed sufficiently Christian, and Smith argues that outreach to people of color is a strategy to expand the organization rather than address a socioeconomic platform of racial justice. Instead, the movement pours resources into missionary efforts in places like the Philippines, Singapore, and South America, where movement leaders intend to replicate the structures and teachings of ex-gay ministries in the United States. In 2002 Alan Chambers made efforts to coordinate work with African American evangelical and Christian churches in the United States by meeting with prominent African American church leaders. Every year, in honor of Black History Month, the Exodus newsletter for February features an African American man who has come out of homosexuality. Exodus consistently showcases men and women of all races in its promotional materials, but those who attend the conference events and make up the program are still predominantly white.

Speaking engagements have become a crucial part of Exodus's work, and Chambers has also cultivated relationships with more prominent religious and political organizations such as Campus Crusade for Christ, Strang Communications, Teen Missions International, Cornerstone Music Festival, Promise Keepers, and Focus on the Family. In April 2004 Chambers took part in a debate on gay marriage at the University of California, Berkeley, and he travels constantly to speak at churches, policy seminars, and other events. In August 2005, *Charisma* magazine, an evangelical publication, named Chambers as one of the thirty top emerging leaders under the age of forty in the American church who will lead evangelicalism into the next decade. Focus on the Family now employs two graduates of the New Hope program in its gender and sexuality division to run ex-gay conferences and seminars, called Love Won Out, throughout the country. Exodus has established partnerships with prominent religious organizations like the National Association of Evangelicals. In the fall of 2003, Exodus had exhibits at the Southern Baptist Convention and the General Council of the Assemblies of God. Randy Thomas, the media manager, represented Exodus at former attorney general John Ashcroft's banquet in Washington,

D.C., and Alan Chambers writes of having had the opportunity to meet President Bush at a Washington, D.C., churches' conference.[28]

The upgrade of Exodus's public image has been expensive. The individual ex-gay ministries function mainly through the fees that program members pay each month, but Exodus relies on donations from individuals and organizations. It is recognized by the IRS as a nonprofit 501(c)(3) organization, and it is a member in good standing with the Evangelical Council for Financial Accountability (ECFA), a Christian financial monitoring organization which has strict guidelines for membership, including undergoing an annual independent audit. Under Chambers, the fundraising aspect of the ministry is more evident, and there are now multiple ways to give money to the organization, including donating stock, supporting AmeriVision (a Christian phone company that donates 10 percent of an individual's long-distance bill to Exodus), making Exodus a beneficiary in a will, matching grants, and transferring frequent flyer miles to Exodus. Despite these new channels for potential financial support, Chambers has written as recently as 2003 that the organization owes $100,000 to vendors because fewer attendees than expected appeared at the 2003 annual conference.[29] According to the newsletter, operating expenses are $15,000 a month over revenues. In 2002 Exodus cut six full-time staff employees to half time and put all plans for Exodus Youth activities on hold.[30] Perhaps for this reason, Exodus also has a specific section on its Web site called "Prayer Requests" where it asks supporters to pray for the ministries and their work. "Your prayers are vital to the success of Exodus. We believe that there is great power in prayer. . . . Exodus ministries worldwide covet your prayers." In the newsletter, writers continue to ask for money for computers, travel, brochures, Web site upgrades, conference displays, and the newsletter. "Twice a week when the staff processes donations, we pray over every check that comes in. We are [as] grateful for the female prisoner who faithfully sends us in her $1.00 every month as we are for the $5,000 check that came in from a man who tithed on the sale of his parents' farm. . . . Would you join us prayerfully, financially and purposefully?"[31] In his personal appeal in the newsletter, called "From Alan's Desk," Chambers writes, "I leave you much the same way I hope to always leave you: utterly desperate. I am desperate for the Lord to do exceedingly abundantly above what I can ask or imagine." However, according to the ECFA, Exodus had a surplus of funds at the end of the 2004 fiscal year. The organization's total income was $925,315 in 2004, and it spent $658,637 on administration, fund-raising, and program services.[32]

Despite Exodus's financial issues, the ex-gay movement has continued to expand into a network of organizations with overlapping but not
necessarily coordinated agendas, including Jewish and Catholic groups,
psychoanalytic organizations, and independent therapists throughout
the world. These include Homosexuals Anonymous; Sexaholics Anonymous; JONAH (Jews Offering New Alternatives to Homosexuality) in
Jersey City, NJ; Courage, a Catholic organization in New York City;
Parents and Friends of Ex-Gays in Washington, D.C.; and the National
Association for the Research and Treatment of Homosexuality
(NARTH) in Encino, California. Non-Protestant and non-Christian
ex-gay ministries like Courage and JONAH have aligned themselves
with NARTH rather than Exodus because of radical differences in religious style, goals, and theology.

Courage is a Catholic organization, with chapters throughout the
United States, which was founded and is run by Father John Harvey, a
Catholic priest. I met with Father Harvey several times at the headquarters on 46th Street in Manhattan, a run-down church with frayed
carpet on the stairs, an office overflowing with piles of paper, and one
good-natured but harried assistant named Tracey. As we sat knee to
knee in a cramped prayer room, Father Harvey, who is eighty-five and
stooped but still lively, explained that while teaching theology in the
1950s, he began reading Freud and found that the priests in his class
knew nothing about homosexuality. After publishing several articles, he
began informally counseling priests, and in 1978 Cardinal Terrence
Cook of New York invited him to establish a spiritual support system
for men and women with homosexual inclinations in the New York
archdiocese. Father Harvey began the first Courage meeting in 1980,
and the archdiocese of New York continues to sponsor him. Initially, he
organized five-day retreats in northern Virginia for priests, which he
called Retreat, Renewal, and Recreation, to help them address their
own homosexuality, and he recalled that from 1978 to 1990 he counseled over 250 priests who struggled with homosexuality. After 1990 he
devoted himself to working solely with laity, although priests still lead
Courage support groups all over the country. Father Harvey makes use
of NARTH, which will refer people to a therapist and a priest, and the
relationship is strong because Joseph Nicolosi, the director of NARTH,
is Catholic and attends many Courage events.

Courage adheres to the Catholic idea that the solution to homosexuality is chastity and community. The Catholic ex-gay movement emphasizes celibacy over heterosexual marriage because celibacy signifies a

spiritual and sacrificial path that is in line with Catholic theology. Courage's official goals are

> To live chaste lives in accordance with the Roman Catholic Church's teaching on homosexuality.
>
> To foster a spirit of fellowship in which all may share thoughts and experiences, and so ensure that no one will have to face the problems of homosexuality alone.
>
> To be mindful of the truth that chaste friendships are not only possible but necessary in a celibate Christian life and in doing so provide encouragement to one another in forming and sustaining them.
>
> To live lives that may serve as good examples to others.[33]

Tracey, the office assistant, tried an Exodus ministry in Canada, but she thought the group focused too much on heterosexuality and marriage. The whole purpose of evangelical ex-gay ministries is to recover heterosexuality through a relationship with God, but Father Harvey believes that there is no way a person will ever eliminate temptations, and his or her goal should instead be to live a chaste Christian life. While Exodus's philosophy agrees with Father Harvey's ideas about celibacy as a necessity on the path to change, it places more faith in the possibility of total conversion and marriage. Father Harvey is skeptical and cautious about the idea of change and marriage, even as he believes in heterosexual marriage as the fullest expression of healthy sexuality, and he is opposed to the idea that if you pray enough, you will "come out" of homosexuality. "I'm not denying that God can work miracles, but many people may not ever come out of their condition. You can't tell someone that he has an obligation to come out of homosexuality—you just put it there as an option." While he believes in the idea of a relationship with God to heal homosexuality, he ultimately does not think this is enough and believes that individuals must grapple with their sexuality by renouncing their sin and electing to lead celibate lives.

Courage is small, underfunded, and less organized than Exodus. Exodus members do not invite Father Harvey to speak at their meetings, even though he has inquired about the opportunity to talk about the Catholic version of celibacy. Although some Exodus speakers attend the annual Courage conferences, they will not collaborate directly, which has more to do with theological differences than their view on homosexuality. While Father Harvey explained that he had faith in ecumenism, he is certain that the Exodus board is unwilling to hear his message. Unlike the evangelical vision of a personal, unmediated relationship with God, Courage believes that priests have the power to eradicate sins, including sins of homosexuality, if a person is truly repentant. Frank Worthen, on the other hand, believes that priests and sacraments are unnecessary intermediaries between believers and God. He refers to the Catholic focus on the Virgin Mary as "the cult of Mary." Despite these underlying theological differences, Father Harvey aligns himself with groups like Exodus rather than Dignity, a pro-gay Catholic group that he calls "Catholic dissidents," because he lacks other options for allies.

In contrast to the theological suspicion of Catholics from people like Frank, Jewish people occupy a more exalted but ambiguous status in the ex-gay movement. Because of the long relationship between evangelicals and Israel, Frank and others consider them God's "chosen people." Evangelical and conservative Christians believe Israel will figure prominently in the events of the apocalypse.[34] For this reason, Exodus has been eager to build alliances with conservative Jewish organizations. Just across the Hudson in Jersey City is the headquarters of JONAH, an organization run by Arthur Goldberg and Elaine Berk for Jewish men and women struggling with homosexuality. Their sons came out to them while students at New York University, and Arthur and Elaine felt they had to develop an ex-gay ministry specifically for Jewish people. Both Elaine and Arthur attended the 2000 annual Exodus conference at Point Loma Nazarene University in San Diego but avoided the charismatic-style praise and worship sessions because of their discomfort with the Christian singing and praying. Exodus attendees paid JONAH a tribute at the closing conference ceremonies when an ex-gay man who was not Jewish but told me he identified with Jews appeared on the stage with a shofar. The evangelical praise and worship band switched gears from soft Christian rock and plunged into a lively rendition of "Hava Nagila."

JONAH states that its purpose is to aid Jews of all backgrounds, ranging from Orthodox to Reform to unaffiliated. "For Jews who are unhappy with a homosexual identity or whose goal is to attain heterosexual marriage and start a family, JONAH provides support, counseling, referrals, and up-to-date information on the causes and treatment of the problem."[35] Arthur Goldberg is a Reform Jew, but he sends Orthodox Jews who call his hotline to Orthodox psychiatrists. His goal is to find a synagogue to sponsor the organization and increase JONAH's network of psychological counseling. While JONAH members do not believe that being gay and Jewish is acceptable, they also "reject conversion therapies that frighten or shame the patient."[36]

Unlike Exodus's leaders, Goldberg is not interested in developing residential programs. The organization's counseling programs emphasize "self-acceptance and achievement of positive goals, involvement in the community, and Jewish religious identity. Our message is a life-affirming one that embraces traditional Torah views as a way of combating isolation and assimilation."[37]

Increasingly the issue of sexuality and Judaism is becoming more widely debated. In 2002 the movie *Trembling before God* received wide distribution and publicity throughout the United States. It sensitively portrayed Orthodox Jewish men and women coping with their homosexuality in the face of a religious tradition that condemns it. JONAH was not mentioned in the film. In anger and disappointment, Arthur wrote a letter to the *Jerusalem Post* that the film perpetuated a "biased and faulty assumption that same-sex attraction and behavior is irreversible."[38] As a young man in the 1960s, Arthur traveled to the American South as part of the civil rights movement, and he employs the language of civil rights to argue that people should have the right to change their sexuality. Even though his ministry work is fueled largely out of personal pain with his son's homosexuality, he claims that he wants to "provide an option for those who want to change in this politically correct environment." JONAH's affiliation with Exodus has created some problems for the group, including accusations from other Jewish people that it is part of the Christian Right. For now, it remains affiliated with NARTH and Exodus until it can form alliances with Jewish groups and psychiatrists.

The ex-gay movement is not only growing in various religious denominations, but Exodus has been expanding outside the United States since the late 1980s. Exodus International is now part of a global alliance that includes Exodus Asia-Pacific and Australia, Exodus Europe/Africa/Middle East, Exodus Brazil, and Exodus Latinoamerica. Many of the international organizations consist of psychiatrists and therapists who use reparative therapy. Before Alan Chambers became Exodus president in 2001, Pat Allan Lawrence directed Exodus International out of Toronto, Canada, and she still coordinates ex-gay programs in the developing world. The international regions mentioned above are part of an Exodus network but function autonomously. Brazil was recently designated its own region because of its extensive network of ex-gay therapists who are not necessarily affiliated with Exodus. In 2001 Frank attended the international conference in Quito, Ecuador, and Exodus materials have been translated into multiple languages for use around the globe.

The ex-gay movement's ability to globalize its organization through the creation of locally run ministries depends upon the global marketing of the U.S.-specific discourses of family values and conversion to heterosexuality. Missionaries have long attempted to Christianize other parts of the globe, but the ex-gay movement is different in that it relies on the premise of sexual dysfunction to evangelize. Exodus representatives like Frank see themselves as sexual missionaries, emissaries fresh from experiences of living as gay men and women, ready to lead others out of what they call spiritual and sexual bondage. As a motivation to other ex-gays to open ministries abroad, Frank writes, "You are in the position of ministering life to a spiritually dead people. Let me challenge you to let your light shine so it can be seen across the channel."[39]

Although Frank and Anita spent four years establishing Bagong Pag-Asa, when they returned in 2001, they found that the residential portion of the ministry had ceased and that there was no real local leadership to run the organization. Exodus Asia-Pacific consists entirely of ex-gay organizations based in Australia, and Exodus has had less success planting ministries that last once the missionaries from North America have returned home. International ministries also flounder because Exodus assumes that men and women everywhere have the resources and ability to commit to leaving their homes and families for up to one year to attend a residential program. The belief that healing from homosexuality emerges from a relationship with Jesus Christ, a commitment to godly relationships with other men, an identification as ex-gay, and a recognition of familial dysfunction presumes that family structure and sexual identification are the same throughout the world. The lack of ex-gay literature produced by local ministries in South America, or anywhere in the Exodus Asia-Pacific region, means that Exodus materials apply a universal conception of sexuality despite very different national contexts.

Despite these limitations, Exodus continues to grow. Even its setbacks and scandals end up generating more publicity for the ex-gay movement. In July 2005, a sixteen-year-old named Zack Stark posted on his Web blog that his Christian parents were forcibly sending him to Refuge, Love in Action's outpatient program for youth, after he admitted he was gay.[40] Zack Stark's postings immediately instigated protests outside the LIA ministry, and the story was picked up by the mainstream press. The Tennessee Department of Children's Services investigated allegations of child abuse at LIA, but it found no misconduct on the part of the ministry. John Smid was interviewed by Paula Zahn on CNN in late July, and Alan Chambers appeared on ABC's *The View* to discuss Exodus's programs for youth. Although the negative publicity damaged LIA's credibility, the event propelled Exodus into the national media spotlight. Chambers and other Exodus leaders have realized that media attention provides an opportunity to promote Exodus's message and to expand the organization.

CHAPTER 2

New Creations

On New Year's Eve, 1999, thirteen men between the ages of twenty and forty-five arrived in San Rafael, California, from all over the country to begin the one-year residential program at New Hope Ministry. Although they were strangers to each other, they began the night by making dinner and finished by praying in the New Year together. The date is deliberately symbolic. In the past, these same men might have celebrated the New Year by engaging in drinking, drug use, and same-sex behavior. This New Year's Eve is a rite of passage, the beginning of what will be a year spent living in close proximity to others, delving into personal issues and problems, trying to conquer various sexual addictions, and hoping to eventually become sexually and religiously transformed. Some arrived believing that within a year their sexual attractions for members of the same sex will have diminished; others simply hoped to conquer debilitating addictions. Many were seeking the camaraderie and sense of community that were absent from their lives. They were joined by eight other men: four were continuing into their second year as leaders in training, and four had completed two years at New Hope and were now house leaders in the program.

At their initial New Year's meeting, Frank warned them, "The kind of miracle I want to discuss with you is not an instant kind of miracle, rather it is a long-term progressive miracle. Many would say it is not a miracle at all, but when God accomplishes something the world says is impossible, it is indeed a miracle." During the evening, the men mingled.

Each was required to speak to every other person in the room, writing down their names, hometowns, and any other facts about them in their workbook. Later, they carted their belongings into rooms shared with one to two other men, deliberating over which bunk would be theirs for the duration of the year. In a few days, they had covered the walls of the rooms with posters and whatever other personal mementos they had to demarcate the space as their own. Curtis's room, for example, was wallpapered with magazine clippings and snapshots of friends.

After the initial euphoria of New Year's, what veteran New Hopers call "the honeymoon period," each man immediately begins a job search in the surrounding area. A sympathetic temporary agency assists in placing the men in local companies where there are other ex-gay men. This is important, because for the first several months of the program, known as phase one, participants are not allowed to go anywhere unless accompanied by two other people. The ministry includes weekly drop-in support groups, an organizational office, and a full-fledged residential program where men take part in group activities, classes, Bible studies, and counseling for a year. The four-quarter "Steps Out" workbook, written by Frank, is the basis for the classes and the structure of the residential program. Men also receive a copy of the "Steps Out" program manual, which lists the program's rules and regulations. By living in a dormitory-style arrangement, sharing living space and household duties, and working full time in the local community, they are to learn how to build healthy relationships with other men. Their one-year commitment to New Hope is designed to teach them coping skills and give them information about the root causes of their homosexuality while acknowledging that the process of change is one that potentially takes a lifetime.

Many are elated to be at the ministry, tentative yet hopeful that they will change. However, Frank also cautions them, "Change is difficult. It involves self-denial, which today is a no-no. The world cannot understand and doesn't want to understand that there are some things so valuable that people will deny their instincts and forgo immediate gratification to gain the pearl of great price who is Christ himself." Obedience to God and acceptance that any conversions they undergo are an unfolding process is Frank's main message. "The place of the homosexual in the church is not acceptance as representing a third order of legitimate sexuality, but acceptance as one in the process of growth and change." Hank seconds Frank's caveat, but he is a more formidable presence because he lives, eats, and spends all his time with the men. His long hair and propensity to go everywhere barefoot only add to the awe he inspires in new men in the program like Curtis, who always seem at a loss for words in Hank's presence. During the orientation, Hank leads the men through a series of requirements for participation: develop a positive attitude, be diligent, keep a journal, share, be celibate, be fervent in prayer, repent, be open and transparent, be committed to the church, and be cautious of seducing spirits.[1] "You have made a sacrifice to be here; make that sacrifice pay off for you. This program is important to you and your future; apply yourself," Hank practically booms. "Do not just try to slip by. You could waste a year of your life and squander what God has provided for you. Not only that, you could inhibit another member's growth. Enthusiasm breeds enthusiasm; lethargy breeds lethargy." Hank's physical and spiritual presence, more than any other, dominates daily life in the program. Because of the heavy responsibility for someone in Hank's position and the tendency for men to demand his individual attention, he is careful to delineate specific boundaries. The "Steps Out" workbook counsels the men, "Do not place heavy expectations on your house leader. To do his job effectively, he must divide his time between all house members; he cannot be exclusively yours."[2] As the year progressed, these boundaries became increasingly difficult to maintain, and often Hank's only respite was the privilege of his single room or his escape to his job.

Attending worship services at Open Door Church their first Sunday in the program was startling for many of the New Hope men. Instead of condemning them, Pastor Mike warmly welcomed the new arrivals from his pulpit, and members of the church beamed at them from their seats. Open Door receives a new crop of ex-gay men every year when the program begins, and the other members of the church were expecting them. Most men who arrived at New Hope defined themselves as conservative Christians who believe that an ex-gay ministry represents their last opportunity to live according to Christian principles after leading lives of what they characterize as sin and unhappiness.[3] In the language of New Hope, they are "strugglers," or dealing with "sexual brokenness." They joined the program because they have been unable to reconcile conflicts between their deeply rooted religious belief that the Bible is the word of God and that it expressly condemns homosexuality and their own sexual desires and practices. Their experiences growing up in conservative Christian churches where they heard dire warnings about homosexuality only reinforced this interpretation. Many arrived with tales of sexual and pornography addiction and anonymous sex in lavatories, rest stops, and parks; stories of loneliness; and suicide attempts. All of them spoke of suffering from guilt, shame, and distance from God. The men used the word *homosexuality* to describe their pasts because it refers to acts and feelings rather than an identity. Only a small percentage of the men in the program ever identified as gay, had long-term lovers or partners, or were socially or politically involved in a wider gay community. Most men eschewed a gay identity and described their sexuality as an experience of guilt about sexual acts, practices, feelings, and desires. Others had left long-term lovers, friendships, and relationships in order to become ex-gays. Hank explained his eleven-year relationship this way: "After many years I just got tired of the contradiction. I would get out of church and I would go have sex with somebody. God said, 'You have to choose between your sin and me. What's it gonna be?' I was never able to deny God. I've tried to justify and it never set well. There was never any question in my mind; I always knew it was wrong." The men also spoke of their expectation that by being at New Hope, their sexual conflicts would diminish as their Christian identity strengthened. They felt certain that it was only through an ex-gay program that they could reconcile their sexuality with their religious belief system through a process of religious and sexual conversion. Having a public intimacy with God and a personal relationship with Jesus would enable them to be new creations in Christ. Their new ex-gay identity would emerge through what they called "an identity in Jesus."

SHOUT TO THE LORD

The men at New Hope grew up with or were familiar with conservative Christian traditions, spanning a wide range from Nazarene, Assemblies of God, Baptist, and Pentecostal to nondenominational backgrounds in Vineyard Fellowships or Calvary Chapels. A few men had upbringings in mainline Protestant denominations like Presbyterianism or Lutheranism. Some left their churches and faith for a time and then rediscovered it. Others attended church at the same time they engaged in clandestine homosexual relationships and sexual practices. The sole Catholic man at the ministry had tried an ex-gay group run by a Catholic church but found that it did not provide enough structure. During his year at the ministry, he was baptized by Pastor Mike and began to describe himself as a "saved Christian." New Hope is adamant about promoting a non-denominational form of Christianity at the ministry. The program book states, "Please don't push your denomination's peculiar sectarian doctrine or dogma on others. New Hope Ministries holds to the simple Gospel presented by Jesus Christ."[4]

Even by defining themselves simply as Christians, the people at New
Hope and Open Door reference a very specific theological belief system.
This includes the necessity for personal salvation through becoming born
again, or saved, faith in the inerrancy of the Bible, and the belief that
Jesus Christ is the Son of God, with whom a person can have an intimate
relationship. The theological tenets of Open Door Church echo these
ideas: belief in the Holy Trinity (Jesus, God, and the Holy Spirit), the
virgin birth, the Second Coming of Christ, and salvation by faith and
grace alone. Open Door's official doctrinal statement reads, "We believe
the essence of the Christian life is a personal relationship with Christ
lived out in the fellowship of the church." The idea of grace is central to
how New Hope and Open Door Church conceive of homosexuality. In
this view, God's grace extends to all people, regardless of their sins, as
long as they ask for forgiveness. Open Door and New Hope understand
salvation as an act of divine grace received through faith in Christ, not
through any kind of penance or good works. When a person is reborn,
the guilt of sin disappears and an inward process of sanctification takes
place as he or she leads a Christian life. The New Hope doctrinal statement
links the issue of homosexuality to this belief system:

> We believe that the Bible is the inspired Word of God and is infallible and
> authoritative in its original writings. We believe that for the salvation of
> lost and sinful man, faith in the Lord Jesus Christ and regeneration by the
> Holy Spirit are essential. We believe that the Bible teaches that all homo-
> sexual conduct is wrong and against God's standards. We believe that
> through making an unconditional commitment to Christ, we are empow-
> ered by Him who gives us victory over homosexual desires and leads us
> into a new life and a new walk that is within His will.[5]

Services at Open Door are informal and spontaneous. At one of my
first visits, Pastor Mike's son, who is the unofficial leader of the Open
Door band, played soft Christian rock songs on guitar accompanied by
a keyboardist, two female singers, and a drummer. Their band toured
Ireland and parts of Europe later that summer as part of a series of
Christian youth events. A disco ball that belonged to the community
center revolved overhead, refracting the light from outside. The lyrics
to "Shout to the Lord" were projected on a screen above us, and the
congregation sang the chorus over and over:

> Shout to the Lord, all the earth,
> let us sing
> power and majesty, praise to the king;
> mountains bow down and the seas will roar

at the sound of your name.
I sing for joy at the work of your hands,
forever I'll love you, forever I'll stand,
nothing compares to the promise I have in you.

The singing was heartfelt and expressive. Brian closed his eyes and extended his palms upward. Curtis shook from side to side as if he were at a concert and frequently lifted his hands in a posture of surrender. This part of the service lasted for half an hour. The singing reached a crescendo, but the band continued, and the congregation repeated the chorus one more time. The program bulletin called it praise and worship, and the intensity of singing was meant to express a deep love for God. Brian and Curtis's participation in worship was much more bodily than cognitive. Afterward, when I asked why Pastor Mike had used a particular word during his sermon, Curtis could not recall what I was talking about. "I loved the worship service," he replied, humming "Shout to the Lord."

With the music playing gently in the background, Pastor Mike had preached a short sermon based around Romans. His sermons tended to be Bible-centered instead of topical. Members of New Hope are encouraged to interpret scripture for themselves and have direct interactions with God. Pastor Mike was an understated and folksy minister rather than a fire-and-brimstone preacher or flashy televangelist. He frequently spoke about the apocalypse and his belief in the Second Coming of Jesus, a belief that some evangelical churches espouse to varying degrees.[6] "The Bible is fuzzy on the end times issue. There will be an ending. I tell people to pick your poison and to be ready," he later explained. The official church doctrine listed at the Open Door Web site states, "We believe the age will end with the return of Jesus Christ to set up His kingdom." Pastor Mike and Frank see evangelizing and sharing their beliefs with a wider culture as a necessity. They often speak of their "callings" to minister to those struggling with homosexuality.

At the end of the service at Open Door, with Pastor Mike's encouragement, several people came to the front of the room for healing prayer. Brian strode forward and leaned over a new member of the program, laying his hand on his shoulder, praying fervently but softly. Ray, in his late forties, wearing jeans and a rumpled shirt, knelt before him with his eyes squeezed shut, also praying. Brian intended his laying on of hands to be caring but casual, so that anyone would feel empowered to step forward to receive healing. Open Door teaches that everyone should receive the baptism of the Holy Spirit. "We believe in the power of the Holy Spirit, his dwelling presence in every believer, and the gifts that he imparts," Pastor Riley explained. "People teach that you're automatically filled with the spirit when you're born again and to a certain degree I believe that your spirit is quickened," said Hank. One of the signs that a person has accepted the Holy Spirit is that he or she receives a prayer language or the ability to pray in tongues. Connected with this ability is a feeling that one has what Hank calls "a prophetic gift of healing. . . . I really believe that the mainstream church is lacking in a dynamic manifestation of the spirit. It's more a religion, [a] head thing, and that has never done anything for me whatsoever. I think everybody should be filled with the spirit." Hank's everyday life is suffused with this practice. Frequently, as he went about his other tasks as the resident New Hope handyman, he would start praying loudly or singing a particularly religious Johnny Cash song, like "Will You Meet Me in Heaven Someday?" He believed that these manifestations of his spirit-filled nature were simply spontaneous eruptions beyond his control, which was further proof to him of the way the spirit moved in his everyday life.

Many men eagerly anticipated the healing portion of the service at Open Door, but overall a communal aspect of worship infused the entire church experience. Pastor Mike asked us to hug and talk to our neighbors, to hold hands, and there was a lot of bumping into each other as everyone swayed to the music. When he noticed my hesitation and stiffness, Curtis grabbed my sweaty palms during praise and worship, forcing me briefly to move along with him. Open Door's mode of worship reintegrates bodily experience into religious life. Being there seemed to allay the men's deeply felt anxieties about their sexuality, and many spoke of feeling ecstatic joy and profound peace after services. It made sense that in a program where physical and sexual contact is strictly regulated, the euphoric and physically intimate experience of worship could serve as a release or safety valve for frustration and loneliness. The repression of all forms of sexuality at New Hope could manifest in the emotionalism of the religious service at Open Door. The lyrics to the last song, projected on the screen from a transparency, read, "Bless our lives, Holy Spirit,/Holy Spirit, fill our lives with peace."

After the services and during the week, men in the program attended Bible studies, men's meetings, and other special-interest groups under the auspices of Open Door. Robert Wuthnow points out that after the 1960s, Christians demonstrated their faith in small, politically oriented groups that transcended denominational and theological affiliation.[7]

Miller writes that, "New paradigm churches tend to be filled with programs that deal with the specific needs of those attending them. It is not surprising, then that small group meetings in homes are at the core or all these movements."[8] Open Door and New Hope are descended from this form of special-interest Christianity, except that they focus solely on issues of homosexuality, which has alienated them from other postdenominational churches. Contrary to the perception that conservative Christian theology and practice are rooted in exclusion, New Hope offers inclusion for those who have been shunned or alienated by both mainstream and conservative churches as long as they acquiesce to the process of change. One man praised Pastor Mike: "When he's really talking about things that are more pointed toward people's lives, he's amazingly open, amazingly supportive. I didn't hear any of the stuff about you're scum, you're going to hell. I was really surprised how supportive he was." In a conservative Christian religious landscape in which homophobia is prevalent, Open Door provides an unlikely haven.

BIBLE BELIEVERS

The idea of a church organized around transforming sexuality has not generally been the norm in most fundamentalist or evangelical religious traditions, which either rarely mention homosexuality or deem it a sin. New Hope and Open Door are part of a wider evangelical tradition, which is a broad category that encompasses fundamentalism and a range of communities, congregations, and movements associated with modern Protestantism. Evangelicalism emerged in the early eighteenth century as a form of "Jesus-friendly Christianity" with what historian Stephen Prothero calls a "unique combination of enthusiasm and egalitarianism, revivalism and republicanism, biblicism and common sense."[9] The revivals of the Second Great Awakening in the 1830s and 1840s provided a new set of religious ideas within Protestant Christianity. In contrast to the Calvinist doctrine that emphasized a fallen humanity and sovereign God, revivalists claimed that sinners could choose salvation and their own spiritual destinies. The evangelical notion of self-determination and agency went hand in hand with individualistic impulses in American society. Evangelicalism's main tenets—that each person can be transformed through conversion, that people have free moral agency, and that inequality is not divinely mandated—altered the ways marginal people in the United States viewed themselves and their social circumstances during the eighteenth and nineteenth centuries. Conversions and revivals had an impact outside of religious life and ultimately represented new forms of democratization in which religious outsiders like women, African Americans, and working people achieved greater access to the public realm and forms of social power. They used the revivals to register discontent with wider economic and social changes brought on by the market revolution.[10] For decades after the Second Great Awakening, fundamentalism and evangelicalism emphasized approximately the same thing: soul winning and orthodoxy. After World War I, evangelical and neoevangelical groups perceived benefits in contact with outsiders and secular culture, while fundamentalists held onto an opposition to secularism and maintained a more separatist stance than other evangelicals.

Generally, evangelicalism in America describes a vast, varied, and interactive aggregation of many different groups, like Pentecostals, charismatics, Vineyard Fellowships, Assemblies of God, and Churches of the Nazarene. Evangelicals believe that people must have an intimate relationship with Jesus and that only an individual desire to follow Jesus will suffice for salvation.[11] The simple meaning of the word "evangelical" refers to the "good news" presented in the Gospels, and many modern evangelicals understand their mandate as spreading this good news and winning souls for Jesus by testifying to their own life-changing experiences. Within evangelicalism, some churches and denominations understand the Bible as infallible, true, and literal, in contrast to a liberal Protestant view that considers the Bible a product of human history and context. For instance, one of Open Door's doctrinal statements reads, "We believe the Bible is the inspired word of God. It is infallible. It is inerrant in the original. It is the final authority for the Christian faith and practice."[12] However, many evangelicals do not actually read the Bible literally, believing there is metaphor and poetry in the Bible.

The historical division between evangelicalism and fundamentalism stems from theological debates about their relationship to God and wider society. There is still discussion among historians about when fundamentalism developed as a movement and as a set of religious ideas.[13] José Casanova writes that fundamentalism emerged as an antimodernist reaction to the disestablishment of evangelicalism from liberal Protestant churches and from American public education. Fundamentalists fought battles on three fronts: liberal modernist heresies in northern congregations, Darwinism in public schools, and Catholic immigration.[14] "The Fundamentals," a series of booklets published between 1905 and 1915, helped define the tenets of fundamentalism. They defended the Bible, conservative doctrine, and the Second Coming of Jesus. However, according to Casanova, "The particular 'fundamentals,' chosen rather arbitrarily, were not as important as the fact of proclaiming some 'fundamentalist' tenet, some taboo boundary which could not be trespassed."[15] These publications produced a body of dogma that was distinct from the rest of Protestantism and helped to consolidate the theological position of fundamentalists.[16]

Historically, popular culture cast fundamentalists as anti-modernist crusaders who advocated a separation from the world and modern society's corruption. This narrative solidified with the Scopes Trial of 1925 in which a schoolteacher, John Scopes, was fired for teaching evolution in a Tennessee public school. The court battle that emerged over evolution and creation and the subsequent representations of the trial in the play and film *Inherit the Wind* created a definitive legacy for Scopes.[17] The trial came to symbolize the triumph of science and empiricism over religion and to embody the defeat of fundamentalism.[18] According to Joel Carpenter, rather than disappear after 1925, fundamentalism continued to thrive in the 1930s and 1940s, and these years were a time of significant institution building by those who defined themselves as fundamentalists and evangelicals.[19] The Billy Graham Evangelistic Crusade and the National Association of Evangelicals inaugurated a new era of neoevangelism. They eschewed religious separatism by working with other religious groups and saw their mandate as influencing the wider culture around them. The 1940s and 1950s witnessed the creation of a variety of evangelical institutions, political action groups, and universities.[20]

For conservative, nondenominational Protestants, many of the distinctions between fundamentalist and evangelical practices and theology have eroded. For churches like Open Door, the descriptive term "fundamentalist" or "evangelical" is less important than their particular set of beliefs and the ways they practice religion and faith as a community. They simply refer to themselves as Christians. Frank and Pastor Mike, for instance, were always reluctant to use either term to describe Open Door. "It really means sticking to fundamental beliefs, but today it means right-wing, and we're not that," maintained Pastor Mike. "We're fundamental in our theology." He describes his church as evangelical charismatic and agrees with the label "postdenominational." "We're a church that always tried to go down the middle, and we got in trouble with both sides. The fundamentalists think, Why would you let gays in your church? The liberals think we're too judgmental." He accepts the Bible as literally true but qualifies his statement, "I have to understand that the Bible has poetry, history, literature, and interpret those things, but I accept it as it stands. The Bible affects lives more dramatically when it is taken as literal truth in a literal interpretation."

Many men in the New Hope program grew up hearing sermons that taught homosexuality was the most horrible sin of all. At New Hope and Open Door they interpret scriptures from Genesis, Leviticus, Romans, and First Corinthians to mean that homosexuality is not God's intent, and Pastor Mike would agree. In the sermons, classes, and Bible studies at New Hope, Frank and Pastor Mike argue that the book of Genesis is proof that sex should be tied solely to procreation, that heterosexuality is mandated by God, and that the aim of sexuality is completeness, or the bringing together of the male and female. The story of Sodom and Gomorrah figures prominently in the conservative Christian debate over homosexuality.[21] Using the New International Version, the New Living translation, or the New American Standard Bibles, conservative Christians traditionally read Leviticus 18:22 as an unambiguous repudiation of homosexual acts. The New International Version states, "Do not lie with a man as one lies with a woman; that is detestable." New Hope's interpretation of First Corinthians includes the use of the words "sexual perverts" and states, "Do you not know that the unrighteous will not inherit the kingdom of God? Do not be deceived; neither the immoral, nor idolaters, not adulterers, nor sexual perverts, nor thieves, nor the greedy, nor drunkards, nor revilers, nor robbers will inherit the kingdom of God." In the "Steps Out" workbook, Frank writes that the Greek words for sexual perverts are *malakoi* and *arsenokoitai*. He translates these terms as "soft" or "weak," and by extension "effeminate," and concludes that the words connote the passive partner in homosexual intercourse.[22] In the Revised Standard and Living Bibles, these terms have been translated respectively as "homosexuals, homosexual perverts and partakers in homosexuality." Frank acknowledges that the basis for New Hope's belief in homosexuality's sinfulness rests on the translation of a few words. However, rather than viewing these translations as the result of the bias of a particular cultural context or religious tradition, Frank believes the translation is a moot point. To him, the Bible is the word of God and is infallible regardless of human error or interpretation.

Most of the men at New Hope read these biblical verses as the inspired word of God and refused to acknowledge cultural or historical context. There were exceptions, like Evan, a seminary graduate spending the year at New Hope. I had assumed Evan was an imposter or spy when we initially met, because his Ivy League education, Methodist background, and progressive political ideas were glaring aberrations at New Hope. His serious, lined face showed signs of time in the outdoors, and he rarely smiled or evinced the emotion of other men in the program. He had written sermons as a theology student, and he was equally well versed in biblical interpretation and postmodern theory, speaking of Judith Butler and John Calvin in the same breath. His nuanced discernment of scripture often led to clashes with Hank and disagreements over Frank's teaching style. "Many conservative Christians believe it just fell out of the sky and it's God's word, and he intended everything there to kind of speak to us in our time and place," he told me. "There's a part of me that holds onto the view that God inspired these texts, that God was active at the moment of their creation and still speaks through them. But I haven't quite figured out how to totally balance that view with the idea that these are historical documents." Lars, a social worker at an AIDS organization, had left New Hope after several years in the program to live as a gay man. At times, he was bitter about the conservative Christian hypocrisy around homosexuality. "I'm very confused, to be honest. I know what it says at face value. It basically says it's not favorable in God's eyes and is sin, in a nutshell; however, there are other things very conservative Christians don't follow anymore, like women not being allowed to talk or wear head coverings, so I'm left to think, if I can't take everything in the Bible at face value, then everything is up for discussion. They excuse things that are convenient for them." His interpretation of the Bible had gradually shifted over time: "Honestly, I don't know what the scriptures say. Before I believed that the word of God was absolute and infallible and you had to do things, and I was willing to do that no matter what the cost. Now I'm not so sure." Unlike Evan and Lars, most men arrive at New Hope believing that when the Bible references homosexuality, it does so in condemnation, and that these isolated verses are part of a larger tapestry of the word of God serving as irrefutable proof that homosexuality is wrong.

Scholars like John Boswell contend that some conservative Christians have reinterpreted biblical scriptures to reflect the political agenda of Christian organizations and that these scriptures are not irrefutable truths. According to Boswell, the word "homosexual" does not occur in the Bible, and no extant text or manuscript contains such a word.[23] He presents evidence that the preoccupation with homosexuality is a result of contemporary politics rather than long-standing biblical injunctions. One of the most powerful arguments for this viewpoint is the fact that Jesus never mentions homosexuality in any form in the New Testament. As Evan put it, "I think it's significant that it wasn't a big issue for Jesus. Jesus never mentions it." Other scholars of sexuality have rigorously demonstrated that modern homosexual identity emerged in the West during the past two centuries, and the category "homosexuality" used by conservative Christians is a modern term placed on a different historical and cultural context.[24] Many of these debates are simply irrelevant to the men at New Hope because the idea that homosexuality is "not what God has planned and not what God wants," as Hank puts it, is the bottom line. The scholarly reevaluation of the scriptures means nothing when a person believes that the scriptures are absolute and immutable truth. As Drew bluntly said, "In Genesis God created man and then he made woman. I believe that Christ walked this earth and that he's real [and] that it's not right. I believe it's a choice."

Frank and other ex-gay leaders also interpret biblical passages to mean that in addition to condemnation, the Bible also offers the promise of liberation. The ex-gay movement's founding statement includes compassion for those struggling with homosexuality, but the ability to feel compassion does not translate into endorsement. The idea of homosexuality as sin is central to New Hope's view of scripture, and the distinction between sin and sinner translates to the difference between sexual behavior and identity for ex-gays. Nowhere do they read the Bible as a way to understand homosexuality as a positive way to live. Dwight, a man from Scotland in his early forties who worked in the New Hope offices, claimed, "So, how I see it is that basically God doesn't want anybody to use their bodies for sex unless it's within marriage. I guess I tend to focus on that rather than on looking just at homosexuality." Marvin Ellison, a Christian ethicist, argues that the Christian tradition has never had a constructive ethic of sexuality that truly affirms and honors the rich diversity of human sexualities.[25] He asks, "What would a progressive Christian ethic look like that regarded homosexuality as a morally good way to be and 'do' sexuality? What difference would it make to focus moral concern not on gender and sexual identity, but on the quality of relational intimacy and whether our connections with each other are just and compassionate?"[26] The idea of homosexuality as a social and moral good was beyond the conception of Frank or any of the men at New Hope. They had fully assimilated the idea that positive sexuality could exist only for married heterosexuals.

Many men at New Hope were quite comfortable with accepting and assimilating a view of scriptures predicated on a starkly polarized moral view of the world. The creation of a moral universe devoid of ambiguity was also a defense against and reaction to reproof and censure for joining an ex-gay ministry. Their experience of being ostracized from their primary community, the church, was critical in their decision to join an ex-gay ministry. Many men endured early rejection as members of their congregations, and others heard messages that homosexuality was a sin akin to murder. Growing up as an active member of an Assemblies of God church in Southern California, Brian internalized these messages from an early age, and they were still the linchpin of his identity. He told me, "It was like, this is sin. You've got to stay away from it, and it's a spiritual battle. It's a war. Spirit forces are raging in the heavenly realm—that kind of thing." Doug, a new arrival at the program, was a heavyset man who had lived in a gay neighborhood in San Francisco for over twenty years before joining New Hope. He remembers sitting next to his high school boyfriend when Jerry Falwell visited as the guest pastor in the Pentecostal church in Oregon where he was raised. "What is significant was he got up on the pulpit and had this list in descending order of who was going to go to hell, and at the top of the list was the homosexuals," he recalled. "So, for the first time in my life, being there in church with my secret boyfriend, we both looked at each other like, oh my God, he's talking about us. Here I am a sixteen-year-old boy and this guy is telling me I'm going to go to hell. And so from that point on, there was no way I could live with the guilt of trying to be a churchgoing Christian and trying to be gay."

Brian remembers, "[In] any kind of example you wanted to give about how bad the world had gotten you included homosexuality." During one sermon while he was a teenager, Brian, in his typically outspoken way, went forward and was bold enough to say that he needed prayer for his struggle with homosexuality. The pastors of his church escorted him into a back office where they attempted to exorcise the demon of homosexuality. "It was very weird, with them pounding on me with their fists. Of course, more than anything, I wanted to be rid of it, so I tried my hardest to participate and to eject this thing out of me. And, of course, they didn't succeed." After pastors urged them to pray more, to fast, to gain more experience in the spiritual disciplines, and to conceal their feelings, many ex-gays simply left their churches. Without exception, this separation produced turmoil, and many ended up rejecting Christianity in all forms until they found New Hope.

New Hope was one of the few places where these men and women, after years of silence and denial, interacted with others who had shared similar experiences, and where their sexual struggle was the central part of their religious identity. Yet their resentment toward their churches lingered and erupted at times. Lars was one person willing to expose the hypocrisy of many Christians who preached love and compassion but practiced something quite different.

> Most of them can't handle the truth. If you're in the church and you're a drug addict, murderer, whatever, guys will come up to you and slap you on the ass. You're one of the guys. But if you state you struggle with homosexuality, you get the whole pew to yourself.
>
> The church has a hell of a long ways to go in accepting people where they are because they hate people who are gay. When I was at church the very last time they were talking about Matthew Shepard and his sin and what a tragedy it was, and I wanted to stand up and say, You are the problem. You're the reason Matthew Shepard got murdered.

I heard Frank and other ex-gay leaders condemn Matthew Shepard's murderers and disassociate themselves from people like Fred Phelps and members of his Topeka, Kansas, church, who protested Shepard's funeral with signs reading, "God Hates Fags."[27] However, neither Frank nor most of the men in the program were willing to go as far as Lars, calling the church to account for preaching words that kill.

THE LORD'S LAND

The first opportunity many of the new arrivals had to share their personal stories and unravel the reasons they ended up at New Hope was at the Lord's Land retreat. A few weeks after spending New Year's Eve together, the men set off for five days at the Lord's Land in Mendocino County, a coastal wilderness area three hours north of San Rafael. The "Steps Out" workbook included a list of what to bring: rain jackets, flashlights, journals, and, most important, Bibles, so that they could find scripture that applied to their life to use during their first testimony. In another incarnation, the Lord's Land had been a hippie commune but was now a Christian retreat center. The center sat deep in the woods, and its roots were evident in the hobbit-style outbuildings concealed by eucalyptus and redwood trees which dotted the compound. The days were divided into quiet time for reflection, group meetings, sightseeing, hikes, and worship. The men met in large groups for two hours in the morning and after dinner, where Frank allotted each forty minutes to give their testimony. In the testimonies, they were to talk about their early family situations, relationship to the church, salvation experiences, and goals and hopes for the future. Each of their "Steps Out" workbooks had pages with space for the testifier's name and any notes that they wanted to take as they listened to each other. They also went on long hikes in an effort to forge bonds within the new group. Frank believes that community is easier to achieve in an austere wilderness setting without the distractions of daily life. He writes in "Steps Out": "The retreat is to be a time of honesty and openness both before God and before our brothers. It is intended to be that first step toward God that opens the door for His intervention in your life. It is a time for bonds to be forged between us as BROTHERS IN THE LORD. These bonds can only be lasting and of value if NOTHING IS HIDDEN, concealed or presented in a deceptive way."[28] Frank warned them to stick to forty minutes for the testimonies, so that "we have 20 minutes to pray over you." Inevitably, even with only two or three in a day's schedule, this part of the day went on for hours, as most men exceeded the forty-minute limit. After all, it was cathartic for many to be able to speak openly for the first time in a group where there was no risk of belittlement or censure. When they returned after a week and we were in the office together, Drew rolled his eyes, recalling how grueling it had been to listen to some men go on and on. No one was able to fit his life story into a forty-minute period. However, Drew also said that no matter how many times he heard men's stories, he was deeply moved by the commonality of so many of their experiences and the isolation and guilt each had endured.

For the men at New Hope, the Lord's Land was the beginning of a healing process that could take the rest of their lives. It was also the initial step in formulating a testimony, which would then strengthen their Christian identities. The forty-minute testimony was part of the longer process of learning to create a life narrative, a testimony about living as a homosexual, being part of a relationship, having sex with men, reaching a crisis point, and slowly being born again until each man could become a new creation in Christ. Eventually, many of them would perform and speak their testimonial narratives in the church, at conferences, and in published materials. Even if the men had been saved previously, the experience of being at New Hope was another born-again experience of renewal and salvation. Through the conversion process, they began to reconcile their opposing frameworks of conservative Christianity and homosexuality as they took on the new ex-gay identity. Ray described his born-again experience as what finally started changing his sexuality: "I remember sitting in a chair and I knew I was in bondage and I was tired of being sick. I accepted Christ as my savior and asked him to come into my heart. I had such a knot in my chest from all the sexual stuff I had done, and it went away. That started my road to God changing me." Curtis frequently expressed frustration at what he considered the secular world's manner of portraying the ex-gay conflict as solely a matter of giving up sexual acts. For him and other men, it is nothing less than a complete reconstruction of religious and sexual selves. "There is no such thing as a cure," Curtis explained. "You learn how to better manage your life, thoughts, and desires and you achieve a sense of wholeness and a better relationship with God."

Despite their disparate backgrounds, the men's testimonies had in common a language of pain. Many described a crisis point in their lives when they were no longer able to conceal their sexual identities and live as Christians. Some reached a point where the conflict became unbearable, and this crisis led to the onset of spiritual conversion. In her study of two Methodist congregations in Chicago and their ideas about homosexuality, Dawne Moon writes that many of the people she met used feelings and emotions to serve as an incontestable form of knowledge, to promote compassion, and to distance themselves from politics. "When members addressed debates using a language of emotion, their emotional experiences with God came to be the only evidence suitable for determining what is right."[29] In their testimonial narratives of pain, New Hope men expressed a sense of detachment from God because of their homosexuality. This feeling of separateness was real and incontestable, and New Hope enabled them to envision only one outcome: to become a new creation through a relationship with Jesus and thus to heal their homosexuality. The ex-gay narratives became a way to stifle other interpretations of homosexuality as healthy, moral, or Christian. Thomas, a gaunt man who looked like he was twenty-five but was actually in his mid-forties, had been through the live-in program when it was still called Love in Action. He recalled the moment of hearing God's voice as pivotal to his decision to come to the ministry:

> I used drugs to anesthetize myself and make myself forget and live with this thing. I always had the application from LIA. It sat in my drawer five years. God was speaking to me, saying there is hope here. I got really strung out. Imagine me fifty pounds lighter—it was scary. I woke up and thought, I hate my life. I just want to die. A spiritual presence came into the room. It said, "I have something so much better for you than this, and I love you and I'm here and I'm waiting." I was so amazed and happy and

I took all the drugs and pornography and dumped them in dumpster and waited for the voice to return. I contacted LIA and said, "Will you take me in the program?"

In some cases, the men acknowledged that their spiritual crises also stemmed from familial and societal pressure and the psychological impact of living as a gay man or woman in a homophobic environment, but they interpreted these crises in ordinary life within a spiritual or religious framework. These crises then lead to the onset of conversion and became the rationale for their belief that there was nowhere else to go but New Hope. Brian had been seriously involved with a man during college, and he spoke warmly of their long-term relationship. Even though during the time they were involved he had left the Assemblies of God church of his childhood and embraced being gay, he felt a constant and nagging sense that something was missing. "So, I had a very fulfilling, completely faithful, monogamous relationship with Ted. I really loved him. Everything about it was great, but I felt that I had sacrificed my relationship with God in order to have it. And it wasn't just something that was in my head. It was in my soul." On a trip to Ecuador, Brian had a spiritual breakdown in which he realized he could no longer continue in his relationship because he felt torn from God. He believed that God was calling to him when he met a Christian woman while traveling who urged him to go back to the church as the solution for his feelings of pain. Upon returning to California, he initiated the painful process of breaking up with Ted and began seeing Joe Dallas, an ex-gay therapist who is a major figure in the ex-gay movement. Despite the counseling, he missed Ted, and to stave off loneliness and frustration, he frequently cruised for sex online and in the park near his home. In his testimony, he defined one particular cruising experience as the turning point that finally led him to New Hope, brought on by the collision of his personal and religious lives. "I went to this cruise area where I had been probably two hundred times before. I was driving around this area and again, something broke, snapped within me. I can remember just sitting on my motorcycle just crying, bawling, loud, in the middle of this cruise area, just crying. I remember thinking, you don't care about me; nobody here really cares about me." As he sat on the motorcycle sobbing, a few people inquired if he needed help, but he immediately roared off, mortified that he had broken down publicly, and determined that he needed more than weekly sessions with Joe Dallas.

Another common thread in the testimonies involved a point of crisis where the men were no longer able to conceal their sexual identities and live as Christians because of shameful public revelations or scandals. Many used the language of recovery, defining these moments as "hitting bottom." "Desperate people. We look for desperate people," Anita explained. Drew had completed the program three years earlier. He grew up in a small rural town in Denmark where there was little anonymity. He occasionally met other men in public parks and restrooms for sex, sometimes traveling to distant towns to avoid detection. One time, the local police initiated a raid to catch men engaging in public sex, and his local paper published his name as one of twenty men arrested for lewd conduct. The humiliation of having this information broadcast to his small town, family, and neighbors was unbearable, and soon after he bought a ticket to the United States and headed for New Hope. "I think this was the one thing in my life I would not want to happen," he explained. "It was totally devastating for me. I remember one night just saying, 'Whatever it takes, I don't want to have this lifestyle.'" Like Drew, Hank was led to New Hope by public revelations of his relationship with another man. Hank battled a pervasive sense of guilt about this relationship that had never dissipated, and while he was working on a military base, the relationship became public. "People started harassing me and making jokes and snide comments. It became common knowledge that I was gay. I was trapped. I couldn't control my behavior. It brought me to a place of a physical, emotional, spiritual breakdown." Drew and Hank could point to one traumatic event in which their own shame and guilt about their sexuality became insupportable. Anita described it this way: "Those who have sinned and suffered the most love the Lord more because they need him more."

Hank, Brian, and Drew believed that their moments of spiritual crisis were induced by God in order to call to the fore their desperate and lost condition. At the Lord's Land, the other men learned to sort out their experiences for the crisis moments, which were examples of God's witness to them. These instances, Frank explained, were God's voice telling them that their lives were empty and that only he could fill and change them. They were necessary steps toward becoming new creations. The notion of being born again implies an appealing "second chance" philosophy by which one's preconversion life of sin and suffering is rendered irrelevant. It paves the way for an entirely new framework for perception and social interaction. The men learn to think about their same-sex feelings and desires as merely sins, not as permanent identities.

As God entered their lives and they became convinced of his presence, the men expressed how it was suddenly clear that their only option was to disavow their homosexuality. The ministry explicitly emphasizes gaining a new ex-gay identity. As part of their "Steps Out of Homosexuality" workbook, the men answer questions like, "Do you feel your new identity is taking form?" "To be a new creation, you must leave the old image behind, is this happening?" The process of religious conversion allows for the possibility of sexual change and transformation. By becoming ex-gay, men at New Hope are able to find a measure of peace with their sexual identities even if they continue to struggle with same-sex desire, attraction, and behavior. The ex-gay label provides a hopeful framework because it places sexuality within the realm of the religious and even supernatural. This removes the bulk of the responsibility from the men themselves and places it in the hands of Jesus. At the end of the Lord's Land retreat, Frank asks the men to read and sign a version of the sinner's prayer. It states, "I have a new life. I have been freed from my sin. Praise you, Jesus! This day I have accepted you."

PRIME TIME

"Deliverance from homosexuality comes from no method, but from a Person," Frank writes in "Steps Out." "It is a by-product of our relationship with Jesus Christ. He alone is our Deliverer. Change is the reward of obedience."[30] The men and women at New Hope are part of a wider evangelical belief system that emphasizes both the divinity and humanity of Jesus rather than creeds or doctrines. They speak of Jesus in experiential terms that place him in their hearts as a friend. Becoming a new creation not only means forging an intimacy with Jesus through prayer, fasting, and other purifying activities but also practicing obedience and submission. Hank told the men at the Lord's Land retreat, "If you are coming into the program to be changed from homosexual to heterosexual, you're probably going to be disappointed. If you're coming here to develop a bond with Jesus, that's what will happen, and out of that change happens." The experiential religious theology of New Hope and Open Door Church asserts that Christianity is Jesus.[31] "Christianity includes church, the Bible, fellowship, but these things are not Christianity. Christianity is Jesus. Jesus must be in your life." Jack, a lanky and earnest twenty-three-year-old from North Dakota, described the way "coming into relationship with Jesus" had begun to transform him. "I would say it was this year of coming into relationship with Jesus that really has been the turning point in my Christian walk. This year it's finally getting into my heart. It's affecting my emotions. I'm crying, which I never used to do. It's amazing how my sexual walk parallels my Christian walk. I'm starting to become more healthy as a Christian as well as a human being, too."

Although they believe in the concept of the Holy Trinity, New Hope members imagine Jesus as the link between humanity and God. Anita explained that because she believes that Jesus was human and divine, she can relate to him as a friend, whereas the idea of God is much more intimidating and inaccessible. She allotted time every morning before her hectic days began when she could spend time alone with Jesus, praying and meditating. She had one area of her small but immaculate apartment, lovingly decorated with plants, where she retreated to be with him. Anita spoke of how trusting Jesus to guide her decisions was the basis of every day. "If I surrender to him each morning, I can trust that he will help me make it through the rest of the day." Every person at New Hope conceded that without Jesus, no one would survive the program, and that his love and grace were unconditional. Curtis sometimes had what he called his "boyfriend days," when he desperately wanted to leave the program and find the perfect man to date. It was always fairly obvious to everyone when this was happening because he would be morose and moody and refuse to take off his Walkman headphones. On one of those days he told me that despite his boyfriend longings, he had to place his faith in God. "No matter how many times I have a boyfriend, that boy will never satisfy me the way God will. How many times I've forsaken God and pushed him away. He's always been there. His grace is so awesome and even now when I screw up, even now when I fall, even now when I sin, he still loves me just as much. And I can never receive that from a person who doesn't know that love." People at New Hope develop an intimacy with Jesus that they perceive as reciprocal and boundless. Hank described the way that faith in his personal relationship with Jesus sustains him as he tried to shed his homosexual identity. "I have to believe that Jesus is in it because if I thought it was just me, then I would have probably given up," he admits. "It's only the belief that he will bless me if I'm here that keeps me going."

The relationship that men and women establish with God or Jesus is not just a reciprocal one of equality, but one of obedience and submission. Frank teaches: "Those who are saved are those who have a RELATIONSHIP with Jesus. They see Jesus as their king, and they obediently serve their king."[32] Submission and obedience to God and religious authority is built into the New Hope program, and Frank informs the men that both virtues are the only road to healing. "Total surrender is saying yes to God every day." Men at New Hope internalize two basic precepts based on biblical readings like Romans 13:1–5: every soul should be subject to those in higher authority, and all authority is from God.[33] Submission to God is also a gendered process. Men and women believe that God has a lordship over their life, and based on their interpretation of the Bible, God's earthly representatives, men, have a similar power. However, submission is not unquestioning obedience to authority but an attitude of the heart. In her work on Women's Aglow Fellowship, R. Marie Griffith describes this as liberation through submission, or the knowledge that a woman is submitting to a man who is also submitting to God.[34] The same idea applies to the new program members and the New Hope leadership. A person is supposed to be so filled and fulfilled by the love of God that submission and obedience do not feel like a sacrifice or imposition, even if this means abstaining from sexual temptations, listening to Hank, and following the New Hope rules. "Desire to serve Him, work for Him, follow Him at all costs. Serving Jesus requires denying self and laying down your life for others. Do not let your bodily desires rule your life," Frank tells new members. However, even disobedience to Jesus is acceptable as long as a person renews his or her faith as a Christian. Having a "boyfriend day" or breaking a rule was permitted as long as it was "offered up" to Jesus and the program leadership. This was the concept of grace that many men found so irresistible. Frank told the assembled at one church meeting, "God has given us free will. If you just surrender and do what God wants, you will change."

In the New Hope members' worldview, God works in their daily lives and speaks to them, overseeing decisions about work, relationships, family, and, most important, sexuality. Unofficially, Curtis's and Drew's other job was to counsel parents, who frequently called seeking advice or help. To prepare them and others who do this work, the ministry runs an informal training called How to Phone Counsel. Anita recommends that counselors pray and consult with God before offering advice, especially in a difficult situation. "Unless someone is standing in the center of the room with a noose around their neck, ready to jump off a chair, there is time to pray," she writes. "Tell the caller, 'Let me pray for you now and then bring this situation before the Lord and see if He will give me some answers for you. Can I call you back in a little while after I hear from the Lord?'"[35] After a few months, Curtis began answering the phones, and he relished the opportunity to avoid his other duties. He would spend hours talking, listening, and dispensing advice to parents with gay children or men deciding whether to visit the program. One day, he eagerly answered the phone but seconds later put down the receiver, looking bewildered. Hoping the call was a prank (a regular occurrence), he explained that the person yelled, "I'm a homosexual! I need help!" and hung up. After that, Curtis's friends in the program who worked elsewhere during the day would preface their calls to the office, "I'm a transsexual and I need help," as one of their favorite practical jokes. "How do I offer that up to the Lord?" he asked Drew.

When it came time for the new men in the program to decide which jobs to accept, praying and talking to God was an imperative part of the process, especially after they returned from Lord's Land and the job search began in earnest. One afternoon, Jack came to the office agonizing over his options. Should he work long hours for a computer start-up company or take a nearby job at a health call center with regular hours? "I need to talk to the big guy," Jack explained to Drew. "I don't think Frank is in his office today," Drew said amiably. "No, I mean the real big guy, up there," Jack replied, raising his eyes skyward. Jack viewed Jesus as both a deity and a friend, occupied and interested in all aspects of his life, whose advice he could seek. After a day of prayer, Jack accepted the position at the health center, and when the computer company ran out of money a few months later, Jack seemed pleased that Jesus had guided him in the right direction. This view of Jesus as an ally, friend, confidante, and guide is a powerful and secure way of living out one's faith, and I heard it over and over. For example, during one conversation with Anita, I told her that I had had a stroke of good luck. My friend could lend me her car for the days I visited the ministry. It had worked out perfectly, because otherwise I would have to catch the bus, which took twice as long. She looked at me and replied, "That isn't luck. That's Jesus."

The men often prefaced answers to my questions with, "I was praying and God told me . . ." When Curtis was returning to New Hope after visiting his family in Canada, the customs official in the Canadian airport almost refused to let him return, but he was certain Jesus intervened to let him through. "I almost didn't want to come back, but Jesus obviously wanted that for me or I'd still be in Canada." Although their trust in his guidance was absolute, they also believed in doing the footwork. Prayer alone wouldn't make a job fall into their laps or get the paperwork done at the office, but knowing Jesus was paying attention and would be there in a clutch is what mattered. The belief that life is not guided by one's own decisions and will but ultimately by a higher force or power has understandable appeal. It alleviates the need to make certain decisions, providing a structure for one's life that leaves nothing ambiguous. In his clipped Scottish accent, Dwight elaborated, "Christianity is saying we can look to God for everything, and if we trust in him, he will guide us. That to me is really exciting, because there are quite a few things that come up, and I don't know if I should do this or not. If I can get guidance from him, it just makes it so much more satisfying to feel I'm doing what he wants." At moments when my research seemed overwhelming and I questioned whether I would ever finish and receive my degree, I caught myself almost envying their faith in Jesus, even if it was impossible for me to share it. Their belief in someone who directs their lives provides a comprehensible vision of the world and locates individual believers safely within that model, even as it flattens and erases nuance and complications.

When Jack revealed that God had instructed him to take the less risky job, I asked how he could actually hear what God was telling him. Jack explained that he did not hear a voice but had a sense after he had decided that it was the job God wanted him to take. Others revealed that they had heard God's voice while praying or meditating. One of the New Hope classes was devoted to the question of how to communicate with God. In response to the question, "Can man hear from God?" Frank tells the men, "We can hear God's voice. Is God's voice always audible? No, but God speaks to us in a variety of different ways."[36] Frank asked the men in the program to describe the ways that God had communicated with them. Some of the responses included a supernatural peace; a word of prophecy given to you; a leader confirming that God has spoken to your heart; a feeling that a sermon was given just for you; a quick jolt to the heart.[37] Frank told them, "The clamor of daily activities drowns out God's voice, but if you go out to be alone with God, you will find that He does want to speak to you. God wants prime time with us."[38]

A few days later, I asked Drew whether he thought Jack took his new job at the health center because it was the one he really wanted, and talking to God was just a way of justifying it. Drew stared at me blankly. There had been a rumor going around the ministry, well meaning but untrue, that I had prayed the sinner's prayer with Anita, accepting Jesus into my heart. "I guess the rumor's definitely not true," Drew said, looking at me. "You just don't get it. Listening to Jesus is a heart thing, not a head thing." I was speaking in a critical and analytical secular language. In the language of New Hope, men and women ask Jesus into their hearts and talk reverently of feeling him working in their lives. In order to maintain their faith in conversion, ex-gay men have to trust Jesus completely. Feelings of desire and attraction for the same sex could linger for the rest of their lives, but the primary motivation to change is Jesus and the fear of losing their personal relationship with him. Hank clearly differentiated between superficial change and real healing, "Change with God is healing, but change without God is just change."

A PRO-GAY THEOLOGY

Despite the belief that a personal relationship with God will heal and transform them, many men realize after a few months or even years that their experiences at New Hope have done nothing to change their sexuality, and they decide to embrace their gay identity. When we met at a restaurant in the San Francisco Centre mall, in downtown San Francisco, Lars, who was in his mid-thirties, was wearing a badge around his neck from his job at an AIDS organization. He described his decision to leave New Hope as prompted by a frustration with the lack of changes in his life from God. "I don't think that what I'm doing is wrong or that my attractions are wrong. If God wanted to take these attractions from me, they'd be gone." He had maintained a personal relationship with God, prayed, and given testimony, but his faith had not induced any sort of sexual change. "I really feel bitter toward God, who has been silent all this time, not giving me the answers I'm looking for. I feel like I gave him every opportunity to heal this one issue, more than most people would be willing to do, and he hasn't done anything by now; maybe it's not that important to him that I'm straight. Maybe he loves and accepts me just the way I am. Maybe I should, too." Lars had participated in the New Hope program a few years before my arrival, and he had his first same-sex experience with another program member during a camping trip. When that occurred, he realized that he needed to try to live as a gay man. Lars had almost formed his own ex-ex-gay community because his roommate, Carl, and his closest friends were men who had also left the New Hope program several years earlier. He also maintained friendships with some of the men who were still at New Hope, like Drew. New Hope had enabled Lars to recognize and accept being gay. This would have been unthinkable while he was working for a Christian missionary organization and dating a woman. The program had been a necessary step in a coming-out process, not the process Frank Worthen envisioned, but a way to recognize that his sexuality was a fundamental part of who he was. He compared his coming out at New Hope to how a teenager feels when first dating, even though he was close to thirty at the time. "It was a passionate, interesting, wild summer of just going on dates with guys and experiencing the whole thing. We were sneaking around doing this, which made it more exciting. Carl and I would go on dates and cover for each other. I felt like I was fifteen years old. I felt like I was experiencing my sexuality for the first time."

Despite living openly as a gay man, Lars still felt unable to reconcile his sexuality with his religious faith. "This has been really difficult in terms of coming out. And I'll be honest; it's still difficult. I felt like by accepting myself as a gay person and exploring my sexuality to date men, I sometimes feel like I can't really choose the faith that I knew and be homosexual. I can have Christianity, I can have faith with my sexuality, but it's a compromised version. It's something very different." Lars felt deep down that he could not experience a full version of Christianity because heterosexuality was God's intent, yet he struggled to reconcile this idea with his own convictions that being a gay man was his fundamental identity. Even if New Hope functions as a site to come to terms with one's sexuality, its effects can be damaging. Lars's upbringing and the program had instilled in him the idea that he would always be estranged from God.

Carl, his roommate, felt differently. If he had residual anger, it was aimed at the ministry's contention that by choosing to live as a gay man, he could no longer have a relationship with God, and the fact that New Hope often disassociates itself from men who have left the program. "The message I felt I received from the program when I was there was one that I have since found to be untrue. Indeed, my relationship with God is burning bright to this very day!" During the holidays, Carl sent Frank a letter explaining that he still loved him, but he had trouble understanding how Frank could believe that he was separate from God because he had accepted his homosexuality. "I have found this place of peace in accepting myself as a gay man and not in leaving it behind. . . . This does not exclude me from my responsibilities to God as far as living a life that is glorifying to him. I pray. I seek God and his will for my life vigorously . . . and yet I am still gay. How do you explain that?" Frank never responded to his letter, although everyone in the office was aware that Carl had sent it, and copies of it circulated via email.

Carl had embraced an identity as a gay man, an identity the ex-gay movement refuses to acknowledge as legitimate, yet he still maintained a close relationship with God. To Frank and the men in the program, this was a total contradiction, because being a Christian meant renouncing homosexuality.

After he left New Hope, Lars began attending a small brick church in San Francisco called Freedom in Christ on Sunday evenings. Freedom in Christ sits along the eastern edge of a sloping park in the Mission District, with views that stretch out over the city and across the bay to the hills of Oakland. On any day, the park is swarming with people: local teenagers from the public high school across the street, undercover police officers, men and women sunbathing, homeless men and women, and dog walkers. Freedom in Christ is similar in style to Open Door Church in its use of expressive praise and worship, hand waving, clapping, and occasional call and response. However, the church is geared toward men and women who are gay evangelical Christians. Founded in 1991, Freedom in Christ states its purpose: to be "a witness to all people in the community regardless of racial, social, sexual, cultural, and other considerations, our primary commitment and mission is to the gay/lesbian communities."[39] The church welcomes Christians who have left the church as well as those who have never experienced a relationship with Jesus Christ and have no church background. It bills itself as a "safe haven" where "healing (physical, mental, emotional, social, and spiritual) can be facilitated through an atmosphere of love and openness and family." Despite Freedom in Christ's place on the other end of the political spectrum, its statement of faith is practically identical to Open Door's: "The Bible is the divinely inspired written Word of God; there is one God in three distinct persons: Father, Son and Holy Spirit; the virgin birth of Jesus happened; His miracles literally took place; Jesus Christ alone is mediator between God and people: sin is universal and salvation is for all who have personal believing faith in Jesus Christ."[40] Pastor Maria Caruana believes that it is possible to be gay and Christian and that evangelicals do not have to join ex-gay ministries as their last resort.

The number of mainline Christian denominations that accept gay people is growing, even while many evangelical and conservative Christian churches are still more likely to uphold the ex-gay message that gays and lesbians must change. Organizations like Affirmation (United Methodists for Lesbian, Gay, Bisexual, and Transgendered [LGBT] Concerns) and the United Church of Christ Coalition for LGBT Concerns are examples of mainline Protestant denominations that defend and welcome gays and lesbians.[41] Yet there are huge fissures even within these denominations, as the ordination of Rev. V. Gene Robinson in 2004 as the first openly gay Episcopal bishop illustrates. Dignity, a pro-gay Catholic organization, was banned from meeting in any Catholic church by the American bishops in the early 1980s and convenes in gay-and-lesbian-affirming churches or community centers. The official Catholic Church doctrine has declared Dignity outside the mainline of the Catholic Church. Yet Father Harvey of Courage still views Dignity as exerting an enormous amount of influence. Many of these denominations continue to decline in membership as independent, nondenominational churches flourish. Nevertheless, LGBT congregations and religious organizations have continued to grow as congregations and as support groups, and recent work like Edward Gray and Scott Thumma's *Gay Religion* has begun to focus on this phenomenon.[42]

If there is a counterpart to the ex-gay movement, it is Evangelicals Concerned (EC), founded in 1971. EC is not a church but an organization dedicated to promoting the idea that conservative evangelicalism and homosexuality are not antithetical. EC has burgeoned into a national organization, with chapters in California as well as in eleven other states. It sponsors Bible study groups, a national conference, and a monthly newsletter with book reviews and news updates on issues related to religion and sexuality. The Bible study is the core of the meetings in EC chapters, but they also function as support groups for men and women who are evangelical and gay. The driving force behind EC is Dr. Ralph Blair, a serious man in his late fifties who runs a thriving psychotherapy practice out of an office on the upper east side of Manhattan. It was difficult not to compare the location and elegance of Blair's office to the haphazard arrangement at New Hope as I sat in the outer room, thumbing through old issues of the *New Yorker*, waiting for my appointment to talk to him. Blair was tall and imposing in a tailored suit, and he spoke with great deliberation about the ex-gay movement and his own work. Like many ex-gay men and women's, his vocation also stemmed directly from his own struggles and experiences as a gay man and an evangelical. He had known he was gay since high school. "During high school and college, I came to a growing understanding of who I was as both gay and Christian and what these two facts meant for my lifestyle. I had committed myself to Christ and it flowed then, that I'd committed myself to either be celibate or to be in a faithful relationship with another guy someday. I then was free to get on with other matters of life, even though I didn't always live up to this."[43] Blair completed his training at Dallas and Westminster Seminaries and worked in campus ministry with InterVarsity Christian Fellowship (IVCF). It was here that his path diverged sharply from that of someone like Frank Worthen. He was ousted from IVCF, which has a very conservative Christian political and social ideology, because he argued openly that a person could integrate Christian faith and responsible homosexuality. After writing a dissertation on homosexuality and counseling, Blair began a job as an assistant professor at City University of New York in 1969. He created the Homosexual Community Counseling Center three years later to provide counseling to gay evangelical men.[44]

On November 2, 1975, Blair met with a nationally prominent evangelical leader who confessed he was gay (he did not divulge this person's identity in our conversations). The leader was determined to found an organization that would formally evangelize to people who were lesbian and gay.[45] They saw this as essential, given their belief that many homosexuals were more concerned with feelings of religious guilt than with legal discrimination or other issues that gay rights organizations were grappling over at the time. Despite some gay-and-lesbian-affirming clergy in liberal churches, evangelical gay Christians had nowhere to turn. Blair left the meeting, and as he walked uptown toward his office, he had his own moment of revelation or crisis. "As I walked north, I thought and prayed about starting a ministry of reconciliation for isolated evangelicals struggling with homosexuality. I remember imagining you who would be coming along in the years ahead, deserving to grow up with better support."[46] He formed Evangelicals Concerned the same year. The name was based on the idea that "ours must be a truly countercultural concern in which there is no disconnection between our sex life and our life in Christ."[47] He held the EC founding meeting during the same week the National Association of Evangelicals was holding its annual conference in Washington, D.C. As Blair passed out his booklet "An Evangelical Look at Homosexuality," Pat Robertson walked through the lobby, snubbing him. The issue of homosexuality was too fraught for the association, which eventually issued a statement asserting that it had no official connection with EC.

From his office in Manhattan, Blair runs five secular groups for gay men that employ psychotherapy and cognitive psychology. Only one of these groups is for religious gay men, which includes a Bible study and a discussion of faith. Most evangelical churches will not sponsor an independent group like EC, and Blair says it is impossible to affiliate with churches because, although the pastor may be supportive, the church membership and laity are not. The evangelicals who speak at EC conferences are generally retired or independently employed—otherwise they risk losing their jobs and the support of their congregations. Similar to the format of Exodus newsletters, the EC newsletter publishes a personal testimony from a man or woman every month. The writer testifies how EC enabled him to reconcile his sexuality and religious beliefs. One man wrote, "EC gave me a vision of healthy, vibrant, reconciled sexuality and spirituality."[48] Blair sends his newsletter to seminaries, colleges, and other religious institutions and contends that EC is well regarded and accepted. Like Frank, he is intent on gaining respectability in the churches. While ex-gay movement leaders assert that churches will not collaborate with them to help people change, Blair argues that there are few pro-gay evangelical churches.

Both EC and the ex-gay movement view their arena of struggle as the church and conservative religious culture rather than the wider political perception of homosexuality and religion. However, Blair has fiercely attacked the ex-gay movement since he debated Guy Charles, a former ex-gay leader who has since renounced ex-gay ministry, on the Barry Farmer radio show in 1976. He publishes anti-ex-gay materials, such as "The Real Changes Taking Place in the Ex-Gay Movement," that argue that ex-gay claims about healing and transformation are deceptive and can be refuted by the testimonies of those who have abandoned ex-gay ministry.[49] Blair meticulously clips and catalogs any news relating to homosexuality, religion, and politics and provides summaries of them as part of the EC newsletter.

Unlike many men I spoke to in the ex-gay movement, Blair contends he never experienced any conflict about being gay and evangelical: "I have long trusted and experienced my relationship with Christ to be on the basis of God's unfathomable love and unconditional grace." He interprets the biblical verses about homosexuality in terms of translation and context. "I have long assumed that it was their ignorance—from within their own personal heterosexual experience and lack of experience of homosexual orientation—that caused heterosexual evangelicals not to see that homosexual orientation is a given."[50] He argues that there is nothing in the Bible that corresponds to homosexuality as we understand it today and that members of the ex-gay movement read contemporary concerns and politics into a text that is removed from its original historical and cultural context.

Blair believes the idea of biological determinism explains homosexuality and frequently writes for the *Independent Gay Forum,* an online journal and community forum that espouses the same viewpoint.[51] He promotes the idea that homosexuality is a genetic and biological condition that is unchangeable, and he maintains that monogamy should be the cornerstone of gay men's experiences, criticizing men and women who do not fit this model. He is intent on combating the ex-gay movement's characterization of all gay males as engaging in rampant promiscuity. He also aims to prove that religious healing does not create homosexual transformation. Only the acceptance of sexuality as fixed will alleviate the religious and sexual struggles of gay men and women. Although EC provides a counter to the ex-gay movement, it has not expanded at the same rate nor received an equivalent amount of publicity.

Blair believes that liberal pro-gay churches are often not theologically rigorous enough for people from conservative Christian backgrounds. He said he disliked attending pro-gay churches because "they don't have much to offer biblically," and he never felt comfortable in a GLBT church like the Metropolitan Community Church (MCC) because he is accustomed to conservative theology, singing, and music. Many of the men and women I met in the ex-gay movement had never heard of EC, but a few had tried MCCs and found them off-putting. Brian, for example, felt that the people he met in the MCC he briefly attended were too focused on justifying being gay. Troy Perry founded the Metropolitan Community Church, a worldwide fellowship of Christian churches with special outreach to the gay, lesbian, bisexual, and transgendered communities, in 1968. Unlike EC, the MCC is now its own denomination, with over forty-four thousand people. It has roughly three hundred churches in seventeen countries across the world. The Metropolitan Community Churches hold to many of the same theological concepts of conservative Christian churches, but members argue that scripture does not condemn "loving, responsible homosexual relationships. . . . Gay men and lesbians should be accepted—just as they are—in Christian churches, and homosexual relationships should be *celebrated and affirmed!*"[52]

There is a significant amount of variation in theology and practice among the individual MCC congregations, despite the Pentecostal heritage of Perry. Depending on the local church and pastor, an MCC could have a Pentecostal, conservative evangelical, Anglican, or New Age focus. In her book on two MCC congregations, Melissa Wilcox argues that the primary purpose of the MCC is identity reconciliation, "to create and sustain a world in which LGBT Christian identity is normative and celebrated."[53] Wilcox shows that, similar to the ex-gay men and women at New Hope, Christians who attend MCCs often frame their choice as living a lie or being true to themselves, but in their case, the MCC is a space to fuse the sexual and religious parts of their lives. Unlike the ex-gay movement, which denies a gay identity, MCC attendees understand their sexuality as essentialist, or innate and immutable. To create an integrated sense of self, the men and women linked their understanding of their sexuality "to an all-embracing non-judgmental image of the divine."[54] Yet she also found a pattern among the MCC congregants: they would attend an MCC for a few years to achieve support for their identities but would then search for a new church that was not primarily GLBT identified once they no longer needed the MCC message of acceptance. In her study, the MCC performs the same kind of identity reconciliation that New Hope provides for some men.

Members of the ex-gay movement and the MCC often debate one another, and the MCC and EC relish the defections of ex-gays to their organizations. A recent prominent deserter from the ex-gay movement is Jeremy Marks, the leader of Courage United Kingdom in London for fourteen years. Over time, Marks slowly shifted his approach from a focus on changing sexual orientation to creating realistic support for gays and lesbians.[55] As a result, Exodus granted him sabbatical leave, and he eventually decided not to return. After years in ex-gay ministry, Marks conceded that despite a relationship with Jesus, his identity did not change. "None of the people we've counseled have converted no matter how much effort and prayer they've put into it. There is much more benefit in the honest view."[56] Marks has not left his wife, but he also grants that his orientation has not changed. He now collaborates with Ralph Blair and Evangelicals Concerned to establish ways for men and women to be gay and Christian.

There are other Christian activists who, while sympathetic to the ex-gay movement, have created organizations to initiate dialogues between gay activists, conservative Christians, ex-gays, and gay-positive Christians. Justice and Respect and Bridges across the Divide are online communities where people respond to each other through what they call "compassionate dialogue." The founding statement for Justice and Respect states, "This project will not seek to adopt any side's political viewpoint, but rather to prayerfully look at the issues and offer reflections and principles so that each one who reads and considers them may reach, prayerfully and thoughtfully, creative alternatives to the caricaturized positions predominant in today's landscape."[57] Tom Cole, director of Reconciliation Ministries, an ex-gay ministry in Detroit, and

Sonia Balcer, an ex-gay woman, write columns about how ex-gays should actively oppose anti-gay violence. To this end, Cole attended a GLSEN (Gay, Lesbian, and Straight Education Network) conference in Ann Arbor entitled Working with Conservative Christians. Cole proclaimed, "[I] stand with GLSEN in my desire to see anti-gay hatred eradicated from the hearts and minds of young people everywhere."[58] Both organizations are striving to create dialogue between pro-gay and ex-gay people, but their respondents are mainly Christians. Given the explicit conservative politicization of Exodus since 2001 around gay marriage and gay rights issues, it is unlikely that Cole's attempts at dialogue will have much impact, even though he continues to serve as a member of the Exodus board of directors.

The attrition rate at New Hope is very high, and despite the emphasis on healing, personal relationships with God, and testimony, the program is still not sufficient for some men. Drew, Hank, and Brian had been associated with New Hope for years, and Curtis, Doug, Ray, Evan, and Jack were determined to finish the program. However, in February 2000, the program received a blow to morale. Tim was a new arrival who had had very little success finding a job or making friends in the program. A small-boned man with dyed blond hair who appeared to be in his late forties, he had a tendency toward exaggeration. He had informed Hank that his thirty-fifth birthday was at the beginning of February, and although no one believed thirty-five was his real age, Hank and the others organized a special dinner with a cake. Everyone sang and made an effort to be congenial. Tim seemed to be in high spirits, and he appeared to bask in the attention. However, two days later he disappeared entirely, without warning anyone. Hank later learned that he had returned to his town in Northern California, but the only explanation anyone received was that the program was too strict. By the end of the year, half of the men who had arrived on New Year's Eve would leave the program, and many were still struggling to find a way to live as Christians and gay men. Tim was the first tangible evidence for many that while becoming ex-gay engenders different forms of religious transformation, the experiences of being gay and Christian may remain unresolvable.

CHAPTER 3

A Refuge from the World

Every night the men at New Hope gather for a communal dinner. The ministry complex is divided into two large apartments by a flimsy wall, with the bedrooms in the back and two large communal living rooms with several fraying sofas, two coffee tables, and chairs in the front. A picture of Jesus clutching a man in a pink T-shirt and jeans dominates one wall, and a detailed schedule for who cooks, shops, and cleans is posted on a whiteboard alongside it. On each side of the apartments, eight to ten men gather around a battered wooden table while the designated cook serves the food. Ray, who has limited culinary skills, has cooked spaghetti and meatballs during my first dinner as a guest. He frantically scoops the pasta and plops some canned peaches on the plate next to it. As we stand around the table, everyone joins hands to pray. Hank says, "Thank you, Lord, for bringing our guest here. Speak to her tonight, Lord; let her know of your presence." Turning to me, he asks, "Can you say a few words?" Surprised and a bit unsure, I stammer, "Thank you for inviting me here and for all your warmth and kindness." Although I did not offer any prayer, no one seems concerned. They are just anxious to eat. During the meal, men share stories from their days at work. Ray supervises adults with Down syndrome at a toy factory, and he talks about how they love to extend the vowels of his name: "Raaaaaaaaay." When someone makes an unkind comment about eating peaches with spaghetti, Ray retorts, "Well, Julia Child was busy tonight." Hank, glaring at Ray, apologizes for the sarcastic quip, since the New Hope rules explicitly forbid "camping," which Frank defines as "the use of gay terms and mannerisms."[1]

Throughout the meal, Hank, whose politics tended to be very conservative, rails against then President Bill Clinton, drowning out any dissenting opinions. Finally, Paul, a slight, soft-spoken man with a lisp that I later learned was a result of a childhood ear injury, quietly but firmly tells him he is being boorish. I had noticed that no one ever defied Hank, and I nervously steel myself for an altercation. To my shock, Hank immediately ceases talking and focuses intently on the remaining peaches on his plate. Before coming to New Hope, Hank and Paul lived together as lovers for eleven years. They owned a house, and Hank was extremely close to Paul's extended family, even working for their family business. Although Paul was deeply in love with Hank, Hank warned him from the beginning that he was unable to remain monogamous. During their relationship, Hank would disappear for days and engage in anonymous sex in rest stops and parks. Both men went through periods of attending church, dropping out and using drugs, and then returning to church, until Hank announced in 1995 that he had decided to try New Hope. Paul was bereft: "As much as it hurt me, when you really love someone you've got to let them go. I helped him pack and loaded up his truck." Paul's life disintegrated, and he became addicted to speed, lost his house and job, and became a prostitute to finance his drug habit.

Hank kept in touch with Paul over the subsequent years, writing regularly about the changes in his life, but Paul swore he would never succumb to what he called the "lies of ex-gay ministry." However, three years later he reached a crisis point, and Paul decided that New Hope was his last resort. He recalled:

I lost the home, our business, lost the military contract of twenty-five years, lost my job. Had to close the house, get rid of our pets. I got very heavy into speed. I became even more addicted to sex. I would trade sex with men for drugs. Sometimes four or five different guys a night to stay wired to do more drugs so I could do more sex so I could do more drugs. God stripped me of everything in those few years. I'm a good worker. I'm a hard worker. I could always take care of myself. Pay my bills, have a good home, very responsible person. But he took away everything I ever stood on within myself. I was still hooked on speed, and I came home one day after another four or five days spin, and I told God I have to give it up.

I started weeping and I cried to God, "God I will not fight you no more. I quit. I can't go on." I went back home and a lot of different situations happened. Over that summer, I made a decision to apply.

After overcoming Frank and Anita's initial reluctance, he was finally accepted to the program in 1999. Hank was already the house leader, but a few weeks before the program began, he had his first sexual fall with another man at a rest stop on his way back from a fishing trip. Hank spent that year at the New Hope community house, a separate building several miles away, where Christian men from the church and men transitioning out of the program live. Frank barred Hank from the program, and Paul began the program somewhat relieved at Hank's absence. Paul had intense nightmares and anxiety attacks his first year, but he had successfully kicked his drug habit and seemed to thrive in the New Hope environment.

Hank returned as house leader as Paul was completing his second year as a leader in training in 2000. Despite his reticence, Paul was a favorite of Anita and Frank, and he forged close friendships with many of the other men, especially Ray. Paul dressed in cowboy boots and flannel shirts with leather vests, and he and Ray lovingly tended the abundance of plants on the porch outside the apartment complex. He admitted to me that he still found Hank attractive—something the ministry leaders knew as well: "I still deal with those issues." However, he was frank about his feelings. "I still love Hank dearly, but not in my twenty-one-year-old eyes. He's a special man, and he's helped me a lot. He softened my heart toward Christianity and God. I don't love him in that way anymore." Inevitably, people compared Paul to Hank, and in his frustration, Paul believed that "God has a twisted sense of humor in keeping us in the program at the same time." Although their situation was difficult and strained at times, Paul felt that New Hope was his last hope, and he refused to quit. "I have nowhere else to go. This is it. If I don't survive here, I'll be dead in a year." Other men echoed Paul's resolve, but no one had ever put it in life-and-death terms. Paul's assertion that he needed the ministry to survive was a much more drastic statement than other men's contentions that ministry was the first place any of them had ever felt they belonged, where others knew who they were and accepted them despite their pasts. Ray called it "a refuge from the world."

Paul, Ray, and other men discover novel forms of religious belonging through the kinship and familial structure of the New Hope program. Even Evan, contrary to his background, eschewed theology in favor of practice. He would often call the New Hope program "living religion," to explain that healing came from day-to-day life in the program, not the classes, workbook, or even church. A live-in ministry like New Hope bases its program on the idea that homosexuals must develop nonerotic same-sex friendships. As I discuss in the next chapter, the program members believe that these friendships and the process of living together communally will fulfill the unmet needs of early childhood and heal their homosexuality. Sexual and religious conversion is inherently a collective process as well as an individual one, based on a person's relationship with Jesus. If the Bible forms the theological basis for prohibitions against homosexuality, the ex-gay program is the place where religious and sexual conversion is practiced. Elements of the program such as Straight Man Nights, the phase structure, the rigorous schedule, and the classes are designed to reinforce an insular ex-gay world, while group activities like sports and camping become collective rituals designed to teach men and women how to be properly masculine and feminine.

In her book *Sex and the Church,* Kathy Rudy criticizes the anti-gay politics of the Christian Right for setting up a heterosexual standard for what constitutes a family. Rudy stresses that "the campaign for family values draws us away from living connected, community-based Christian lives to a more isolated and separated form of living."[2] She argues that the church must provide structures similar to what she finds in gay communities in which people organize their social-sexual lives on a communal and friendship model. "In many of these worlds, allegiance to the entire community is often more vital and meaningful than any particular coupling within that community."[3] New Hope embodies Rudy's idea in that it builds structures for religious belonging in which same-sex friendships become more important than eventual marriage or procreation. The program becomes a sacred place, set apart in time and space from men's previous lives, where they develop a collective consciousness as ex-gays and a sense of religious belonging.

For many men, the most meaningful part about living at New Hope is having the sense that they finally belong somewhere. Darren, a forty-five-year-old man who is now married with three children, completed the program in the 1980s. He recalled, "I just loved it. I had been alone for so long and suddenly I had all these friends. And they were going through the same thing I was." Hank referred to finding a sense of community as a coming-out process after being in the closet. "I always had to hide until I came up here. I think being in the closet is an extremely, extremely stressful thing. Not only do you have to hide, you have to pretend you like something that you don't like. My closet was becoming my coffin. Because when you're in the closet, the only voices you hear are yours and the devil's. I was never able to receive respect or intimacy or friendship from people because I was always hiding. It just about killed me, it really did." He continued, "I didn't feel accepted by the straight world, and I was mostly in religious circles and definitely didn't feel accepted there. It was this nonbelonging, and the gay world was so anti-Christian, I didn't feel like I belonged there either. There was no little niche where I belonged." Describing his feelings after his arrival five years prior, Drew told me, "I felt I was at home. I had that connection with guys for the first time where I was living with them and close to them but not in any sexual way, and that was something I never had ever before." Basic things that other people take for granted in friendships are often highly valued by men who come to New Hope. Dwight had lived alone while working as a surveyor in foreign countries. He eventually became so neurotic and isolated that he forbid people to enter his house for fear of contamination. He joined New Hope in his late thirties, and he now feels his life is healthy and that he can interact normally with people: "I love being with people I can identify with. It is such a haven for me. To be known for who I am—not to have to live that double life anymore with the church. It is very healing. I can't tell you." The men at New Hope expressed a palpable sense of relief upon arriving at a place where secrecy, alienation, and self-hatred are no longer necessary. For many, this is the first time they have been able to overcome alcohol and drug problems, keep a job, maintain accountability, and build stability in their lives.

At the same time they speak of belonging, members of the ex-gay movement perpetuate the idea that the "gay lifestyle" is inherently harmful, empty, promiscuous, and dangerous, and many men in the program assimilate these ideas. The idea of a residential program is to build a site of belonging in opposition to the notion of a gay community while idealizing heterosexual dating and marriage. Yet while the leaders of the ex-gay movement state that heterosexuality and marriage are eventual goals, ex-gay men and women in the program contradict this idea. As part of their queer conversion, they take on an unstable identity—ex-gay—that resists a binary heterosexual or homosexual definition. Contrary to the Christian Right notion of family values, the men and women affiliated with New Hope forge extended ex-gay networks and accountable relationships with other ex-gays, eschewing a privatized notion of marriage and family. Long after they have exited the program, many of their primary relationships are with other ex-gays.

HOMOSEXUAL HOMOSOCIALITY

"The way out of homosexuality is relationships," Frank writes in the "Steps Out" program manual. "Here you will be joining a group of men whose focus is on the life-changing power of Jesus Christ. Together you will become a team, discovering godly relationships with people of the same sex. During your program year, you will no longer have to face the challenges of life alone, unsure, and insecure."[4] The idea that same-sex friendship leads to heterosexuality is predicated on the assumption that most of the men coming to New Hope have no experiences with healthy friendships or relationships. New Hope re-creates a family atmosphere, setting up a kinship network for people estranged from their families or friends: "The program is intended to be a signpost, pointing the way to a better life. Our family atmosphere is designed to help you grow into Christian maturity through exposing the deep, non-sexual roots of homosexuality and providing truths that can help transform the way you relate to others."[5] Although the men might grate on each other's nerves, as the dinner exchange between Hank and Paul attests, the program enables the men to build a commitment to each other through the creation of family bonds.

The residential program is the place where homosocial bonding between ex-gay men occurs as collective "living religion." Scholars have broadly defined homosociality as the bonds between persons of the same sex or the unity of gender sameness in the absence of the other sex. Gender-segregated institutions, like the military and sports teams, are examples of the sites where homosocial bonding occurs. Ostensibly, in these contexts, homosexuality functions as the inverse of homosociality, so the two can never be present at the same time. Men can bond with one another because they are presumed to be heterosexual. In contrast, the New Hope residential program is an attempt to reconstitute and affirm the power of masculinity and heterosexuality where homosexuality is already presumed. Scholarship on homosociality in the United States has tended to focus on men and has linked the emergence of homosocial worlds to crises and panics around masculinity and the social and political power of women at different historical periods.[6] At the turn of the twentieth century, articles like "The Alleged Effeminization of Our American Boys" in 1905 and "The Feminizing of Culture" in 1912 exemplified circulating cultural ideas about the excess of female influence in the three most sacred spheres: home, school, and church. "Step by step women are taking over the field of liberal culture and it is not through the generosity of men that liberal culture has come into the possession of women; they have carried it by storm and have compelled capitulation."[7] All-male worlds emerged as part of an Anglo-American middle-class ideology of strenuous masculinity and out of a certain nostalgia for a romantic notion of the frontier past as urban life came to dominate work and family organization.[8]

The theories behind residential living at New Hope are part of this longer trajectory of male homosociality, and the program emphasizes that male bonding in sports and outdoor activities will reaffirm masculine gender identity and resolve the unmet needs of early childhood that New Hope leaders believe caused members' homosexuality in the first place. The men at New Hope are not encouraged to form female friendships but to build them with other men in the homosocial context of the residential program. The problem with the homosocial model is that one heals homosexuality through relationships with people to whom one could potentially be attracted. This means that the leaders are careful to discourage same-sex desire. Reasons for dismissal from the program include "sexual misconduct, sexual activity with other program members, leading others astray, drug and alcohol problems, disrespect toward leadership, unpaid rent and an uncooperative or unteachable spirit."[9] Hank is usually the one who mediates problems of sexual attraction or sexual falls, but as his own fall after the fishing trip demonstrates, he is also not immune. When a program member has strayed or had a sexual fall, that member must confess his sin to the house leader and then to the rest of the men. Unwillingness to share these sexual falls with the group is anathema to the program. If the sin is recurrent and every avenue of help has been exhausted, the person is expelled from the program.

STEPS OUT: THE RESIDENTIAL PROGRAM

Part of belonging at New Hope means adhering to a rigid structure and perpetual surveillance. Idleness and free time are discouraged, and the schedule can be grueling. The men are encouraged to be accountable for others' behavior and to report any indiscretions in weekly house meetings. For men who hid their homosexuality as children and later as Christian adults, the community accountability structure is essential. "I saw the correlation between having accountability and acting out sexually," Drew explains. "It was more the relationship with other people that was nonsexual where the healing was coming from. I didn't have this drive to go out and find men to have sex with." In this way, the men at New Hope learn to belong to the culture of the ministry. Although some refer to being in the program as "doing time" and complain about the isolation and rigorous schedule, for many it is the day-to-day interactions with roommates, with Jesus, and with other people that make the program appealing.

New Hope reproduces itself because a few men who complete the one-year program stay on for another year as leaders in training. After a second year, Frank may choose these men as official house leaders. Hank, who had been at New Hope for over seven years, was often referred to as "our model of masculinity." His gruff attitude and background in the army enhanced his reputation. Yet Hank would become highly emotional at the slightest provocation, and he was sympathetic to the men in the program, who were dealing with everything from homesickness to sexual temptation. Still, his appearance had earned him the name "Mountain Man" from Curtis, who was very clothes conscious and tended to be severe about the fashion choices of other men in the program. Hank had great authority in house matters as the second in charge. His responsibilities ranged from monitoring the progress of each man in the program to determining whether a video they watched was sufficiently Christian. Despite his strictness, he still managed to maintain a sense of humor about his more mundane duties, like keeping the kitchen supplied with dishes and food. Tupperware disappeared from the house at an alarming rate, and Hank was convinced the men brought the containers to work where they forgot them. One afternoon I found him gleefully writing "Ex-Gay Ministry" in large black letters on every item in the house. "Let's see who brings them to work then," he said, laughing.

House leaders mediate between the men and Frank within the New Hope hierarchy. Sam, a quiet and sensitive man from Massachusetts in his late thirties, and Scott, also in his thirties, acted as the assistant house leaders in the chain of command. Sam and Scott had been affiliated with the program for over two years and were each responsible for half of the men in the program. Drew and Dwight made up the rest of the leadership team. Although house leaders act as disciplinarians, counselors, and friends, they are not licensed therapists. Their skill resides primarily in their experience of the same sexual conflict as the men at New Hope and their completion of the program. Personal experience is the prerequisite for a position of authority. The stress of living in such close proximity to other men and feeling responsible for them can become overwhelming.

Hank's predecessor left after five years to live as a gay man, and it can be disappointing and even devastating for everyone when a man leaves the program unexpectedly, as Tim did in February.

A REFUGE FROM THE WORLD

At New Hope, men work all day at various jobs in the surrounding area. When they return from work and finish dinner, they sing and pray together in an adjoining room as part of praise and worship. Scott, who possesses a clear and rousing voice, usually leads the chorus. He attended Jerry Falwell's Liberty University in Lynchburg, Virginia, and traveled all over the world with Falwell as a member of his choir before admitting he was gay. Scott has been affiliated with the New Hope program for three years and has an inexhaustible store of self-deprecating jokes. New Hope manages to have skilled musicians like Scott almost every year, and that year there were two philharmonic-level violinists in the program at the same time. When new members come to the program, Frank expects each man to become part of the New Hope men's choir and perform at church. Singing is one of the only musical outlets, because secular music (other than classical) is not permitted in the house. In addition, the men can only watch videos that are G or PG, and they are encouraged to rent Christian videos from the local Christian bookstore. They cannot use the Internet because of the availability of pornography, chat rooms, and other places to meet men. The reason for these restrictions is Frank's inherent distrust of the influence of popular culture as a potential "stumbler," a slippery slope that might lead to a sexual fall. Frank believes that television and radio can contaminate the purity of mind they are attempting to achieve and can even have potentially satanic influences. He writes, "Our desire is that the live-in program be a refuge from the world."[10] Anita also speaks openly about avoiding television because she fears that even images of couples kissing might incite her own impure thoughts.

On Monday and Thursday nights, everyone participates in devotions where they are supposed to spend time with God by praying, studying the Bible, or journaling. Frank considers this period of absolute silence essential for having a life in Christ. Next, there is a two-hour class taught by Frank or Hank from the four-part "Steps Out of Homosexuality" workbook. The classes range in subject matter and include prayer, personal sharing, and discussion. They cover addiction, theology, and theories about the origins of homosexuality, masculinity, dating, and the "gay lifestyle." Each section contains numerous Bible verses that relate to each topic. On Tuesdays the men attend smaller Bible study groups lead by house leaders to build closer bonds. They bring accountability sheets to the Bible study meetings, and if anything forbidden has transpired—acting out, looking at pornography, phone sex—the men discuss it and later share it with the rest of program. Curtis and Jack also attend the meetings and social events of a Christian youth discipleship house sponsored by Open Door. Most of the men at New Hope are in their thirties or older, and Curtis and Jack, both in their early twenties, find the youth group to be a welcome reprieve.

On Wednesdays, there is a house meeting where people can air grievances, relate the worst transgressions from their accountability sheets, and discuss practical matters of running the house. These meetings can last for hours if something significant has occurred. On alternate Wednesdays, the men join together for suite prayer or roommate prayer. The rooms in the house are organized like a college dormitory: two or three men share a small room with bunk beds. Ray has decorated his room with pictures of wolves, his favorite animal, while Hank keeps his room practically bare. At group prayer, the men tell their suite-mates what they need prayer for, and the others commence praying. At one point, Curtis admitted to his three suite members that he was homesick and felt like he wanted to leave the program. Knowing this, Jack and other suite members prayed specifically for him that week. Later, when he developed a crush on a young man he met at the 2000 annual Exodus conference, the group prayed for weeks.

Frank still leads a drop-in group on Friday nights for men who are struggling with homosexuality or sexual addictions but will not commit to a residential program. This is a tradition that extends back to the 1970s when he first began the Love in Action program. The New Hope leaders grudgingly take turns hosting this group, but Frank keeps the drop-in independent from the residential program because he believes that outsiders also attend drop-in to "cruise." Although he never skips a week, even Frank is skeptical about the group's utility. One day he came into the office searching for a replacement for a broken lamp in the drop-in meeting room. With his typical drollness he commented, "They'll have too much fun if it's dark at the meeting." Even after Drew scolded him, Frank continued to repeat the joke while chuckling. When the television program *Will and Grace* aired a spoof about ex-gay ministries in August 2000, Frank wrote several letters to NBC in protest. The men were not allowed to watch it on their television, but they nonetheless avidly debated its implications. The most amusing part of the show occurred when the ex-gay leader at a group meeting says, "Whoever thinks this is just a gay pick-up group can leave right now," and on the show, everyone jumps up and exits. Frank believes the show created a farce out of his real concerns for the drop-in group even while he maintains the ability to joke about it.

On Saturday mornings, the men complete stewardships, which entail cleaning the house or surrounding area. In the afternoon they have a group outing, and during the year, the men went on dozens of excursions. Every Saturday afternoon, two or three men load gigantic bags of potato chips and other bulk foods into the two New Hope vans, and as soon as they finish, everyone clambers in, and they drive off for the night. Frank treats the men in the program like part of an extended family and often acts as if he is a proud father. Drew says, "Frank just loves to get the guys in the van and go places." Although Curtis goes reluctantly, preferring the shops in the San Rafael mall to the forest, many of the other men relish the hiking and camping. However, even the outdoors is not a refuge from the world. On one previous camping trip, Drew told me, the New Hope men inadvertently set up camp alongside a group from a Bay Area gay and lesbian outdoor club.

The weekends were also dedicated to church, and attendance at Sunday services at Open Door is mandatory regardless of a person's religious background. After a few months, men were required to stack chairs, usher, or serve coffee. Drew and other men at New Hope frequently assisted Maureen, a quadriplegic woman at the church, by physically carrying her to services and around town. Despite her inability to use her hands, she had written articles for the New Hope newsletter for twelve years, typing with her mouth. She was lively and sharp-tongued, and many of her articles concerned the problems women have in maintaining friendships with ex-gay men. After hearing Hank's testimony at Friends and Family Weekend, she joked, "How many more of these do we have to hear?" Many years earlier, she had fallen in love with a man at Love in Action who cruelly told her no one would ever marry her. In 2001 she moved to Boston to marry a Christian man who was also partially paralyzed. Drew and other men from the ministry accompanied her.

To be accepted into the New Hope program, men must first spend a weekend visiting the San Rafael site. This is an initial screening process so that the house leaders can determine if the person's intentions are genuine, and the applicant can witness how the program works on a day-to-day basis. Afterward, an applicant pays $20 to fill out an extremely detailed and lengthy application form. There is a section entitled "spiritual information" in addition to the standard personal data, where applicants must answer whether they have been born again and what being born again means for them.[11] They must also provide a list of the churches they have attended and discuss their level of church involvement. The next part asks whether the applicant or his parents, friends, grandparents, or spouse have been involved in what they call "occult practices," such as astral projection, astrology, Eastern religions, hypnosis, magic, metaphysical healing, numerology, palm reading, psychic phenomena, reincarnation, Satanism, séances, witchcraft, or yoga. There is a chart where the applicant can pencil in "P" for past involvement or "C" for current.

In the section "Homosexual Issues," the application asks whether the person has been sexually involved with people of the same sex and the dates of the encounters. "Approximately how often do you engage in sexual sin with another person?"[12] The application also includes a comprehensive list of sexual activities that the person can check off, including pornography, compulsive masturbation, voyeurism, mutual masturbation, heterosexual sex, exhibitionism, sadomasochism, bestiality, prostitution, pedophilia, long-term relationships, urolagnia/coprophilia, drag/cross-dressing, telephone sex, and anonymous sex. The applicant checks off who these encounters have occurred with: unknown people, non-Christians, people already known, family members, and Christians. "Would it make a difference if someone had committed mutual masturbation with a Christian versus a non-Christian?" I ask Drew. He responds that the idea is to have as thorough a sexual history of that person as possible and that the ministry operates under the premise that the more questions asked, the better. If the applicant was sexually abused or molested, he is supposed to list the dates and by whom. Finally, the applicant must provide three spiritual and three practical reasons why he wants to overcome his homosexual desires.

There is also a biographical writing requirement of three to five pages, where men are supposed to include information about their families, past homosexual involvement, salvation experiences, and involvement in a charismatic movement. If accepted, the man will learn to refine this personal history, first at the Lord's Land, and then over the course of the year. No application is complete without the essay and a letter of reference from someone affiliated with a religious organization. International applicants also have to answer questions about living in the

United States and their English-language skills. New Hope has received applications from people in Germany, Ireland, England, Indonesia, and India but often must turn them down because of visa requirements. Drew had to forgo returning to Denmark for three years in order to qualify for a green card and because of the atmosphere regarding immigration after September 11, 2001. The foreign men who do come to the program—including Drew, Dwight, and Curtis—volunteer in the New Hope offices for a small stipend since they are unable to work legally.

Detailed job experience and financial information is also required, and men with a significant amount of debt are not accepted. In 2001, to participate in the program, an applicant had to pay $1200 upfront for a security deposit, program books, and the first month's rent. The monthly fee was $850 to cover the cost of a shared bedroom, ten meals a week, all utilities, phone calls, and household necessities. The program does not have the financial resources to provide scholarships. In order to prove that he can afford the program, the applicant must disclose his financial information and credit history. At the end of the application process, there is a lengthy release of liability form, which explicitly states that the applicant will not sue or try to attach the property of New Hope to any lawsuit. The liability form also makes this caveat: "I am aware that the Steps Out Residential Program is not a substitute for psychiatric treatment, psychotherapy, therapeutic counseling or any other form of therapy, in general or otherwise. I am voluntarily participating in the activities of New Hope with full knowledge of the fact stated herein; and I hereby agree to accept complete responsibility for my own psychological, mental and emotional well being, and any and all risks attendant thereto."[13] New Hope sends rejection letters if it learns that the person applying has mental health issues. The ministry often finds that men accepted into the program suffer from personality disorders and other mental illnesses that it is not equipped to handle. Two men from the 2000 year left after six and eight months because the ministry believed they needed professional care and counseling. One man believed he heard different voices and fantasized about himself as a biblical figure who was destined to save Israel. As the admissions counselor, Drew urges unsuccessful applicants to live in a roommate situation, learn how to relate to other men, establish accountability with their local pastor, and become involved in a singles' group.

New Hope is actually more flexible about rules than Love in Action in Memphis. Applicants to LIA are required to have a full psychological evaluation by the clinical director and to complete several personality tests; a Minnesota Multiphasic Personality Inventory (MMPI-2) with 567 questions; and a Myers-Briggs Type Indicator test. Questions on MMPI-2 are designed to interpret the applicant's personality type. You can answer true/false to statements that range from "Someone has it in for me" to "Evil spirits possess me at times" to "I would like to be a florist."[14] One rainy afternoon, Curtis and I sat at a table in the offices and decided to fill it out, answering true to the questions we found most absurd. By the time we had finished, we were convulsed with laughter. However, the clinical director of the LIA program has a PhD in clinical psychology, and he analyzes and evaluates these tests quite seriously. At an information session about LIA at an Exodus conference, John Smid claimed that the extensive psychological testing enables LIA to determine the full extent of addictive behavior in a person. At the LIA program, there are no doors on the rooms, the men must wear short hair and modest dress, and there are military-style cleanliness checks of the men and living quarters. Hank once told me that with his bare feet, goatee, long hair, and confrontational attitude, he would not have lasted one day at LIA.

At New Hope, some men who need extra preparation elect to enroll in a preprogram that begins in September rather than wait until the program officially begins on December 31. Their first three months overlap with the last three months of the previous year's program, and they have the option of leaving in December. When applicants are accepted, Drew sends an official letter with logistical and spiritual information. Drew warns them that now that they have decided to participate in an ex-gay ministry, their temptations will be greater than ever before. "When you take a stand for Christ you can be sure that Satan isn't happy; it is important that you ask God for protection during these weeks."[15]

DOING TIME

After my first dinner at New Hope, Evan and I sat outside. He was interested in my graduate program and what books I had read in queer theory and gender studies. As we talked, he smoked, and I hardly noticed until Ray yelled from an open window that he was breaking the rules. Evan shouted back, "It doesn't matter. She's a girl." Many men smoke, but the program condemns this practice because Frank and Hank believe that two men sharing a cigarette can be semi-homoerotic and can lead to a sexual fall. There was an incident at the house a few years earlier when two men who were smoking together began kissing.

Because of his refusal to quit smoking and confrontational approach to leadership, Evan often found himself on the receiving end of Hank's ire. New Hope's program manual states that "a positive attitude of humble submission toward authority" is a necessity for progression in the program.[16] Evan often complained that Hank seemed to think he was "God's representative on earth."

New Hope calls its rules "protective parameters" and uses a phase structure to regulate the men. No matter how long a person has been in the program, he is always required to sign in and out, and there is never a time when his whereabouts are unknown. The program closely monitors his time and activities, because men come in to the program with addictive patterns related to pornography, sexual compulsion, relational detachment, and emotional dependencies. The parameters change when it is apparent to Hank, Scott, or Sam that a person can handle new responsibilities and freedoms. The three meet with Frank frequently to evaluate individuals' progress and decide whether they are eligible to move to the next phase. Each man in the program has at least three evaluations throughout the year, where the house leaders explain areas where they see growth and provide suggestions for improvement. For instance, Hank held Evan back in phase two because he arrived at Bible study one night after ingesting a fifth of vodka. Evan was exasperated with his progress, and he resorted to drinking. Other men who did not share in accountability groups or participate openly were also unable to move on to the next phase. Frank writes, "We have consistently seen that those who do well in our program have teachable spirits and willing, obedient hearts. You must be willing to share openly and enter into the group discussions to fully understand and apply the principles being taught."[17]

The phase structure has four periods, generally lasting three months each. If any of the requirements of a particular phase are violated, that person must return to the previous phase for at least one month. During phase one, men in the program are required to travel in groups of three to "promote healthy same-sex bonding while reducing the risk of unhealthy emotional dependencies."[18] The idea is "safety in threes." When a person cannot be alone with another person, he is less likely to have a sexual fall. Men also have a curfew of 10:30 P.M. every night. In phase two, the curfew is extended to 11:30 P.M., and the men can travel in groups of two. They are also allowed to rent movies for the house and receive unmonitored phone calls and visits. During the day, Curtis, Drew, and I could walk up the street to buy sandwiches for lunch because of Drew's status as the office manager, but we were unable to go without Drew until Curtis reached the end of phase two. During phase two, Curtis had halfheartedly attempted to convince Frank and Anita that I counted as a program member, to no avail. If the three months in phase two pass uneventfully and a man is successful in his evaluation, he reaches phase three and can travel alone and receive a weekend away with clearance from leadership. It is only in phase four that the men are permitted to spend a day in San Francisco with another person and a clear itinerary. Although New Hope is only forty minutes away, San Francisco is strictly off-limits, and because they rarely visit, the city, barely visible across the Golden Gate Bridge, has an aura of danger and allure. When Curtis finally met me for a long-awaited shopping excursion in downtown San Francisco at the end of the year, he seemed slightly disappointed. Lessons from the workbook and hearsay had instilled the idea that as soon as a person entered the city, offers of sex and other temptations would abound.

During the first two phases, Hank, Sam, and Scott monitor the men's contact with friends and family outside of the program because New Hope wants men in the program to rely on other ex-gay men for friendships and support. To this end, visits from friends and family are discouraged but still allowed for at least the first three months. The house leaders also approve all incoming and outgoing phone calls, which is almost unnecessary because privacy is impossible with only two phones in the main dining areas for the entire house. Men in the program are also forbidden to have contact with friends who are still "in the lifestyle," or living as gay men. Frank writes, "Influence from friends who are not walking with the Lord can be discouraging and harmful to you."[19] By forcing men to temporarily sever contact with the rest of the people in their lives, New Hope reinforces the boundaries of the world of the ministry.

To head off potential sexual attraction, the "Steps Out" program manual tells men to dress modestly, and it is forbidden to sleep in the nude. The leadership asks people to give up wearing clothes that might "stumble someone else or keep you linked with your past."[20] The program manual provides examples of inappropriate clothing, including "short shorts or tight pants, tank tops, spandex or biker pants, and cut-off or half-shirts."[21] No one can join a health club or gym. The program book also outlaws hair coloring, but Curtis kept his hair meticulously bleached and dyed throughout most of the year. He also provided free weekly haircuts at the house, and he even dyed Jack's hair once. No one reprimanded him or seemed to think anything of it, and Anita teased that having an in-house hairdresser made her feel like someone "rich and famous."

The other area in which New Hope is explicit about rules is with what the program manual calls "the gay image." According to the program manual, "camping (the use of gay terms and mannerisms) is not permitted, neither are gay jokes or innuendos. Your house leaders will ask you to stop any behavior or manner of speech that glorifies the gay image."[22] This explains why Hank reprimanded Ray, a consistent camp-rule violator, at my first house dinner. Frank believes that sarcastic conversations and humor are relics of a man's homosexual past. He urges them to learn "new, Godly ways of communicating." Despite anti-camp regulations, Ray never failed to elicit laughs from everyone, even if he was talking about the miserable childhood he spent in foster homes or the accident that left him with a broken hip, which still gave him trouble. His humor in the face of misery was a means of survival, and his initial difficulty securing employment meant that he would often come to the office during the day to pass the time. Once, when they were reminiscing about the wide variety of jobs they had held, Drew described being an undertaker, "I worked in a cemetery with three hundred men under me." Without missing a beat, Ray replied, "You had three hundred men under you. I never had that many."

The men in the program measured time by phases, and many made allusions to "doing time." While the program emphasizes that the regulations foster close relationships, the rules eventually caused men to feel confined. Curtis especially chafed against the restrictions, and he often equated being at New Hope to being in prison because he was not permitted to go anywhere. Unlike the other men who had jobs elsewhere or lived at the community house, Curtis worked all day at the ministry and strolled across the street for dinner at the house. The only reprieve from the ministry came from walking Anita's scruffy white dog, Corky, up and down the cul-de-sac between the offices and apartment complex, never out of sight of the ministry. He often described his period of being in the program as part of a trial that God had set out for him. Other men also made comparisons to being in prison—"We have to endure for now and soon we'll get out," Sam once explained. By March, Curtis had already begun planning his last day of the program in December, when we would meet in San Francisco. The program restrictions and schedule eventually took their toll in other ways. Many men griped that they had put on weight since the program began because they were sublimating sexual desires into gustatory ones. Curtis grumbled, "All we do here is eat. Everyone has gained ten to fifteen pounds this year." When the weather grew warmer, Drew and Curtis spent their lunch hour power walking around the neighborhood.

By April, Curtis was becoming increasingly upset and finding the protective parameters of the program overly rigid and confining. The youngest man in the house, he had never lived on his own and found the experience demanding. After Sam blamed Curtis for encouraging a flirtation with his roommate, Curtis was practically in tears. The next day he complained of an upset stomach, and when it worsened he checked himself into the hospital. Instead of a hardship, he told me that his week away was a respite from the routines and rules of New Hope. When it came time to return, he was depressed and reluctant to leave the hospital. While hospitalized, Curtis was placed on morphine; the doctor also gave him prescriptions for Vicodin and laxatives. The first day back, Curtis neglected to fill his prescription, and Sam berated him for being irresponsible. Unable to face another day at New Hope, Curtis decided to engineer a way to return to the hospital. He swallowed enough Vicodin to make himself sick and ended up vomiting all night. He claimed he did not want to kill himself, but the idea of another day in the program was unbearable. After he returned to Canada a year later, he characterized that time as "the worst month of my life." His complaint about the program was that he was never alone. The homesickness, rules, emphasis on the group, and lack of privacy became insupportable after awhile.

CRISES IN MASCULINITY

With all its quirks and elaborate phase structure, the program's main purpose is to rebuild masculinity through bonding with others as part of homosexual healing. New Hope's program is based on a model that homosexuality is a conditional response to past hurts and unmet needs from the same-sex parent, and if a boy perceives that he is rejected from his father, he will look to any other man to affirm him. The boy thus develops no sense of his own manhood and seeks masculinity through sexual relationships. Nonsexual relationships forged through homosocial living are the answer to reclaiming lost masculine potential. Frank writes, "the need for affirmation through sex will diminish as we come into right, Godly relationships with others."[23] The men at New Hope read in the "Steps Out" workbook that the lack of models for manhood and masculinity when they were children caused their homosexuality.

New Hope also views lesbians as wounded by men and therefore unable to embrace femininity or womanhood, as I discuss in the next chapter. The ex-gay model characterizes lesbian relationships as controlling, jealous, manipulative, and codependent due to the abuse lesbians have supposedly suffered.

The main proponent of this view is Alan Medinger, head of Regeneration Ministry and a close friend of Frank and Anita. Medinger, now in his late sixties, left his wife twenty years earlier to live with another man but eventually returned, and now they both direct the ministry in Baltimore. His book *Growth into Manhood: Resuming the Journey,* which is geared toward use in ex-gay programs, is a must-read at New Hope. At the Exodus annual conference in 2000, the bookstore sold more than one thousand copies in two days. Medinger believes that a return to traditional gender roles is the cure for homosexuality, and he disapproves of women taking leadership roles in ministry. To function as heterosexual, Medinger argues that a person must have what are conventionally defined male or female attributes. "Healing involves coming to a comfortable acceptance of our own manhood or womanhood," he writes. "We start to feel right about ourselves as men or women, and we rejoice in our manhood or womanhood. . . . What a process of liberation this is, and it goes hand in hand with victory over the behavior."[24] Ex-gay literature views masculinity and femininity as the same across categories of race, cultural context, nationality, and class. For instance, Medinger contrasts masculine and feminine characteristics: "The masculine faces the world: it is oriented to things; it explores; it climbs. Its energy is directed toward the physical: measuring, moving, building, conquering." In opposition, the feminine "looks inward toward feeling, sensing, knowing in the deepest sense. Its energy is directed toward relationships, coming together, nurturing, helping."[25] Even though Medinger acknowledges that men can exhibit some feminine qualities, he writes that men must be predominantly masculine to be heterosexual. Homosexuality is not just "an excess of the feminine but a deficit in the masculine."[26]

According to Medinger, when a person is able to relate to both men and women, their homosexual desires will diminish. "As one becomes comfortable with both men and women, as one feels oneself equal to other men and women, and free to relate to women as a man, and free to relate to men as a woman, the excessive neediness fades away."[27] Medinger employs the argument of biological determinism when it is convenient for explaining gender, a cultural construct, but not when it might support the biological underpinnings of homosexuality.

In a workshop he conducted at the annual Exodus conference in 2000, this one called Recovery and Coming to Terms with the Culture, Medinger reiterated many of the themes in his book: the basis of gender roles is in a person's physical body; gender roles stem from biological and physical characteristics like differences in strength and brain structure in men and women; God created these differences, and therefore men and women should act accordingly. He even cited studies to prove that women's brains are different from those of men and therefore function in a more integrated manner.

During the months that Frank devotes to the concept of masculinity in New Hope classes, the men read a book called *Crisis in Masculinity* written by Leanne Payne, head of Pastoral Care Ministries. Payne believes that homosexuality stems from a wider societal malaise, a crisis in masculinity: "When enough individuals are out of touch with the masculine, a whole society is weakened on every level of existence."[28] She recounts helping a man named Richard with his homosexuality by laying her hands on him in order to have him "yield up those sins and compulsions of which he was most ashamed."[29] Payne teaches that a man like Richard is cut off from his masculinity, but he can partake of Jesus's masculinity and be affirmed in his own through prayer.[30] Payne believes that men must learn to be in union with Jesus in order to recapture their masculine identity. During a visualization exercise, she has men imagine that their masculine bodies are transposed onto the body of Jesus.

Next to Drew's desk is a watercolor painting of a rugged Jesus dressed in jeans, his biceps bursting out of a work shirt. As with the literature on muscular Christianity around the turn of the century that transformed images and ideas about Jesus from a long-haired effeminate man to a robust, muscular, carpenter figure, Payne sees Jesus as a masculine workman and role model.[31] Frank teaches the men at New Hope that "masculinity equals Christ, Christ equals masculinity."[32] During the New Hope classes, men answer questions about their masculinity based on Payne's ideas: "Has your masculinity remained affirmed? Are you able to initiate? Has there been a 'touch deprivation' in your early life? Has this resulted in 'skin-hunger'? Does the 'guilty child within' still control you and keep you from becoming free to express your masculinity?"[33] Even the men's desire to look at pornography is blamed on a lack of masculinity: "It is a vicarious way of seeking and finding masculinity. For someone who has no inner mental picture of himself as a man, it provides such a picture through identification with another."[34] Frank teaches that fathers transmit masculine strength to sons, and this masculine affirmation is what separates a male child from his mother. When a father abdicates his role, the son is left to find that affirmation among his peers, and peers become a second source of rejection. The deprivation of "father-love, father-touch, and father-communication" erupts in compulsions to touch and be touched by other men sexually.[35] Although some men at the ministry like Drew and Hank are skeptical about the books by Payne and Medinger, others have found that they accurately represent their lives. Denny, a former member of the program who now attends seminary school but visits the program, explains, "I fought very hard to fit into the masculine world. . . . It's like my dad put up a 'No Trespassing' sign, and I've waited all my life for him to say the trespassing sign is down. It still hurts. I think for me the core brokenness is basically a broken-hearted kid whose wounds have never been healed. It's overcoming a broken heart of feeling emasculated." Medinger's and Payne's books encourage men in ex-gay programs like New Hope to seek out the sources of emasculation and lack of "father-love" in their lives. Later, they incorporate these examples into their testimonial narrative to explain the causes of their homosexuality.

A MALL OF MASCULINE MEN

One afternoon toward the end of phase two, when Curtis and I were walking back from lunch in downtown San Rafael, a truck stopped alongside us at a red light, and the driver emitted an enormous belch. Curtis turned to me with disgust and said, "And you wonder why I have trouble getting in touch with my own masculinity." Drew and Curtis often questioned me about things that supposedly masculine men did, like sexually harass women. What did men say when they harassed women? Did they yell? Whistle? Drew told us about a married man in the program several years earlier who would lean on the porch railing of the New Hope apartments and yell at women as they walked by. Drew and Curtis joked that to become heterosexual, they would have to learn how to harass women, too. For them, learning to be a man was an elusive process, rife with stereotype and pitfalls, and they were constantly questioning just what this entailed. "What it means to be male has become more confused in our culture, and men are a lot more insecure about it," Evan would say. Medinger's and Payne's work revolves around the idea that there is one way to be a man, and that masculine behavior necessarily connotes manliness, linking a lack of a secure gender identity to being homosexual.

Curtis would often express frustration because he did not exhibit the manly traits that Medinger described. The idea that he could be assertive and confident without enjoying sports was hard for him to accept. One day when he was feeling particularly down, he spoke about how he was never going to enjoy the camping trips on the weekends, and that he would always be more interested in hair and fashion. The only thing he ever felt good at was styling and cutting hair, and he dreamed of returning to Canada to be a hairdresser. We talked about how masculinity was not necessarily what you did, but how you felt about yourself and your self-confidence. There were a thousand other ways to envision masculinity and femininity that Medinger never covered, I told him. A week later, Curtis confided that he had initiated a long talk with Hank after our discussion. "It's in your heart what matters, not whether you're a football player," he explained. Doug, who was close to Curtis, had been a popular football player in high school even while he had his secret boyfriend. He liked to tease that his mere example was enough to help Curtis learn how to be masculine. One night we were discussing playing basketball, a frequent weekend activity for the men. Doug turned to me in front of several men and said sardonically, "Didn't you tell me you were so glad to interview me after having all those vanilla interviews with the wimpy guys who got beat up in P.E.?"

As part of the residential program, men are supposed to have relationships with other men who have similar backgrounds and problems. Once they have gained confidence from this experience, the ministry encourages them to initiate relationships with other Christians who are not struggling with homosexual feelings or behavior. Yet, Curtis would wonder aloud, how was he supposed to meet "masculine men" when he was stuck in the New Hope offices all day? Hanging around with Drew and me did not suffice, and technically, female friendships were against the New Hope rules, although no one seemed to take note. Jack also bemoaned his lack of heterosexual friends, "I wish that we could go to this mall of masculine men and find nonstruggling men, even people who are dealing with regular heterosexual problems." Many ex-gay men express a sense of feeling unequal to straight men, and they are fascinated by how straight men act and think. Some of them almost seemed to view straight men as an altogether different species. At the Exodus conference at Point Loma Nazarene University in 2000, a Christian college perched on a peninsula overlooking the ocean in San Diego, clean-cut students in khakis and button-down shirts served food to the ex-gay conference attendees. The students were unfailingly polite; they were not even allowed to smoke or hold hands with a woman on campus. As we waited in line for lunch one day, Ray stared at them with genuine puzzlement. "You know what I wonder about? I look at those straight guys, and I wonder what they're thinking about all this. I wonder what goes through their minds." There was unmistakable long-ing mixed with envy in his voice.

The demythologizing of heterosexual men is supposed to reveal that ex-gays' same-sex desires stem from envy of what they perceive they lack. Frank teaches, "We search in other men for those characteristics that are unaffirmed in us. We are envious of the traits, abilities, attri-butes of others."[36] Ex-gay psychiatrists and therapists like Joe Dallas write that a homosexual moves from comparison with other men to admiration to envy to eroticized envy to same-sex attraction. If men can eradicate the envy and comparison parts, they will no longer feel attracted to other men. Drew firmly believes that viewing straight men as ordinary people with insecurities and foibles has contributed to his own sense of masculinity. "A lot of it's, you're envious of their mas-culinity, they're better educated than I am, they play sports, all the things I didn't feel I measured up to. So, I'm finding the more I get to know other guys in a more personal way, I don't feel as less of a man."

New Hope's main solution to the need to identify with heterosexual men is called Straight Man Night. Men from Open Door and the sur-rounding area come to New Hope and answer questions about what it means to be heterosexual and masculine. The meetings are designed so that ex-gay men realize that they have common ground with heterosex-ual men. Drew says, "I used to believe that straight men were an entirely different breed from myself. The program helped me see how many sim-ilarities we actually have. We have the same insecurities. It helped me get over this idea that I'm a freak of nature." As part of a "Steps Out" workbook lesson, men pose a series of questions to the straight men vis-itors and write down the straight man's response. Some of the questions include:

Were you ever afraid that you might have homosexual tendencies?
Did you and any of your friends experiment with homosexual sex?

They also ask questions about the straight men's relationships with their fathers, and when they first began to have sexual feelings toward the opposite sex. No one discusses what it is that makes a person "straight," but the criteria usually seems to be marriage. The questions continue,

> What physical aspect of the opposite sex turns you on?
> As a Christian, how do you deal with lust?
> Do you compare your body with other men?
> What limits do you have in showing affection toward other men?

Some of the questions are quite personal:

> How important is the sexual side of marriage?
> To what extend are your sexual needs met?
> Can a man ever fully understand a woman?[37]

The idea that straight men have points of identification with the men at New Hope is a radical idea for many. Dwight explains, "Learning to live with other men has started to heal my emotional needs, and it's helped me start to see men as no big deal, which I think must be a step on the way to healing." At the end of the night, the New Hope men fill out evaluations of the straight male visitor to determine if he should be invited back, and they answer whether they learned anything significant. "There are a lot of things *I* could teach straight men," Curtis griped after the first round of interviews, "like how to dress."

RITUAL MASCULINITY

By focusing on masculinity as achievable through practices and performances, Medinger and the ex-gay movement inadvertently acknowledge that masculinity and femininity are socially constructed rather than innate. The tension between men's performances of masculinity and their innate masculine potential permeates the New Hope program. For Medinger, part of learning to be a man means "doing the things men do."[38] In his book, Medinger writes that when ex-gay men withdrew from playgrounds, ball fields, and tree houses as children, they "withdrew from the very ground of which [their] manhood was to be formed."[39] Medinger urges men to participate in sports as a way to rediscover their masculinity, and at his ministry, men play on a softball team. During Medinger's annual conference workshop, several men asked him insistently, "Do I have to play sports?" When Medinger replied, "Yes," another asked, "Can I just watch them on TV or do I really have to take part?" During the year, the men at New Hope white-water raft, hike, and camp. They play sports every Sunday and often pray before and after the games. The practices of basketball or camping become sacred rituals in the service of developing a new identity. The idea is that if they first recuperate their gender identity through masculine ritual practices like basketball, heterosexuality, masculinity's natural correlation, will soon follow. For many, climbing a mountain or scoring a basket is a transforming religious experience. Scott, who was not physically fit or particularly adept at sports, reminisced about climbing Half Dome in Yosemite National Park. Upon nearly reaching the top, exhausted and out of shape, he collapsed and cried as other hikers streamed past him. The men prayed for him instead of offering physical assistance. They believed that he had to conquer the mountain alone in order to achieve masculine godliness. He described reaching the summit as "A moment of feeling redeemed by Jesus as a man." Each year the men climb the same mountain as a rite of passage.

Although the men acknowledge the fallacy that playing sports will make them masculine, and some are critical of Medinger's rigid concepts of gender roles, they also concede that doing stereotypical masculine activities has been important to them even if it is not causally linked to their homosexuality. In one of our conversations, Brian explained: "If you've grown up always feeling inadequate in that regard, having success playing a team sport and feeling equal to other men is a really important process. That made sense to me—that if you've always felt unvalidated in something, it is important to feel you can go out there and do it." Others have said that playing games they were always afraid of as children eliminates their feelings of not being able to perform without being ridiculed. Some men, like Hank, experience masculine affirmation in their jobs. "One thing that has helped me is my job. I weld, construct, [wire] electrical, patch roofs, tear down walls. There was a time when I would never have been able to do this. It has built my self-confidence, my sense of masculinity."

GAYLAND

Around my birthday, Drew invited me to dinner at New Hope, and after we had finished, the men sang as he carried out a cake decorated with a rainbow flag. Surprised, I asked about the decoration, and he laughed and admitted that because my birthday fell on the weekend of the gay pride parade in San Francisco, there were only rainbow-decorated cakes available at the bakery. Hank asked me if I had ever been to a gay pride parade, and I said I had watched it several times and even marched in the New York City dyke march with friends in 1993. Most of them had never been, and a discussion ensued about gay pride and what took place at the marches. They were astounded that the parade was not just naked men having public sex, which is what they had heard from Frank. Just as the ex-gay movement intrinsically links masculinity and femininity to sexual orientation and preference, so that gay men are weak, passive, and effeminate and lesbians are aggressive and masculine, New Hope creates a monolithic vision of what it means to be a gay man or lesbian. To many men in the program, the gay community is static and bounded, a place where promiscuity, drug use, and general hedonism are rampant. In their conception, only marriage offers an alternative to their loneliness or unhappiness.

Most men at New Hope were never part of a gay community, and most never even self-identified as gay. Their experiences with homosexuality consisted of sexual behavior rather than a cultural, political, or identity affiliation with other gay people. Coming mainly from rural backgrounds and small towns, many had never lived in places where there were large numbers of gay people. Others lived a fairly closeted existence, even though they were in sexual relationships with other men. The lack of connection to a gay community or gay identity was almost universal among the men at New Hope, and it explained why their sense of religious belonging at New Hope was so important and profound. Evan explained how at the religious college he attended the idea that a person could become part of a gay community was inconceivable.

> My freshman year, we had a pastor at the temple, and I went and talked to him and said, "I think I may be gay." This guy was like, "Evan, why do you think you're gay?" He asked if I'd kissed a woman, and I said, "Yeah," and he said, "Well you're not gay. I've known some really hard core cases and you're not like them." There was a gay-lesbian student group on campus and I asked him if I should go to it, and he said, "Why would you do that?"

Doug was one of the few men who had lived in a gay neighborhood and had predominantly gay friends for his entire adult life. He had also participated in AIDS activism. During a fifteen-year span, he lost his three best friends to AIDS, and before each one died, they rededicated themselves to Christianity. Feeling betrayed because their common bond had been their antagonism toward their Christian upbringings, Doug eventually decided that he could no longer cope with his sadness and guilt. He longed for what he calls "the American dream" of children and family, which he felt was impossible with another man. Within a half-hour of alerting friends he was considering an ex-gay ministry, they were at his house and ready to chain him to a door to prevent him from leaving. After three years at New Hope, his political views are the polar opposite of what they were, and he no longer has contact with any of his friends from his previous life.

Doug was an exception. Some men enter the program before they ever experience a same-sex sexual relationship, and many, like Lars and Carl, have their first sexual experience in the program. For Curtis, who had almost no sexual experience with other men, all his knowledge of what it meant to be gay came from information in the "Steps Out" classes and the stories from men in the program. While some men find New Hope a refuge from the world, Curtis learned more about sexuality than he would ever have been exposed to in his hometown. He often referred to New Hope as "gayland," because everything in his life revolved around the issue of his sexuality. "For most guys coming here is like an umbrella or shelter or a safe haven. For me it's opening my eyes to the world. I've learned more about being gay here. With the knowledge I have now, going to a gay bar, I can pick up any guy I want because I know what they will look for." The idea that there are various ways to live as a gay person, just as there are as a heterosexual, is difficult for many of the men to grasp.

One of the reasons for the "success" of men like Hank and Doug is that they had relationships with other men before coming to New Hope. They have been in relationships, have had countless sexual experiences, and have decided they were empty and meaningless. Frank says, "The strange truth about change is that often those who have been the most involved, the most addicted, those who may have cross-dressed or undergone a sex-change operation are the most motivated." Doug, Hank, and Frank also speak of having crises as they neared middle age. They felt that as they grew older, their chances of having a relationship were growing slim. Frank admits that he was "washed up in the gay lifestyle" before he had his conversion experience on the way to the gay bathhouse in 1973. He acknowledges that the circumstances for his being saved were related to his personal situation. "I had been depressed for a long time and I just felt bitter. Some of my friends had committed suicide because their best years were gone, and they didn't want to put up with the bad years. It was a depressing time for me at that time. I was suicidal because it was over for me and it was hard to take. It was hard to adjust to being older." However, Doug and Frank's fear is not unique. Increasingly, scholars have devoted more time and research to the issue of aging for gay men and lesbians.[40] These studies found that many gay men enter recovery and support groups to cope with the social and spiritual problems that accompany aging, but that most do not see becoming saved as a Christian or repudiating their sexuality as the necessary solution. Ex-gay ministries are not the only option for gay men who want to fulfill the need for connectedness to a community in a complex and radically individualized society.

However, in the "Steps Out" workbook, Frank teaches that the only way to have a social world as a gay man or woman is through the bar scene. "For the most part, the gay community surrounds things that aren't really community-building activities. It's dead-end type stuff." The "Steps Out" workbook describes the "gay lifestyle" as revolving around a "ghetto area in an urban environment. Lifestyles may be covert or overt depending on whether the person is out or living a double life."[41] The lessons at New Hope depict neighborhoods like the Castro in San Francisco as hedonistic and completely oriented around sex. Frank writes, "In urban areas, the lifestyle goes on twenty-four hours a day. There is always the desire for the new, exploration, new people, new places. The need for expanded stimulation leads to fetishes, partialisms, S.M. and other forms of sensuality."[42] During a class, Frank asks the men to enumerate the reasons they chose to enter the gay lifestyle. Some of the responses were to fulfill the need for acceptance or belonging, to function socially, to build one's self-esteem, to find one's identity, and to find protection from the attacks of the straight world. When the men did not find belonging, social groups, self-esteem, identity, or protection while living as homosexuals, New Hope became the only alternative.

The ex-gays' lack of involvement in gay communities and the character of their sexual relationships as anonymous or closeted bolster their idea that monogamous or long-term relationships are impossible for gay men. "I always felt like a freak in the gay community because I didn't go to the bars night after night. I wanted a soul mate," Doug explained. The workbook teaches that there is something intrinsic in being gay that prevents men from sustaining long-term relationships, but it rarely discusses the constraints of a homophobic society or the legal restrictions on gay couples. The men at New Hope often argued that lesbians were more likely to have long-term partners because their relationships were about friendship rather than sex, and therefore they were not constantly seeking out new sexual encounters. Curtis took these messages as absolute truth. "The chance of having a guy who is going to stick by me until I'm eighty is slim to none. As much as the gay community pushes that they're normal people who want normal lives, how many relationships in the gay lifestyle stay monogamous? How many can say they've been together for twenty-five years or more? The straight community isn't that wonderful but I can cite more than one example." The notion that it could be positive, healthy, or desirable to be nonmonogamous as a homosexual or heterosexual was unthinkable under New Hope's ideas of family and marriage. Similarly, many men seemed to believe, despite the evidence to the contrary, that once married, people are always faithful and monogamous. The terms of the debate disallowed for the possibility of a nonpathological view of a person who had multiple relationships, and I often found myself falling into the trap of defending a monolithic "gay community" by arguing to men at New Hope that many people have monogamous, long-term relationships.

Hank and Paul's relationship had also disintegrated over the question of monogamy. While Hank refused to be monogamous during their eleven-year relationship, Paul recalled that he would have chosen to be faithful. "I would have enjoyed being faithful. I'll be honest. I fell in love with Hank." When Hank would disappear for days, Paul admits that he would sink into depression and eventually started seeing other men to retaliate. "Many hours I sat there and waited and worried and wondered. After awhile I said, you go do yours and I'll do mine. But to be honest, I would have rather it had been just him." Even men who had left the program and were dating other men felt frustrated by their experiences. Lars seemed disillusioned and jaded. A friend who was part of a long-term couple that he respected had recently made a pass at him. "There are a lot of men in partnerships, and they have other relationships. I don't really want that; I don't want to play that game. I want to meet someone and fall in love. And have the fairy tale. And sometimes I get so frustrated I think if I can't have it with a man, then I'll have it with a woman, damn it." He spoke of feeling like an anomaly in a gay community that he perceived as placing no value on long-term relationships. "I would like to think that a person could be monogamous. It would be great. I'm not sure," Lars said dejectedly. "All the guys that I've known who have been together ten, fifteen years, they have an open relationship, and that's something that I've had trouble with."

Part of the men's notion of gay male relationships as only promiscuous or nonmonogamous stemmed from the experiences of people they knew. Some men who left the program counteracted the repression they experienced at New Hope with extreme promiscuity. Jared, who had

completed the program years earlier, moved to New York and continually had unprotected sex with men. Although he admitted that his greatest fear was contracting the HIV virus, he had unprotected sex with men
he met online and at sex clubs. "I don't know if this is years of repression coming out or the way I'm dealing with the anxiety of not knowing if what I'm doing is right or wrong. I'm not always safe," he
explained. "I've had unprotected sex with guys I know are HIV positive
and that scares me. The most traumatic experience of my life would be
having to tell my mom I'm positive." However, rather than attributing
his behavior to something intrinsic in gay men, he acknowledged how
much the disapproval of his family and the guilt it engendered in him
contributed to his behavior. Speaking of his estranged mother and step-
father, he explained, "The only thing that would make that difference
would be if my parents were to say, 'You know what, Jared, we love and
accept you no matter how you live your life, and you're always welcome in our home.'" He continued, "If I could hear those words from
my parents it might change things. I would be open to a long-term relationship, to embracing that."

Men like Jared and Lars who defined themselves as gay were more
likely to argue that gay male problems with monogamy had more to do
with society and less to do with being gay. Lars cited the lack of social
structure and support that creates difficulties for gay men and women
to stay together. "We can't get married and be recognized by society and
have the full benefits of insurance and whatever else. And because we
don't have that, it's kind of like you're always in a dating relationship. I
blame it on that more than I blame the gay life." Lars was consumed by
fears that he could never find commitment in a gay relationship. "One
of my biggest fears about the gay life is to end up being alone. I would
like to fall in love with a woman and have a family. If I'm honest with
myself, it's because of the social structure we live in." It was a common
theme for all the men that monogamy was the only way they could envision organizing their lives. Part of this stemmed from their religious
ideals, but the idealization of monogamy is not just limited to ex-gays.
Prominent gay men advocate the importance of monogamy and long-
term relationships for gay people as a means of gaining respectability. In
a society where monogamy, marriage, and long-term partnerships are
state sanctioned and rewarded, it was difficult for men at New Hope to
imagine other ways to envision relationships and community. Even as
they found solace in each other, they frequently invoked marriage as a
utopian ideal.

A STEP TOWARD MARRIAGE

Most of the men in the New Hope program say they eventually want to get married, and many in the ex-gay movement consider it to be the final proof that change is possible. In conversations, they were prone to fantasize about marriage as the ultimate panacea and seemed to think that once married, they would have no other problems. Brian expressed these sentiments, "I want to get married. I want a woman to hold in my arms every night when I go to bed. I want to be a protector to her and to fulfill that role. I want to have kids that sit on my lap and call me Dad and kiss me and that I take care of. I want that." Frank and Anita have been married since 1985, when they were set up on a date by Barbara Johnson, the same woman who introduced Frank to the people at Melodyland. In the early 1980s, when Anita realized her son, Randy, was gay, she contacted Love in Action, and the package of testimonies they sent her were the primary motivation for her involvement in ex-gay ministry work. When she moved back to Los Angeles a few years later, she went on a date with Frank to Disneyland. "It wasn't love at first sight, but we grew to love each other." Frank tells a different story: "I knew right away I wanted to marry Anita. I thought, I don't want to lose this person. It was love at first sight, which I don't recommend to anyone. I wouldn't recommend any of the things I've done to other people." Frank had been an ex-gay for eleven years, and he had even been engaged to a woman from Open Door Church who ended up with another woman. Frank recalls, "I was so inept in any kind of relationship with the opposite sex. They were just from another planet. When I was in the gay lifestyle I never related to women at all."

Anita's hesitation faded when she began to sense that that their marriage was a spiritual or even supernatural matter. "I think God told me that this was the man I was going to marry, but I felt like Frank deserved somebody that adored him, not just somebody who obeyed God," she recalled. "I told God that for me to marry Frank he was going to have to put the love there and change the way I felt about him, and he did." After their initial meeting, Open Door Church invited Anita to visit so they could determine if she would be an appropriate match for Frank. The idea of simply dating was irrelevant; the relationship was measured only in its potential for marriage. It is a tradition every Easter for the entire congregation at Open Door to march down the main street of San Rafael holding a cross in procession. "I liked Frank, and I didn't want to mess this up, so I told the woman at Open Door Church, 'Oh, sure,

I'd *love* to parade around town on Easter.'" Despite Anita's initial reservations, she spent a weekend at Open Door, and soon after decided she was meant to be a part of the ministry and church. Frank and Anita became engaged that weekend and married a few months later. Open Door members supplied food and a cake because Frank and Anita had no money, and everyone danced to the praise and worship band.

After sixteen years of marriage, Frank and Anita behave like an affectionate old-married couple. When they discuss the early years of their marriage, Anita tells Frank, "I made you a fun person." At the 2001 Friends and Family Weekend conference, she publicly recounted a story about how Frank wanted them to have children, even though he was fifty-five when they married. Her response was, "As long as you live and don't leave me with a gay teenager to raise." One evening, Anita and Frank invited me to dinner at their favorite Chinese restaurant in Tiburon, a picturesque town on the water in Marin. Anita lovingly fussed over Frank as he ordered, chastising him for choosing spicy food. Afterward we strolled down the streets, window shopping and peering into expensive stores while Frank retrieved the car. Anita sighed as we stood in front of a boutique displaying a blue dress and matching coat. "If only I'd married a rich man, but I didn't. I married a man of God. I'd need to lose some weight before I could wear that anyway." To Frank, marriage is the culmination of the ex-gay experience:

> If you've submitted, the Lord will put you through a period where you don't know who you are. You lose your identity for awhile. Then, finally, your heterosexual identity begins to emerge and you think, I could do that. I could have a relationship. You really want somebody who is going to be yours. You can have it in marriage. To me it just became very desirable to have a lifetime partner. Somebody to share your life with, and it's been just wonderful. It's almost sixteen years. I got everything I ever wanted.

Anita has taken it upon herself to dispel the myths surrounding marriage to the men at New Hope and to caution men about attempting to date women too soon. She is realistic about marriage, and although her relationship with Frank is solid, she does not recommend it for most ex-gay men. To the question, "When am I mature enough to marry?" she answers, "When you do not see marriage as the answer to your homosexual problem. When you rid yourself of the fantasy of marriage and accept the reality. Being willing to pay the cost of marriage and put forth effort to make it work."[43] She teaches a class to the New Hope men called A Step toward Marriage (Formerly Called Dating) on how to relate to women and eventually find a dating relationship after the first year in the program. She advises the men to even avoid using the term "dating" because it conveys commitment and romantic interest: "If you have no romantic interest, then do not imply that one exists through using the wrong terminology."[44] In his book, Medinger advises men to practice some of the traditional male courtesies to women, like opening doors, standing when a woman enters the room, and helping her with her chair when she sits down.[45] Whereas Medinger counsels, "Start to treat her as 'the weaker vessel,' who is deserving of special honor and consideration," Anita is much more egalitarian and blunt.[46] In the past, many women in Open Door Church have misinterpreted the New Hope men's attentions for romantic interest. Anita seemed concerned about imparting this to me early on in my research. "Are you fishing?" she asked one day in the office. "Fishing?" I answered. "Yes, are you interested in dating one of the guys in the program? They seem sweet and sensitive, but they're not attracted to women romantically." I replied that it had never crossed my mind. "Well," said Anita, "if you are interested in any guy at the ministry, I could tell you who would be a good choice." She had never asked about my sexuality, and I often wondered if she thought I was gay or straight. I revealed that I had been dating a man in San Francisco for the past several months. Although I had mentioned it to Drew and Curtis, by the next week my status had traveled through the New Hope gossip hotline. "I hear you've got a boyfriend," Ray said at dinner. "When can we meet him?"

In the past, Christian dating provided a way for ex-gay men to avoid any sexual activity with a woman. Of the women he dated before coming to New Hope, Lars disclosed, "It was a safe thing; because the relationships were Christian and based on Christian principles, premarital sex just wasn't an option. And that was a safety thing for me that protected me, because being with a woman just freaked me out." He describes how the relationships with women alleviated the stress of being gay in a homophobic world. "There was something about the relationship that was comforting. I think it was because it earned the support of family and society and religion and so it made me feel like I was doing something right. Something that was normal and expected. But there was always this yearning to be with a man, and that was powerful." Lars's experience raises the complicated issue of sexual attraction and sex in marriage, which the ex-gay movement has just begun to confront. Medinger writes, "Most male overcomers I have encountered continue to differ from other men in that they do not become sexually stimulated by the sight of a woman's body."[47] He admits, "I don't know the reason why, when so many other changes take place in the man overcoming homosexuality, this one generally doesn't."[48] Many ex-gay men like Darren say they are not attracted to women in general, just their wives. According to Evan, at an Exodus workshop I was not allowed to attend entitled Sex in Marriage, Alan Chambers told the men that it took nine months after his wedding before he was able to consummate the marriage.

Despite their obsession with marriage, most men felt that to have a wife and not experience sexual attraction for her would be intolerable. Curtis was particularly vehement on this point: "I will not live a double life. I would rather be gay than do that because it would be so horrible for the woman. I'd feel so bad for her. That would be so cruel, and that's why I never had a girlfriend because I would never put her through that. I could never pretend I have feelings for her." Many men like Brian believed that although they had never experienced sexual attraction for the opposite sex, marriage would enable them to be attracted to their spouse through mutual love. The societal approval that marriage receives would transform love and respect for their wives into sexual attraction. Even Curtis held out hope, "I may not ever be like that raging heterosexual. But once I get to know my wife more, it becomes what God has intended for a man and a woman. I'll start seeing her differently. I'll start having those feelings for her. That's what I want. That's what is important. I don't have to be attracted to all these women—that's not my definition."

The general idea in the ex-gay movement is that lust in general is destructive, even in a heterosexual context, but that lust for a wife is acceptable. As noted, Alan Medinger concedes in his book that even after marriage, many ex-gay men do not experience sexual arousal from the sight of their wives. "For now, I believe it is practical to assume that the sight of a woman's body will not be a source of sexual stimulation for us. This is the only clearly noticeable difference that I have observed between homosexual overcomers and men whose attractions have always been heterosexual."[49] On the other side, Frank explains the idea of a psychic or sexual response toward women as something godly. "God will bring a correct response to the opposite sex, but He will never, ever lead us into lust."[50] When men ask whether they will ever be attracted to the opposite sex, Worthen tells them that "by the world's standard, no, but by God's standard, yes." However, Anita warns the New Hope men not to discount the element of physical attraction in their choice of a potential spouse. She counsels that there is a physical side to marriage: "Don't rely on promises of physical change, such as, 'I plan to diet.'"[51] Anita warns the men not to try to "remodel" the women they date by buying them clothes or changing their hair. Darren recalls that in the early years of his marriage he constantly fussed over his wife's appearance until she grew incensed. In addition to telling men to make sure they are emotionally, intellectually, and spiritually compatible with a woman, Anita also gives candid sexual advice. In one class, she explained to a wide-eyed audience that men achieve orgasm more easily than women, and for men not to feel pressure to perform because women "are more interested in intimate times of touching, cuddling, verbal communication than orgasm." She writes, "the man who thinks a woman should achieve orgasm by penetration alone is also wrong. Most women must receive their excitation before penetration."[52]

THE BONDAGE OF SELF-PLEASURING

Officially, the ex-gay movement considers masturbation to be a sinful activity. However, the men admitted that everyone in the New Hope program masturbates regularly. Medinger permits men to masturbate as long as they are fantasizing about women: "For most men whose primary sexual attractions are homosexual, the creation of heterosexual fantasies is often such hard work that it does not produce the escape that we associate with lust."[53] As "hard work," masturbation becomes a tool for developing opposite-sex attractions, but Medinger cautions men that masturbation has the capacity to enslave and that a person could "fall into bondage to it."[54] A workshop at the annual conference in 2000 called The Bondage of Self-Pleasuring highlighted this concern. The teachings at New Hope attempt to balance premarital chastity with the arousal of heterosexual desire through masturbation, while acknowledging that masturbation can lead to homosexual fantasies. The accountability sheets that men fill out each week are designed to regulate these illicit fantasies by making them public. According to Medinger, ex-gay men can go beyond what is considered appropriate Christian sexual behavior in dating to see if their level of sexual arousal has changed. He suggests that in addition to kissing and holding hands, ex-gay men should even embrace a woman with full-body contact to see if he feels "a surge of sexual arousal." If not, he should seek further healing before pursuing marriage.

Sexual advice is actually long overdue in ex-gay circles. Women who date or are married to ex-gay men are one of the new groups that ex-gay leaders are attempting to reach at conferences, and Anita allocates counseling time to these women. Nevertheless, wives of ex-gay men are the most neglected subset of the ex-gay movement, and although these women are beginning to speak publicly, there are few testimonies from their perspective. At the 2000 annual conference, Exodus held a workshop called Sex in Marriage for the Wife of a Sexually Broken Struggler, led by John and Wynema Barber, who direct a ministry in Atlanta. Wynema had been shocked to discover that during the fifteen years of their marriage, John had had multiple affairs with men. Now the two of them run a ministry that focuses on sexual compulsions, and he considers himself ex-gay. Wynema dominated the workshop, and at times she seemed to regard John with exasperation.

Almost all of the sixty people gathered at the workshop were women from their mid-twenties to fifties. There were also three young couples wearing wedding bands. After Wynema's testimony, women's hands shot up with questions. One woman asked what to do about the fact that her husband was not sexually attracted to her body. Wynema answered that it was a difficult question, because "He's the mirror from which you reflect your femininity." Another woman from Indiana inquired whether it was her Christian obligation to have sex with her husband, despite the risks of sexually transmitted diseases. "As Christians we feel an obligation to give ourselves to our husband sexually, but we have to protect ourselves. Educate yourselves," Wynema told her. To another query about whether a woman should have sex with her husband if she knows he is having sex with men, Wynema said marriage should not be a reward-and-punishment system, but that Christ will keep a marriage balanced. "God created us to meet those needs that they have." However, Wynema confessed that if she knows her husband has had a sexual fall, she refuses to be sexual with him for a long time. Her anger was palpable: "It used to be that if he wanted to have sex, I would have sex and perform, and it *was* a performance." A younger woman told Wynema that sometimes women want to have sex as well. She wanted to know how she could satisfy her own sexual needs. After a few moments of silence, Wynema told her that masturbation was acceptable as long as she fantasized about her husband, but that the woman really needed to pray to God for guidance. Despite the lack of attention to women's sexuality in the ex-gay movement, there are hundreds of Christian books about women's sexuality and intimacy. One prominent evangelical women's group that emphasizes women's sexuality is Intimate Issues. Their Web site reads, "Do you want to discover the beauty, holiness, and fun of sex as God intended? Do you want hope and healing for your intimate relationship? The Intimacy Ignited Conference breathes the fire of passion into a couple's intimacy through fresh teaching on the Song of Solomon." One satisfied couple who used an Intimate Issues book wrote, "We discovered that God's Word is holy *and* hot . . . filled with invaluable wisdom for our sexual relationship."[55]

Although Alan Medinger and Frank describe sexuality in marriage as godly, the women at the conference workshop testified to a neglected perspective. There is also no material on the experiences of husbands and boyfriends of ex-gay women, no workshop entitled Sex in Marriage for the Husband of a Sexually Broken Struggler. Frank believes that despite the pain wives of ex-gay men experience, these men have a special ability to be husbands because of what they have endured. "Because the ex-gay is somewhat unsure of himself and his ability to handle a marriage, he enters into marriage without the callousness so often found in the 'Macho' man."[56] Frank argues that ex-gay men are extrasensitive to their wives because they have first-hand knowledge of the pain that results from disrupted families, and they make sure their children receive love and affirmation. Anita sometimes dispenses this advice to the women she counsels: "Go find a man who will appreciate you."

THE "EX-GAY GHETTO"

Despite the focus on marriage and dating, most men remain single and affiliated with ex-gay ministries. For them, the friendships and sense of belonging that they discover at New Hope is sufficient. Frank writes that the "gay lifestyle" is insular and limited, but ex-gay life often mirrors his account of gay life. While ex-gay leaders like Frank condemn the gay lifestyle, men and women who complete ex-gay programs often move on to create friendships and social worlds that revolve around their experiences of being ex-gay. The ex-gay movement uses the term "ex-gay ghetto" to describe men and women who remain in ministries and support groups indefinitely. After years in the New Hope program, many are fearful about the next step and choose to stay at New Hope because of the cohesiveness of the program. Often men return to the places they had lived previously but find that applying the lessons of New Hope to a non-Christian world is unrealistic. Some choose to spend another year at the program or live in the New Hope community house nearby, where they have fewer restrictions on their lives. Denny recalls that after he left, "I went through a major depression. When you leave there you almost feel institutionalized, your life is so controlled and regimented, and then you go to having all this free time and not having things or people to fill that time with and you think, How did I cope before?"

At the Exodus 2000 conference, Andy Comiskey, one of the keynote speakers and founder of the Living Waters ex-gay program, addressed the issue of ex-gay "ghettoization." "The ex-gay world is a dead sea surrounded by other ex-gays. There is a deceit that our well-being depends on our ingrown community."[57] He exhorts the men and women to move beyond the ex-gay identity. "We are not a people group, just a group of strugglers. We don't want another false identity. God forbid our gathering become grounds for another false identity." Comiskey urges ex-gays to leave the ministry and create new communities in churches. For Comiskey, ex-gay friendships encourage the gay self, and ex-gay people need "identification with those who don't share [their] vulnerability." The message from Comiskey and other ex-gay leaders who witness people returning year after year to Exodus conferences is that they must assimilate back into society. For many, this can be a forbidding task. After the conference, Hank and Drew discussed Comiskey's message at length. Both Drew and Hank had been at New Hope the longest—for five and seven years, respectively—and they may have been feeling defensive. They feared becoming addicted to the ministry itself, the site that is supposed to help them cure their addictions: "I don't want to be addicted to this ministry, where I can't leave this shelter or this bubble. I think that's a danger that people can get caught up in if they're not careful. I don't think God wanted people to become eternal New Hopers. I think we need to get the healing we need and move on," Drew said.

Toward the end of the year, when men reapply for a second term because they want to become a leader in training or want more time in the program, there is a period of panic and doubt. The leadership team cannot allow everyone to stay, because of limited space and resources. Many become anxious when they feel their time is winding down, and this leads to sexual falls. Suzanne, the leader of Grace ministries, recalls that after two years in the women's residential program in the 1980s, many of the women could not bear to depart. One night she caught Anne Paulk, before she was married, and Jeanette Howard, the house leader, on the verge of having a sexual fall until she intervened. Anne Paulk has publicly told this story to illustrate the difficulties of leaving ex-gay programs. Others have fears about becoming isolated again after finally having relationships and friendships with other men and women. Paul told me, "My fears about leaving here are about going back to the incredible loneliness—that's what drove me so much to what I was doing, I was just very, very lonely." New Hope encourages men to attend the Friday night drop-in group if they still need some accountability. Evan was another person who longed for intimacy with another person but was doubtful about finding it at New Hope or as a gay man. "Then there's trying to find a place of healing in the straight world and not being understood. Not really feeling like I fit. Feeling like I don't belong in the straight world, I don't belong in the gay world. After all these years there's the despair of 'Will it change?', of never finding intimacy, of having a taste of what intimacy would look like and never finding it. Despair of 'Will I ever find it?'" A year after returning home, Curtis wrote in an email, "I don't fit in the straight community at this point and I don't fit in the gay community. I'm getting ridicule from the gays and the straights."

One morning in the middle of the summer, I arrived at New Hope as usual. When I entered the office, a pale and shaken-looking Drew told me that Paul had died the night before. Paul had been in Ohio on a business trip for the hardware company where he worked, and a hotel employee discovered him in his hotel room. I remembered Paul's explanation in his interview, "If this doesn't work out, I'll be dead in a year." He had struggled to cope with living in a residential program with Hank, but he also appeared more confident and hopeful. Recently, he had become a leader in training, mentoring other men, and Frank had urged him to give his personal testimony in public. A few months before, the very thought terrified him, but he was becoming accustomed to the idea. In his interview Paul claimed he no longer harbored any illusions about his same-sex feelings: "I feel within myself that it's something I'm going to be dealing with until the day I die." The official word from Anita and Frank was that he died from a heart attack, but at the request of his family, no autopsy was ever completed. Since coming to New Hope, Paul had suffered from severe anxiety attacks, and I asked Drew whether it was possible that his guilt or shame about a sexual fall or his stress in a tempting situation far from the safety of the ministry had triggered his heart attack. Drew professed that nothing had been found in his hotel room, and he really did not think anything like a sexual fall had occurred. Hank later expressed his belief that Paul's heart was worn out from drugs. The night of his death, Paul had called New Hope from Ohio and asked insistently to speak to Sam, who never received the message.

At his memorial service at Open Door Church a few days later, the congregation sang "Amazing Grace" and held hands across the aisles. Hank sat alone by choice in the middle of the auditorium with empty folding chairs surrounding him. In her tribute, Anita remembered how Paul taught her to be "less religious and more real." A female colleague gave a moving eulogy about his gentleness, his love of gardening, animals, and children. Scott stepped up to speak, and he was the first to mention that Hank and Paul had been lovers and that Paul had struggled with drug addiction and prostitution. As he talked, his voice broke; he started sobbing and was no longer able to continue. Adam, a former member of the program who now plays music for the Open Door band, placed his hands on Scott's shoulders for support, and Scott managed to tell us how much he loved Paul; then he was overwhelmed by crying, and Adam led him away. All the men in the program assembled at the front of the room to sing Paul's favorite song, "Knowing You." Scott, somewhat recovered, led them as they repeated the chorus. "You're my all, you're the best, you're my joy, my righteousness, Jesus." The service concluded with the song, and we slowly filed out to head home.

A few days later, Drew, Curtis, and I went on a walk at lunch. I expressed surprise that the ministry had not closed for a few days after Paul's death and that, except for Scott at the service, people did not appear to be outwardly grieving. I felt confused because public emotionalism and disclosure was usually part of the fabric of everyday life at New Hope, but the day after Paul's death, everything had continued as usual. Anita entered the office, hugged me, and said, "It's awful," but before I could respond, she immediately asked for help with her Palm Pilot. Instead of discussing Paul, Curtis relayed a conversation with a friend from home. Only when Sam visited the office and played a song that reminded him of Paul did anyone mention his death. Perhaps, people were mourning in private or they were concealing their distress in my presence. During the walk, Drew divulged that many of them believed that God had decided it was Paul's time to go, and that comforted them. I wanted explanations for Paul's death, and they felt God was explanation enough. For the men in the program, the rituals of daily life at New Hope provide an antidote for despair and isolation and form the material and religious basis for community. Out of these experiences, they invent new ways of religious belonging to an extended network of people who have experienced the same things. New Hope had kept Paul from prostitution and drugs and provided him with support and friendship, but it may have been that without New Hope, he could not survive. His death came to epitomize the perils of placing so much faith in the New Hope program and the idea that an ex-gay ministry is the only place to experience community that a person cannot imagine another place where he might belong.

CHAPTER 4

Arrested Development

In May 2000, Frank and Drew flew to Chicago to picket the annual conference of the American Psychiatric Association (APA). As they demonstrated, Frank held up a sign that read, "I am no longer gay . . . It's Possible!" The other fifty protesters included Bob Davies, the president of Exodus International, and Mike Haley, a New Hope graduate who works in the youth and sexuality division at Focus on the Family. Mike marched with his wife, Angie. The sign over their baby stroller proclaimed, "My daddy changed . . . Now I exist . . . It's Possible." Members of the ex-gay movement were in Chicago to protest the APA's formal declaration that reparative therapy for homosexuals is unethical. In March of the same year, the APA Board of Trustees issued a position statement that the APA opposes any psychiatric treatment, such as reparative therapy, which is based on the assumption that homosexuality is a mental disorder or that a patient should change his or her homosexual orientation.[1] Frank and Drew were there to assert that this decision violates their right to change and that it increases the risk that ex-gay ministries and ex-gay-supportive therapists could lose their licenses. Frank explained, "Our aim is to move the APA toward reconsidering their stand on therapy for gays with unwanted homosexual feelings. Our stand is that it is not helpful or right to force people to accept the gay lifestyle when it conflicts with their conscience."[2] The refusal of the APA to even reconsider its position on reparative therapy continues to be a source of great frustration for Frank and others who have sought to make Exodus a professional organization for over twenty years.

In somewhat of a twist, in 1973 the annual APA meeting in Honolulu was also rife with protest and interruption. However, the protestors in 1973 were gay activists demanding that homosexuality be removed from the second edition of the APA's *Diagnostic and Statistical Manual of Psychiatric Disorders* (DSM), its official book of mental illnesses. This protest was successful, and after struggling for years with the APA on this issue, gay activists finally forced it to acknowledge that gay men and women could live as well-adjusted individuals. The APA reversed decades of psychological thought and practice that posited homosexuality as a pathological condition and disease. In the intervening twenty-seven years, a shift had occurred in the political and medical landscapes. The activism of gay organizers in 1973 and ex-gays in 2000 illuminates how the medical and scientific professional establishments continue to occupy a significant role in the debate over change, cures, and sexuality.

The ex-gay movement has reconfigured psychological, psychiatric, and sexological models and theories about the origins of homosexuality and lesbianism in the postwar period through its own medical institution, the National Association for the Research and Treatment of Homosexuality (NARTH). NARTH employs psychoanalytic and developmental theory as the basis of reparative therapy to explain how homosexuality arises as a condition due to a distorted sense of gender identity. It argues that homosexuality is a temporary condition or a problem of "arrested development" that can be cured through reparative therapy and gender-affirming ex-gay ministries. The ex-gay movement often deploys these models in opposition to research that argues that homosexuality is biological or even genetic. Since the 1990s, the question of whether homosexuality can be cured, changed, or repressed has hinged on whether it is inborn (biological) or learned (developmental). The ex-gay movement has a stake in these debates, even as men and women in the ministries subvert both models.

Arguments about change have not been confined only to the ex-gay movement but have also been formulated in different ways by a constellation of shifting historical actors. In one arena, there is a long history of research on sexuality, including therapeutic and medical interventions by sexologists, psychiatrists, and psychoanalysts. These disciplines granted medical and scientific sexual theories power and validity. However, medical and scientific discourses were not the final arbiters in the debate around sexual change. Homophile reformers, lesbian feminists, gay rights advocates, and queer activists as well as ex-gays and conservative Christians have formulated their own models of sexuality and change that have interacted with and challenged medical and scientific discourse. They provided their own definitions of sexual change before and after the APA decision as part of a cacophonous public discourse about sexuality, sexual identity, and sexual practices. The ex-gay movement's use of medical/scientific and therapeutic models is refracted through these various discourses, people, and historical moments. This is evident in the way ex-gay men and women have learned to understand their own family histories and the possible causes for their homosexuality.

HOMOSEXUALITY AND THE POSSIBILITY OF CHANGE

In May 2000, when Frank, Drew, and others protested the APA Chicago meeting, Robert Spitzer, a medical doctor from the New York Psychiatric Institute, was also present. Spitzer had been a member of the original Committee on Nomenclature that removed homosexuality from the APA's DSM in 1973. He found himself riveted by the stories of ex-gay men and women who felt that the APA was infringing upon their right to change. Spitzer began listening to the activists' stories, and soon he was meeting with Exodus movement leaders. By the summer of 2000, he had commissioned a study of sexual-orientation change, working directly with Exodus ministry leaders to find potential subjects. When I first met him, he was at the twenty-fifth annual Exodus conference in San Diego, California. I had attended a session called Homosexuality and the Possibility of Change, led by Rob Goetze, the head of Free to Be Me, an ex-gay ministry in Toronto. The room was jammed with approximately seventy men and women, but one-third filed out as soon as the speaker announced this would be a workshop on research studies on change. Goetze espoused two unpopular views. The first, "Just because change is possible doesn't mean it's mandatory; we can't revile those who don't change," was received with some shock. The next, that the ex-gay-commissioned studies on change were flawed, elicited loud guffaws. After he criticized a survey NARTH published as well as a popular book entitled *Homosexuality and the Politics of Truth*, by Jeffrey Satinover, a supportive psychiatrist, several people accused him of being pro-gay. This workshop was not what people had expected, and many felt threatened. Goetze's group had painstakingly sifted through all the major studies and felt that none of them accurately demonstrated change. When an audience member accused Goetze of being disloyal to the ex-gay movement, he replied that his desire was for the ex-gay movement to produce unassailable research. Then one of the men in the audience asked Goetze what he thought of Spitzer's study, and Goetze replied, "Why don't you ask Dr. Spitzer? He's sitting right next to you."

Exodus had paid for Spitzer to come and experience its annual conference as well as to find potential interview subjects. Throughout the day, Spitzer kept referring to himself as their distinguished guest, and the other people in the audience treated him like royalty. Exodus could not believe their windfall: the former champion of the 1973 APA decision was now actively supporting the idea that homosexuals could change. Spitzer was in his seventies, with white flyaway hair and a slight hunch to his shoulders. When I first met him at the conference and introduced myself, he was initially dismissive, but as I told him about my research he grew more interested, asking if the men and women at the ministry liked me. A few minutes later, we bumped into Anita and Curtis, and Spitzer was surprised at my familiarity with them. It was obvious that Spitzer had actually met and talked to very few people in the ex-gay movement. After that, he invited me to join him and the members of JONAH for lunch. Arthur Goldberg and Elaine Berk had come from New Jersey to meet Exodus leaders and attend workshops. Also joining us was a man from the San Francisco area named Derek. Derek was stocky and appeared to be in his twenties, although he later told me he was forty. He was not Jewish and had never been to Israel, but he claimed that he felt like a Jew. He carried a shofar in a sling on his back everywhere he went during the conference.

After lunch, Spitzer talked about his feeling that aside from the ministry and workshop leaders, most of the men and women at the conference were not succeeding in changing their sexuality. He felt that those people who had really experienced some kind of sexual transformation would not be attending an Exodus conference because they would have moved on with their lives. Spitzer and I had just encountered Hank, who was in charge of conference security, and he kept interrupting our conversation to speak into a walkie-talkie. Two men I had never met approached as Hank, Spitzer, and I talked. One of them turned to Hank and said in reference to the other, "Hank, he keeps asking me to tell him if he's pretty." Hank was noticeably irritated. "Men are handsome; women are pretty," he responded gruffly. "Well, I don't care what you think," the other man responded. "I am pretty."

Spitzer appeared slightly baffled by the evangelical style of the five-day conference, which included hundreds of workshops and morning and evening worship services in an auditorium. He found the Christian aspects of the conference and ex-gay movement in general difficult to understand (he is a self-described atheist Jew), but he liked the music and worship style, even calling it seductive. For him, the idea of religious transformation was illogical and without sufficient scientific rigor. "I can't believe a perfectly intelligent person would then start talking God this, God that, God told me," he griped. He supported a psychological model for curing homosexuality, and was certain that homosexuality was tied to a person's gender identity. He claimed his study was driven by his belief that the APA does ex-gays a disservice by not recognizing that some people do change, and he agrees with the conservative Christian idea that all people are innately heterosexual. While he supported gay rights, he believed there was truth to the ex-gay movement's assertions about the emptiness of the "gay lifestyle" and that the APA committed a major error when it legitimated this "lifestyle" in 1973. Spitzer and I attended a workshop later that day entitled Developing a Secure Gender Identity. The man and woman leading it had us join hands as a group and pray for our masculinity or femininity. A few hours beforehand, Spitzer had been lambasting the entire religious process, yet there we were, uncomfortably clasping hands in a circle with everyone else. Not participating would have been strange and awkward among the Christian participants, who were hugging, crying, and sharing intimate feelings.

Spitzer's final study on ex-gay men and women, published in May 2001, attempted to show that men and women actually experience sexual change in behavior and desire.[3] As a result of this study, Spitzer experienced problems with his department at Columbia University. Many of the other psychiatrists and MDs believe it is poorly executed as well as politically suspect. Some presume the study is his bid to replicate the media and professional attention he received after the 1973 decision. When I met him again in the fall of 2000 in New York at an academic conference, it was obvious that he was already somewhat marginalized at Columbia. His musty office was at the end of a hall in a building that evoked all the gothic stereotypes associated with psychiatric treatment. Over lunch, he had admitted to experiencing difficulties in finding respondents for his study, and he had warned ex-gay leaders that if they did not refer more people, he would be unable to write a positive study for them.

Spitzer's study founders on the question of how to measure sexual change and what constitutes sexual orientation. His survey method entailed interviewing someone for thirty minutes over the phone and guiding him or her through a questionnaire. His final sample included 143 men and 57 women, including self-identified Christians and a small percentage of Jewish and Catholic subjects. He based the study on the assumption that as a person's homosexual feelings lessen, their hetero-sexual feelings intensify. Two-thirds of his respondents resided in Cali-fornia, and 80 percent were Caucasian. In order to prove that people experience significant change in terms of fantasy, desire, behavior, and identity, his criteria included only people who had been out of the "gay lifestyle" for five years. Inevitably, Exodus had sent him the names of men and women who direct ministries, which raised questions about how people represent themselves if they feel a responsibility to legiti-mate the ex-gay movement. Spitzer's notion of change also hinged on the idea that subjects would report sexual thoughts and behavior accu-rately and truthfully. Aside from statistical questions about age, sex, race, and religion, the majority of the study asked about the frequency of sexual behavior and desire. Some sample questions included: "In the past year how often did you use pornography? Considering all the things that go into being homosexual such as sexual attraction, fan-tasies, behavior, romantic and emotional intimacy, lifestyle and identity how would you now rate yourself? Do you fantasize about the same sex during masturbation—how often?"[4]

When it came to *why* people wanted to change, the study had fewer questions. Rather than open-ended inquiries, respondents were pre-sented with choices. Seventy-three percent answered that the gay lifestyle was "unsatisfying," a term Spitzer presented on the question-naire. When asked whether "your homosexual relations were emotion-ally painful," only half responded in the affirmative. The other yes-or-no questions asked whether a subject wanted to change because of a belief that homosexuality is "unnatural" or because it conflicted with their religious views. In setting aside the centrality of religious belief, Spitzer ignored a crucial element in the way men and women conceive of their sexuality and the forces—social, cultural, religious, and personal—that drive them to want to change. He neglected to address how it is possi-ble to measure the term "sexual orientation" when it is variously defined over a lifetime.

When Spitzer released his results around the time of the 2001 APA conference in New Orleans, Ariel Shidlo and Michael Schroeder,

New York–based psychologists, also released their own study, arguing that conversion therapy is ineffective and potentially harmful.[5] They had been interviewing men who attempt reparative or conversion therapy for over five years. Their study found that of 202 men who had received therapy to change their sexual orientation, 178 reported that their efforts had failed and that they felt harmed by the attempt to change. In a series of press releases, the National Gay and Lesbian Task Force compared the two studies as "snake oil versus science."[6] Spitzer issued a public press release in the *Wall Street Journal* on May 23, 2001. He acknowledged that complete change was uncommon and wrote that no one should use his study to justify a denial of civil rights to homosexuals or as support for coercive treatment.[7]

Despite Spitzer's personal views on homosexuality, he pointed out that a person's sexuality can fluctuate over time. He wrote in the editorial, "The assumption I am now challenging is this: that every desire for change in sexual orientation is always the result of societal pressure and never the product of a rational, self-directed goal."[8] Yet can anyone separate a person's desire to change from the religious, cultural, and political environment in which they live? Spitzer divorced the results of his study from its wider political implications, making an argument that science is separate from its social context. He also believed that the ex-gay movement was not politically invested in proving that change occurs. Regardless of the efforts of Spitzer or the ex-gay movement, the APA has not reversed its stance on reparative therapy. In 2000, it strongly aligned itself against conversion therapy. "Recent publicized efforts to re-pathologize homosexuality by claiming that it can be cured are often guided not by rigorous scientific or psychiatric research, but sometimes by religious and political forces opposed to full civil rights for gay men and lesbians. . . . In the last four decades 'reparative' therapists have not produced any rigorous scientific research to substantiate their claims of cure."[9]

Spitzer's study is emblematic of mainstream debates about change and the ex-gay movement, which tend to revolve around proof about whether people change. The leadership of the ex-gay movement embraced Spitzer's work because it provided them with scientific legitimation. However, biological and psychological studies have failed to address the ethical, religious, and political questions of why people choose to change. Spitzer failed to acknowledge that many of his subjects were compelled to join ex-gay ministries or counseling primarily because of the stigma, shame, and guilt imposed on them by their families and religious upbringing. Many ex-gay men and women experience the transformation of their religious and sexual identities as a process of conversion, which cannot be measured by Spitzer's study. Yet some gay rights activists are also invested in medical or scientific studies to prove that gay identity is immutable and unchangeable. In 1986 the psychiatrist Richard Pillard published a study on twins to demonstrate that there was a genetic link for homosexuality.[10] Then in the early 1990s, Simon LeVay, a gay scientist, completed a study that claimed to have found a difference in one area of the brain between gay and straight men.[11] By 1993 Dean Hamer's study, which claimed a direct genetic marker for homosexuality, was broadcast throughout popular media as the discovery of the "gay gene."[12] Many scientists and scholars have criticized these studies for flaws in methodology and results. In each case, it was unclear whether scientists were measuring same-sex desire, sexual orientation, sexual acts, or behavior. The idea that there is a difference between thinking of sexuality in terms of sexual (particularly genital) acts and theorizing sexuality as a deeply ingrained feature of a subject's feelings, self-definition, and social functioning did not enter mainstream debate.

Jennifer Terry writes that we live in a historical moment when the promise of genetics dominates most social and political issues.[13] Many people believe that violence, depression, and even sexuality can be attributed to genes or biology and therefore medicated and treated. The homosexual biological studies of the 1980s and 1990s appeared within this cultural context. Vernon Rosario has noted that if homosexuality is socially and historically constructed, the search for a "gay gene" is the quest for a genetic basis of a sociohistorical construct.[14] It is the claim that homosexuality is inborn that has mobilized liberal gay rights activists since the 1990s. Wary of biological determinist models, queer activists and others have argued that civil rights protection should not be founded on a claim of innateness, naturalness, or immutability. After all, the world has not eradicated racial discrimination just because scientists can argue that race is genetic. Terry writes, "The labeling of any sexual activity or identity as immoral or criminal is a matter of religious, cultural, and legal convention and tradition, not transcendental 'naturalness.'"[15] Perhaps, as others have argued, citizenship, acceptance, and rights should be achieved through social rather than biological means.[16] This was a stance gay liberationists and lesbian feminists advocated in the 1970s as a response to an earlier period when scientists tried to prove that homosexuality was an innate identity.

INVERSION, PATHOLOGY, AND DISORDER

Debates about the psychological and biological basis of homosexuality date to the late nineteenth century, when European sexologists began to write about the invention of a distinct type of person—labeled at different times and by different people as the homosexual, intermediate sex, invert, urning, and third sex.[17] Scholars like Michel Foucault acknowledged that same-sex behavior has existed forever, but their work illustrates that during the late nineteenth century there was a shift from legal and criminal classificatory schemes that used labels like "sodomite" to categorize men by sexual acts to the invention of a distinct homosexual person. The sexologists in this period renamed what had been considered sinful or criminal behaviors as conditions of identity. They were galvanized by the idea that homosexuality or sexual inversion was congenital and therefore a medical condition, arguing that their research was intended to remove the criminal stigma from sexual inversion and treat it within the realm of medicine and science.

However, the category of "homosexual" did not just arise as a result of research carried out by sexologists. Although historians have demonstrated that medical and scientific discourse classified the homosexual/invert/third sex, they have also debated whether the imposition of these discourses was an attempt to control preexisting communities of same-sex men and women.[18] John D'Emilio argues that industrial capitalism created the conditions necessary for the emergence of a homosexual community and identity during the late nineteenth century, and that processes of urbanization created the space for an autonomous personal life for men and women, which had been unimaginable before.[19] The basis for all of these arguments is that homosexuality as a category and identity—describing men and women with erotic interest in others of the same sex—is historically and socially contingent. Although what are now called homosexual practices may have existed for thousands of years, the category and identity "homosexual" has only existed since the late nineteenth century.[20]

The sexologists who researched and classified homosexuality assumed that it was a biological phenomenon. Sexology was premised on the belief that moral character and psychological features were tied to biology. The early sexologists like Karl Ulrichs (1825–95), a lawyer in Germany who coined the concept of the "urning" to describe a masculine man with sexual attractions toward other men, and Magnus Hirschfield (1868–1935), a German-Jewish psychiatrist, both used biological arguments in order to argue that urnings, members of the third sex, homosexuals, and others were not diseased or criminal.[21] They sought to utilize science as a tool to effect social change and were significantly invested in arguing that homosexuality was part of the natural variation of human sexuality because they considered themselves homosexual. Hirschfield, especially, used the concept of the third sex to describe a whole range of sexual intermediate types, like hermaphrodites, androgynes, and transvestites.

Richard von Kraft-Ebbing (1840–1902) also advanced the biological argument for homosexuality. In his work *Psychopathia sexualis: A Clinical Forensic Study,* Kraft-Ebbing included a massive classificatory scheme based on detailed case histories for what he considered all the major sexual perversions. However, Kraft-Ebbing's views on perversion shifted over the course of his lifetime, and he later argued that perversion was a disease rather than a crime, helping to shift the focus from criminality to pathology. His other contribution was to link an insecure gender identity to the homosexual condition.[22] Most explicitly, he coined the term "mannish lesbian" to describe a woman characterized by cross-gender behavior.[23] The case studies collected by Kraft-Ebbing, Hirschfield, and Ulrichs focused only on men, but Havelock Ellis (1859–1939), whose own wife had erotic interest in women, was one of the first sexologists to collect female case studies. Like the sexologists who preceded him, Ellis hoped to supply evidence for the idea that homosexuality was not a crime but a physiological abnormality. He accepted the distinction between acquired and congenital homosexuality, a dichotomy that continues to overshadow the debate about sexuality and change today. The idea that there was a biological basis for homosexuality, and that homosexuals should not be subject to criminalization, united the diverse theories of these sexologists.

Although psychological, psychoanalytic, and psychiatric approaches gained prominence after Freud, they never completely eclipsed the biological approaches, as the recent gay gene studies attest. However, Sigmund Freud's work in *Three Essays on the Theory of Sexuality* shifted research on sexuality and homosexuality from biological determinism toward psychoanalytic and later psychological approaches. Freud characterized homosexuality as a natural feature of human psychosexual existence and asserted that all men and women had homosexual drives and tendencies. He also located the causes of homosexuality in the psyche rather than in anatomical or congenital origins.[24] Homosexuality, according to Freud, was a problem of mental health. Some of his psychoanalytic theories concluded that homosexuality in boys was generated by an intense attachment to the mother during the Oedipal phase, a deep attachment to a father or older male, or competition with siblings for the mother's attention.[25] Based on his concepts of the Oedipal complex, fear of castration, and hatred of the father, he argued that homosexuality was an arrest in development along the road to full heterosexuality. Freud's work still placed heterosexuality as the norm, but he analyzed it in the same way as homosexuality.

Freud opposed isolating homosexuals from the rest of society, and he emphatically stated that homosexuals were not diseased. Adamantly opposed to the criminalization of homosexuality, he also disagreed with the idea of therapeutic treatment to cure it. "To undertake to convert a fully developed homosexual into a heterosexual is not much more promising than to do the reverse, only that for good practical reasons the latter is never attempted."[26] Freud rejected the moralism of therapists and analysts in the United States who viewed homosexuality as an illness.[27] Despite Freud's opinions, after his death many psychoanalysts and psychiatrists in the United States revised his theories to argue that homosexuality should be treated and cured.[28] This became the basis of the APA designation of homosexuality as pathology in the DSM.

Even though psychiatric and psychoanalytic approaches continued to be significant from the 1910s to 1940s in the United States, there were still researchers who focused on biological factors. In the 1940s, scientists in the field of endocrinology theorized that hormones were the chemical agents of masculinity and femininity, and endeavored to explain homosexuality as a result of a hormonal imbalance.[29] Later, in the postwar period, psychiatry popularized human sexual behavior as either healthy or sick.[30] Some of the treatments for homosexuality at this time included the use of electroshock therapy and aversion therapy as well as castrations, hysterectomies, and lobotomies.[31] The political climate mirrored the psychiatric view of homosexuality, and the idea of a "homosexual menace" that imperiled national security reached a crescendo with McCarthyism.[32] Despite the emphasis on repression, World War II released Americans from their homes and into military service and work. Sex segregation in each of these realms aided in the formation of exclusively gay communities, which fostered private and public identities for gay men and lesbians, a reprieve from the stifling political and medical climate surrounding them.

Alfred Kinsey's work moved studies away from biological toward sociological methods. Kinsey focused solely on behavior and defined same-sex experience as "contact resulting in orgasms."[33] Homosexuality was a set of behaviors, not an identity or a psychological or physiological type.[34] With the creation of the "Kinsey scale," he argued that any sexual behavior fell within the normal span of human sexuality, and therefore the idea of a cure was irrelevant. Unlike developmental theories of homosexuality that originated with Freud, Kinsey argued that there was no noteworthy difference between the families of heterosexuals and homosexuals. Although some scientists scorned his work, Kinsey was widely read, and his findings may have helped validate the lives of many gay men and lesbians living during a period when bar raids and police harassment were still part of the grim reality of everyday life.

Whether influenced by Kinsey or not, homophile movements emerged in the United States in the 1950s, like the Mattachine Society in 1951 and Daughters of Bilitis (DOB) in 1955.[35] Founded by Harry Hay, a communist and leftist radical, the early Mattachine Society emphasized the idea that homosexuals were an oppressed minority and explicitly denounced police harassment in its magazine. Mattachine eventually shifted from a platform of Marxist-influenced radical militancy and the idea of homosexuals as an oppressed minority to one of accommodation and equality through integration into mainstream society.[36] However, these homophile movements would be crucial in later battles against the APA and in the emergence of gay-liberation movements in the 1970s. Future manifestations of these same movements would oppose the idea that homosexuality was biological and that it was a pathology that necessitated therapeutic treatment.

When the American Psychiatric Association formally classified homosexuality as an illness in 1952, the notion that homosexuality could be treated became a touchstone of psychotherapy in the 1950s and 1960s, despite Kinsey's findings. Irving Bieber and Charles Socarides, psychiatrists whose work formed the basis of reparative therapy, championed the idea of homosexuality as a pathology and a developmental mental disorder. In 1962 Bieber published a study that used information about 106 homosexuals and 100 heterosexuals to argue that homosexuality is a result of "highly pathologic" parent-child relationships and early life situations.[37] Bieber's male-centered Oedipal and pre-Oedipal theories of the pathological development of homosexuality argued that homosexuality was a result of traumatic early life experiences. According to Bieber and Socarides, psychoanalysis could cure up to 50 percent of "strongly motivated obligatory homosexuals."[38] Reparative therapy, the idea that therapy can repair early life traumas, became the basis of counseling at the National Association for the Research and Treatment of Homosexuality.

Bieber's and Socarides's psychoanalytic theories were as essentialist as many biological studies. They saw homosexuality as a transhistorical and transcultural phenomenon of specific parent-child dynamics. In this model, psychoanalysis emphasized that sexual orientation was somehow embedded in the body from an early age. Reparative therapy's goal was to rediscover a heterosexuality that was "natural and innate." Both Bieber and Socarides used their findings to argue that a stable, long-term gay relationship was unattainable. They stressed that heterosexuality meant solace and enrichment, while homosexuality only wrought "destruction, mutual defeat, exploitation of the partners and the self, oral-sadistic incorporation, aggressive onslaughts, attempts to alleviate anxiety and pseudo-solution to the aggressive and libidinal urges which dominate and torment the individual."[39] Charles Socarides, himself the father of a gay son,[40] also argued in a series of articles published in the 1960s that homosexuality was a severe illness, accompanied by psychotic manifestations like schizophrenia or manic-depressive mood swings.

According to Socarides, the crucial period of time for the development of this pathology was during the first three years of age, when a male child was supposed to establish an identity separate from his mother. The failure to do so hindered the emergence of a secure gender identity. Therefore, all male homosexuals are characterized by a "feminine identification."[41] Psychologists used these assessments in the early 1970s as rationales for brutal treatments such as aversion therapy.[42] To accomplish aversion therapy's objective of attaching unpleasant feelings to pleasurable stimuli, gay men were given shocks or nausea-inducing pills while viewing pictures of handsome men.

The theories of Bieber and Socarides remained prominent well into the 1970s, when the controversies at the APA meetings erupted. While other practitioners classified homosexuality as a behavioral abnormality, most professionals in the APA agreed that it constituted pathology. However, there were dissenting professional opinions during this time, like that of Evelyn Hooker, a psychologist who was convinced by a gay client to conduct a study of his friends. Her ensuing friendships with gay men and subsequent participation in gay rights struggles provided her with a different perspective than most clinicians. She actually had relationships with gay people, and she made the important argument that homosexuality did not affect the psychological well-being of an individual.[43] Hooker maintained that society should end the stigmatization and exclusion of homosexuals rather than promote treatment. Judd Marmor, a psychiatric practitioner, also joined Hooker in her critique of the APA's view of homosexuality as pathology. Marmor disagreed with Freud's ideas about bisexuality, stressed that homosexuality was the sexual orientation of a minority, and argued that homosexuals constituted a distinct identity group.[44] Finally, Richard Green, a psychiatrist at UCLA, challenged the right of psychiatry to define homosexuality. He wrote an article entitled "Homosexuality as Mental Illness" in which he questioned, "When is a pattern of behavior a life style to be considered by philosophers; when is it a social phenomenon to be considered by jurists or sociologists; and when is it a disease to be considered by physicians or other healers?"[45] Today, Green is the author of a study on "sissy boys" that asserts that American boys suffer from a "sissy boy syndrome," which places them at high risk for becoming homosexual.[46] Despite his earlier sentiments, he now argues that boys should act in "gender normal" ways.

Hooker's findings and her affiliation with the Mattachine Society in addition to the work of Marmor and Green made these researchers natural allies for gay activists opposed to the psychiatric models of pathology. Gay activists contested the idea of pathology in a series of protests in the early 1970s. They attacked not only the APA as an organization but the unassailable status of science in defining who and what was considered deviant or normal. Gay men and women understood quite well the social consequences of being labeled and defined by others. Their dispute with the APA challenged the authority and power of science to classify homosexuality as a disorder.

THE APA DECISION AND ITS DISCONTENTS

Studies like those of Hooker and Marmor spurred on the growing gay rights movement initiated by the Mattachine Society and the Daughters of Bilitis. Not only had the psychiatric profession classified homosexuality as pathological, the state had also criminalized homosexual behavior throughout the twentieth century. As the homophile activist movement grew, many gay men and women condemned the criminal sanctions imposed on homosexual conduct. Homophile activists also contested the therapies many had undergone to cope with being gay. One man recalled that "the few insights I gained during analysis were nothing compared to its overriding message—I was inherently impaired because of my sexual orientation and that if I could not change it, I was doubly a failure."[47] The years 1961–65 signified an increased militancy in the homophile movement on the East Coast. Led by Frank Kameny of the Washington, D.C., Mattachine and galvanized by their participation in the bus boycotts and freedom rides of the civil rights movement, members of the D.C. branch began to address employment discrimination and other issues that the older, more cautious part of the movement had eschewed.[48] ECHO (East Coast Homophile Organization), the Janus Society of Philadelphia, and the New York Mattachine also took a more radical stance against the medical establishment. Kameny declared, "The entire homophile movement is going to stand or fall upon the question of whether homosexuality is a sickness."[49] These activist groups became direct-action oriented while the old guard sought to live discreetly. By 1965, the movement had splintered over whether it should address the individual or the community, whether homosexuality was a sickness, and whether it should be civil rights oriented.

At the same time, the Daughters of Bilitis (DOB) also witnessed increased radicalism through the leadership of Del Martin. DOB had an ambivalent relationship with the feminist movement that was emerging in different incarnations around the country during the mid-1960s. Members of DOB debated whether to organize as part of the feminist movement with groups like the National Organization of Women (NOW) or with the homophile movement.[50] Many saw lesbianism as the embodiment of feminist principles and argued that regardless of the outcome of the homophile movement, women would still be second-class citizens. At the same time, lesbian-feminists who formed diverse groups throughout the United States like Radicallesbians in New York, the Furies in D.C., and Gay Women's Liberation in San Francisco saw their sexual identities as a choice connected to their feminist politics.[51] By the early 1970s, feminists and lesbian-feminists were defying a binary gender system and traditional concepts of masculinity and femininity. Their suspicion regarding and antipathy for biological and psychiatric studies stemmed from their beliefs that women's roles were constructed by society. The idea of the personal as political expressed how power inequities in society were replicated in women's daily experiences. Feminism politicized sexuality and gender in a way that homophile movements did not and situated it within the realities of power inequalities between men and women.

When the Stonewall uprising occurred in 1969, homophile activists had moved beyond the civil rights integrationist approach into what became gay liberation. Unlike the more cautious, assimilationist homophile activist groups like Mattachine and Daughters of Bilitis, the gay liberation movement analyzed structural racism and systematic oppression rather than simply prejudice. Members connected their group to black power, feminism, and third world struggles, incorporating ideas about pride, power, and identity. New groups like the Gay Liberation Front (GLF) employed innovative strategies including guerrilla theater, marches, rioting, and demonstrations in an increased move toward visibility.[52] For these activists, biology was not destiny, and male and female roles were learned, not rooted in biology. Structural forces and homophobia were the sources of oppression for gay men and women rather than genetics.

Given gay-liberation activists' negative experiences with the psychiatric, psychoanalytic, and medical professions, their next obvious target was the APA. In 1968 gay activists picketed the American Medical Association (AMA) meeting in San Francisco, where Charles Socarides was speaking. They demanded to have a voice at these professional medical meetings. Their presence made clear that they would no longer merely be the objects of medical research but subjects, speaking back to the medical profession. Frequently during this time period, gay activists picketed public lectures by psychiatrists who spoke about the disease of homosexuality. In 1970 activists protested the annual APA meeting in San Francisco by using guerilla theater tactics to interrupt Irving Bieber during a panel on homosexuality. Activists also disrupted a session on the use of aversive conditioning techniques for homosexuals by yelling "torture."[53] The ensuing uproar forced the APA to rethink its policy of refusing to allow gay people to appear at the conference. By the following year, the APA had approved a panel that included Frank Kameny and Del Martin. They spoke about personal experiences of legal discrimination and social exclusion and showed that gay men and women could and did live happy and healthy lives. The next year, the same panel included Judd Marmor and Dr. Anonymous, a gay psychiatrist whose identity was hidden under a mask and cloak to protect him from losing his job.[54] By the end of the conference, Kameny informed the APA that gay protesters wanted to present their demand for the deletion of homosexuality from the DSM to members of the APA Committee on Nomenclature.

Robert Spitzer was a member of the APA Committee on Nomenclature in 1972. After meeting gay activists, he arranged for a formal presentation of their views before the committee at next year's meeting in Honolulu.

He was impressed by the activists' and gay-supportive psychiatrists' arguments and became instrumental in pushing through the demand that homosexuality be removed from the DSM and declassified as a pathology. Spitzer zealously assumed a leadership role by arranging a panel discussion for the meeting that would represent both sides of the issue and by writing a position paper on the topic. The panel, which was chaired by Spitzer, included Bieber, Socarides, Green, and Marmor.[55] During the panel, Bieber argued that "removal of the term from the manual would be tantamount to an official declaration by the APA that homosexuality is normal."[56] Marmor's presentation asked, "But why claim that heterosexuality is mankind's preference?"[57] Spitzer's conclusion argued for the removal of homosexuality from the DSM, but he was careful not to state that it was a normal sexual variation. In his concluding remarks, Spitzer asked that the APA create a new classification for homosexuality, defined as "sexual orientation disturbance."[58] He drafted a civil rights resolution for the APA that opposed discriminatory legal practices that were justified on the basis that homosexuals were mentally ill.

When the APA committee voted to remove homosexuality from the DSM, gay activists and psychiatrists celebrated, but many still expressed reservations about the committee's conclusions. Spitzer refused to wholeheartedly support the view that homosexuality was a normal variant of human sexuality, even calling it "suboptimal" in his paper. The board had approved the removal but created the new category of sexual orientation disturbance. In 1975 Spitzer developed another term, "homodysphilia," that applied to homosexuals who were distressed by their sexual orientation, without consulting the members of the task force on homosexuality.[59] He later altered the classification to "dyshomophilia," lumping it with fetishism, zoophilia, pedophilia, voyeurism, and sexual sadism—much to the chagrin of Green and Marmor. At the end of the controversy, what remained clear was that Spitzer steadfastly clung to the idea that the DSM needed a category for homosexuals who were "distressed" by their sexual orientation.

NARTH AND REPARATIVE THERAPY

Psychiatrists like Bieber and Socarides who voted against eliminating homosexuality from the DSM echoed Spitzer's insistence on retaining a pathological definition for homosexuality. Their work was instrumental in the creation of the National Association for the Research and Treatment of Homosexuality in 1992. NARTH provides scientific validation for Exodus and functions as professional venue for like-minded psychiatrists.[60] NARTH members are licensed psychotherapists, psychiatrists, and medical professionals who, by virtue of their credentials, have some influence within certain psychotherapy and medical institutions. NARTH's president is Joseph Nicolosi, PhD, who is also the director of the Thomas Aquinas Psychological Clinic in Encino, California. Nicolosi is a psychologist who was closely involved in Spitzer's 2003 study and referred many of his patients to him. According to their promotional materials, NARTH's primary goal is to make psychological therapy available to all homosexual men and women who seek change.[61]

NARTH provides an international referral service of both religious and secular licensed therapists offering sexual reorientation treatment in the United States, Canada, Europe, and Australia. Professionals in the NARTH network "defend the right to pursue change of sexual orientation" and are sympathetic to the goals of the ex-gay movement.[62] While most therapists use counseling to eliminate anxiety, worthlessness, and self-blame which arise from sexual and religious conflicts, ex-gay therapists assume that homosexuality is an unwanted condition and use psychotherapy and other methods to trace its basic causes and help men and women to live heterosexual lifestyles. They also sponsor an annual conference, publish the monthly NARTH bulletin, lecture, distribute literature to college and high school libraries, and practice as therapists and counselors. Part of their research consists of designing surveys to demonstrate that change is possible for homosexuals, as well as psychological literature documenting treatment success.[63] NARTH is closely tied to the ex-gay movement, and Nicolosi participates in the Exodus annual conference as well as smaller ministry conferences. He also counsels many men who attend ex-gay programs, and several men at New Hope worked with Nicolosi and NARTH-affiliated therapists before coming to the residential program. Despite the fact that it bills itself as a scientific organization, NARTH has a religious aspect. Nicolosi is a practicing Catholic and endorses the religious component of ex-gay ministries. The NARTH materials claim that there is a wide range of philosophies represented among affiliated members, including Catholic, Jewish, Mormon, Baha'i, Protestant, and Muslim.[64] Nicolosi also includes his own testimonial narrative on the NARTH Web site and in materials to explain his purpose. "I'd like to tell you why I stand up for what I believe," he writes.

> We live in a culture where tolerance, diversity, and the right to define oneself are valued very highly. Today, people who want to live their lives as "gay" are free to do so. That's their right. But there's another sexual minority I'd

like to tell you about. These are the men and women who—despite having some homosexual feelings—believe that humanity was designed to be heterosexual. Homosexuality will never define "who they really are." The major professional groups—the American Psychological Association and American Psychiatric Association—(the "APA's")—have abandoned these people. That is why I am standing up for what I believe.[65]

NARTH's psychiatrists, psychoanalysts, teachers, and social workers actively seek to legitimate reparative therapy through the publication of literature on the developmental models of homosexuality. They utilize Bieber's and Socarides's theories of arrested development and gender deficits to explain the causes of homosexuality. Nicolosi's most well-known book, *Reparative Therapy of Male Homosexuality: A New Clinical Approach,* is one of the standard texts for ex-gay therapists. He names gender deficits as a primary cause of homosexuality and explains the process of psychotherapy for homosexuals, addressing issues like ego strengthening, self-assertion, and the need for mentors. Nicolosi conceptualizes male homosexuality as a problem of incomplete masculinity, and he writes that "disenfranchisement from males—and from the empowerment of one's gender—leads to an eroticisation of maleness. The resultant homosexuality is understood to represent the drive to repair the original gender-identity injury."[66]

NARTH purports to be a referral organization for people who desire counseling, but it does not hide the fact that its function is also explicitly political. Nicolosi writes, "we want to clarify that homosexuality is not 'inborn,' and that gays are not a people, in the same sense that an ethnic group is a people." According to their statement of purpose, NARTH stands ready to "advise government, educational, and mental-health agencies as well as the media and religious groups on issues pertaining to homosexuality."[67] To justify NARTH's political work, Nicolosi writes, "This does not mean that we will never editorialize about such issues in the pages of our publications, discussing the relative merits of the important social matters of our time, such as gay marriage and adoption, as well as the psychological and psycho-social implications of those issues."[68] In fact, in 1996, Charles Socarides, Benjamin Kaufman, Joseph Nicolosi, Jeffrey Satinover, and Richard Fitzgibbons coauthored an op-ed in the *Wall Street Journal* advocating reparative therapy for gay men using a patient rights argument:

> Suppose that a young man, seeking help for a psychological condition that was associated with serious health risks and made him desperately unhappy, were to be told by the professional he consulted that no treatment

is available, that his condition is permanent and genetically based, and that he must learn to live with it? How would this man and his family feel when they discovered years later that numerous therapeutic approaches have been available for his specific problem for more than 60 years? What would be his reaction when informed that, although none of these approaches guaranteed results and most required a long period of treatment, a patient who was willing to follow a proven treatment regime had a good chance of being free from the condition?[69]

Nicolosi uses the term "non-gay homosexual" to differentiate between the idea of homosexuality as a political and sexual identity, and "homosexual" to denote someone with homosexual desires and behaviors who does not identify with the label of "gay."[70] Nicolosi believes that men and women with homosexual identities have been duped into believing they are gay by pro-gay activists and the "gay-influenced" psychiatric establishment. As his previous testimony demonstrates, he is applying the arguments of science, religion, and rights to argue that ex-gays are a minority who deserve the opportunity to receive treatment, even while he denies that gay men and women are a legitimate identity group, subject to full citizenship status.

New Hope and other ex-gay ministries incorporate NARTH's theories of homosexual development into their classes, and they are the basis for the residential live-in program. However, Nicolosi's ideas about repairing gender deficits originate in a book called *Homosexuality: A New Christian Ethic* by Elizabeth Moberly. Moberly's book is so dense and unreadable that one man produced his own "Cliffs Notes" version of the book so that other men and women at New Hope could comprehend it. Yet it has nearly taken on the status of sacred text at the ministry. According to Frank, Moberly was a celebrity at Exodus meetings in the early 1980s, and in the New Hope archives, there are photographs of her receiving a makeover and haircut from an ex-gay man. Moberly believes that Nicolosi stole many ideas from her book and that he has received undeserved acclaim from the ex-gay movement. After Frank and other leaders refused to acknowledge or validate her accusations of plagiarism, she ceased coming to Exodus meetings, and she is not affiliated with NARTH.

Moberly, like Nicolosi, argues that the greatest need for the homosexual is to develop nonsexual same-sex friendships that will fulfill the unmet love needs of early childhood.

The solution to same-sex deficits is to be sought through the medium of one or more nonsexual relationships with members of the same sex. The

> healing relationship must be gender specific because of the nature of the problem. . . . The same-sex attachment is itself therapeutic. . . . The homosexual is not to stop loving members of the same sex but to meet his or her psychological needs deeply and completely without sexual activity. The same-sex relationship is to be so fulfilling that same-sex deficits remain no longer and the relationship itself is outgrown.[71]

According to Moberly, homosexuality is the result of incomplete sexual and emotional development that emerges from difficulties in the parent-child relationship.[72] Every child has specific emotional needs that the same-sex parent must satisfy, and when there is a rupture in the same-sex parent relationship, these unfulfilled needs become eroticized at puberty. Therefore, in all homosexual relationships, each partner is seeking to fill emotional and physical deficiencies in the relationship with the parent of the same sex. Homosexuality is a reparative drive to correct this deficit through the medium of homosexual relationships. Moberly writes, "there is a child searching desperately and helplessly to renew a much-needed relationship that was severed in the past."[73]

Rather than using the term "homosexuality," Moberly coined the phrase "same-sex ambivalence." She also created the term "defensive detachment" to explain the way a child refuses to identify with a parent of the same sex. The ideas behind reparative therapy are particularly appealing to ex-gay men and women because they assert that homosexual needs are normal even if the sexual expression of them is not. She maintained that homosexuality was only a condition and not a sexual orientation. Moberly's theories removed the focus from sinfulness and gave men and women an explanation for why they were homosexual. Jeff Ford, a former ex-gay ministry leader who has since renounced the ex-gay movement, recalls Moberly's impact. "It seemed to offer a new ray of hope. It took the emphasis off repression and sublimation and actually encouraged gay men to attempt to meet their legitimate needs for same-sex love in non-erotic ways."

Evan credits Moberly with giving him hope after several suicide attempts. "Where the change took place was after I read Moberly's book. Then I could finally say I'm homosexual because I realized I wasn't stuck. It didn't terrify me anymore." After reading Moberly's book, he was convinced that the path to heterosexuality is a search for gender identity and the fulfillment of psychological needs. Moberly created the term "emotional dependency" to describe the dependency ex-gays have on members of the same sex. She claimed that the dependency stemmed from the deficiency in parental relationships. "This impulse is essentially motivated by the need to make good earlier deficits in the parent-child relationship."[74] To fill the emotional void left by the parent, homosexuals become addicted to food, drugs, alcohol, or sex. When this does not suffice, a homosexual develops an emotional dependency on another person. Moberly characterized same-sex relationships as having "an all-consuming, even obsessive need to be with the love object." Frank writes that a homosexual often takes on the mannerism of dress and speech of the person he is emotionally dependent on, calling it a form of "idolatry."

Moberly's idea that a good nonsexual relationship with a member of the same sex is a cure for homosexuality became the rationale for the ex-gay residential programs. She removed the pressure from ex-gay men and women by arguing that relationships with the opposite sex were not the solution to homosexuality. "Attempted heterosexual relationships, or social contact with the opposite sex, are not the solution to homo-sexuality, since increased opposite-sex contact can do nothing to fulfill same-sex deficits."[75] Opposite-sex contact was completely ineffective in fulfilling same-sex deficits. She criticized the focus on sexual behavior at ex-gay programs and the idea that marriage would cure homosexuals. "Marriage is a mistaken solution for homosexuality, since opposite-sex contact cannot remedy same-sex deficits."[76] Even therapists did not escape her criticism: "Therapists, whether secular or Christian, may try to block such fulfillment [of same-sex needs] in the name of cure."[77] As a Christian, she insisted that men and women not pray about hetero-sexuality directly but about the "fulfilling of homosexual needs." Moberly deflected possible criticism by conceding that not all men who experience same-sex deficits end up as homosexuals. She granted that there is a spectrum, in which biological and genetic factors shape whether someone is gay.

Moberly never actually treated ex-gay patients, so her theories were purely speculative, and yet ex-gay-supportive psychiatrists and psychol-ogists at NARTH and elsewhere continue to base their counseling prac-tices on her book. These concepts have also trickled down to the local level. Many of the ex-gay men and women at New Hope and Grace learned to shape their specific experiences into ideas of early familial problems or a lack of masculine or feminine identity. Men and women appropriate the lingo DD (defensive detachment) and ED (emotional dependency) to talk about sexual attractions or early-childhood experi-ences. Evan told me, "I struggled with ED. I would meet somebody and basically obsess about them. I didn't know it was ED until I went into the group. That's when I realized, 'Oh, that's what that is. That's why I do all that stuff.'" Hank also used the Moberly framework: "It's a reparative drive. I'm attracted to what I feel that I'm not. So I can get from them what I think they have so I have it also. That's the bottom basic dynamic that's involved."

The few men at New Hope who are unable to reconcile their family background with Moberly's model often feel confused. Curtis would frequently ask Frank why he was gay when he has had a close relationship with his father his entire life. After reading Moberly and discussing the theories in class, Curtis eventually decided it was because most of his friends in high school were women. His problem, he explained, was that he had always tried to please women because of growing up with two sisters. He observed them undergo difficult experiences with men, and he began to identify with them to the extent that he desired to be a woman. That desire was what had caused him to become sexually attracted to men. Paul told me, "I get confused when I come here because so much of what is taught does not relate to me. My father was there for us. He took us hunting and fishing and camping. I've always had best buddies growing up. I didn't have a domineering mother." Moberly and NARTH provide a rational and origin for a homosexual condition based on family relationships and incomplete gender identity. Yet they function only as models. Frank urges the men at New Hope to find ways to plug their family experiences into Moberly's theory even if their pasts do not mesh with the idea of reparative drives and defensive detachments. As Curtis's evolving ideas about his own life demonstrate, the longer men remained in the program, the more they incorporated reparative theories of sexuality into their own testimonial narrative about their sexuality.

MONSTER ENMESHMENT

Ex-gay developmental theories about early family experiences and defensive detachment are almost nonexistent for women, and the small amount of literature on families tends to blame mothers for creating effeminate sons and masculine daughters. While women receive far less theoretical and practical attention in the ex-gay movement, none of them seemed disturbed by this neglect. As with the long history of psychological and biological research on homosexuality, the ex-gay movement, in conference workshops and literature, often compares women's experiences to those of men, who serve as the norm. Although Moberly's

theory primarily addresses men and masculinity, she makes conciliatory gestures to the question of lesbianism. "A defensive detachment
from the parent of the same sex implies blocking of the normal identi-
ficatory process. This may [in some instances] be expressed in effeminacy in the male homosexual and quasi-masculinity in the female
homosexual."[78]

Moberly wrote that all gay men are effeminate and all gay women
are masculine-identified or butch, echoing the misogyny of sexologists
like Kraft-Ebbing, who created the category of the mannish lesbian.
Because of the persistence of these gender identity models, New Hope
and the ex-gay movement in general cannot account for homosexual
men who feel masculine or lesbian women who identify as feminine.
The ex-gay literature does not address alternative ways that gender
interacts with sexual identity, ignoring the existence of a femme or a
butch gay man. Moberly writes that "In the woman, there is the search
for a mother-substitute to make up for previous deficits in mothering,
whether or not this is consciously realized to be the goal of the relationship."[79] Many women believe that a lack of a feminine role model
or being told they were masculine is directly responsible for their homosexuality. "When a father says, 'I want you to think like me, not like
your mom,' what does the child hear? The child hears, 'Being a woman
isn't that great. Thinking like a woman is kind of dumb and stupid.'"[80]
Starla Allen, who is a prominent ex-gay speaker and an ex-lesbian,
writes primarily about ex-gay women. She spoke at New Hope's annual
Friends and Family Weekend conference in 1999, where she argued that
a close relationship with a father can cause a girl to disidentify with her
mother. When a girl is separated emotionally from her mother, her perception of a mother's rejection can also lead to first defensive detachment, then to the acquisition of a masculine gender identity, and finally
to lesbianism.

Since ex-gay theories about lesbians presume that all lesbian women
are masculine-identified and must study how to become feminine, many
workshops address this issue. These workshops tend to stress the idea
of femininity as drag: applying makeup, growing one's hair, wearing
skirts. Like Medinger's ideas about the practices of ritual masculinity
for men, the idea is that the performance of femininity will repair gender
deficits and restore heterosexuality. Practices like putting on makeup,
walking in heels, and donning skits connect a woman to an untapped
femininity within. Suzanne, the leader of Grace, remembers being at
New Hope in the residential program and working during the day in a

customer service job. She recalls that one of her watershed experiences was when her female coworkers escorted her to the nearby mall and insisted on her buying a purse. For Suzanne, this symbolized the pinnacle of femininity, "As I learned to apply makeup and wear my hair long, I began to shed my homosexual identity."

I attended a femininity workshop at an Exodus annual conference in Orlando, Florida, led by Lori Leander, a woman in her thirties with frosted hair and bright red fingernails. She made a point of immediately informing the ten women in the audience that she was married and that her husband worked for Focus on the Family. Anne Paulk was sitting beside me with her baby daughter on her lap, wearing a yellow dress. Leander asked us to define femininity, and Paulk answered that women are "soft, warm, nurturing, while men's bodies are hard and muscular." Leander agreed and placed a transparency on the overhead projector listing feminine characteristics: *nurturing, weak, relational, soft, gentle, responsive, sweet, expressive, charming, delicate, sensually receptive, prudish, and quiet.* Her list of negative female traits included *spiteful, smothering, weepy, clingy,* and *wishy-washy.* She praised Anne Paulk as an example of true femininity: "Anne radiates femininity. She's like a princess with her Tiffany jewelry and perfect makeup." She next instructed us to "find our identity in Christ" and to look to Jesus to discover our true identity. "You need a heart change. The only way is to go before the Lord. Your heavenly father wants to be your daddy." Yet all her own examples of femininity were physical, and she constantly referred to her Lexus car and her extensive wardrobe. At the end of the workshop, she provided us with a four-page handout with tips on skin care, makeup, hair, and clothing: "Hose should never be worn with a hole or run. Color should be the same or lighter than shoes. Try and match your hem line. Purse should match shoes or at least blend. The higher the heel, the more flattering it is to your leg. Accessories can make or break the outfit."

At another workshop in San Diego called Developing a Secure Gender Identity, Christine Sneeringer, an ex-gay woman from Florida, wearing a dress and pink cardigan, also told women to focus on the outward aspects of femininity. Sneeringer, however, admitted she had difficulties resisting the men's department at stores, and that her New Year's resolution was to stop wearing men's jeans. She imparted practical tips on moving away from being a "gender-detached woman" that were almost identical to the ones Leander had shared. "Avoid using nicknames like Chris and adopt the feminine sounding version of your names."

Her final advice: "I'm still not crazy about pantyhose, but being a girl is fun." Curtis and I exited the workshop and headed to the Hawaiian Fiesta Barbeque, one of the nightly conference events. The conference program suggested that we wear festive clothing, and we finally located Drew, Doug, and James, another man from New Hope, perched on a bench surrounded by tiki torches. James, bearded and wearing glasses, had dressed in a bright orange shirt, and the others had on short-sleeved button-down shirts with the same variation of bright-colored flowers and prints. "What are you wearing?" Drew asked, noting my predominantly black outfit. "She's a Hawaiian in mourning," James replied. "No, she's rebelling against developing her secure gender identity," Curtis responded.

Some women who had been in the Love in Action residential program resented the ex-gay movement's ideas about femininity. Laura, a forty-six-year-old woman, recalls her time in the New Hope residential program. "Some of things frankly ticked me off, [like] when they had those makeup sessions. 'We just want to show you how to put makeup on,' this and that. Most of us wanted to; some of us didn't." She laughs as she continues, "What concerned me was that we didn't try to put a pretty bow on the package when there was rotten fish inside. You can't just do the outward behavior. The bottom line is that you've got to want to change in your heart." Other women refute Medinger's ideas about the appropriate roles for women as responsive and passive. Diane is a former Love in Action program member who still attends Church of the Open Door and participates in New Hope Ministry. She is a lean woman in her late thirties with long brown hair. She believes that she has healed her homosexuality without adopting traditional feminine attributes. Fixing cars has always been her greatest passion, and after a workshop on femininity in which the leader told her to stop tinkering with cars, she stalked out angrily: "I'm like, wait a minute, who decided what femininity was, what masculinity was. I am very mechanically inclined. That is not technically a femininity trait, but I'm sorry, I've always been that way even before I went into the lifestyle. You have to accept yourself for what you are." Like many other women who believe they are in the process of conversion, Diane's identity is primarily religious. "First I considered myself a lesbian, then a woman who struggles with lesbianism; now I consider myself a woman of God."

In addition to the rigid notions of femininity, ex-gay literature also describes lesbian relationships as emotionally dependent, or "monster enmeshment." According to Starla Allen, lesbian relationships feature envy and idolatry because a gay woman seeks traits she admires but lacks in another woman, and then what Allen and her coauthor Patricia Allan call "emotional cannibalism" ensues.[81] Lesbian relationships also involve "possessiveness and self-centeredness."[82] Suzanne described her previous long-term relationship this way: "We made a lifetime commitment to each other, but the dependency was so intense it went its natural course into defensive detachment so we went to physically [and] emotionally abusive screaming and yelling." Now married with three children, she goes on to say that women's emotional involvements are "slimy, sticky, dramatic, and intense."

When Frank founded Love in Action in the 1970s, he admits that he was oblivious to women. The first women's program began in 1979, and Frank characterized it as "a total disaster." A married couple with two children directed the program. The wife, who had been an ex-gay for several years, fell in love with another woman in the program and divorced her husband. When Frank married Anita in 1985, New Hope initiated another program for women. Frank admits, "I couldn't handle it. Different issues. I had no idea what their issues were." Anita says part of the reason New Hope cancelled the women's program was that it was too emotionally draining for the women who ran it. She implied that the women's program had more drama and conflict than the men's program because that is the very nature of women. When she learned that I regularly spent time with many close female friends, she began warning me that friendships between women were generally unhealthy and emotionally dependent. I responded that I thought some degree of emotional dependency was an element of all friendships and not necessarily negative or destructive. A few days later, with a look of concern, she handed me a pamphlet on emotional dependency to take home and read.

In the wider ex-gay culture, the literature on women's emotional dependency renders lesbianism completely asexual.[83] The ex-gay movement explains the difference between homosexual men and women as sexual versus emotional. Ex-gay literature describes men as sexual predators, while claiming that women experience little or no sexual attraction for one another. Describing her previous lesbian relationship at New Hope's annual conference, Starla Allen told the audience, "Sex was the last thing I wanted. Mine was mostly emotionally dependent. That was what broke up most of the relationships—emotional dependency."[84] Women affiliated with New Hope seem to have internalized this view of women's sexuality. Jan, an ex-gay woman who completed the New Hope program in 1989 when it still had a women's residential program, told me that she believes the sex drive is much higher in men than women. "There are men that need it twice a day. Men have a tendency to desire sex because they're more visual. Sex addiction would apply more to a man."

After years of sponsoring books and theories about gay sons, Exodus is just beginning to address issues around lesbian daughters. At the 2000 annual Exodus conference, a workshop for parents of lesbian daughters was sparsely attended, and as the only person under forty, I received some curious glances. Jim and Terry Vratny of New Heart Ministry in Boulder, Colorado, convened the meeting by sharing their personal testimonies. Terry Vratny blames her daughter's lesbianism on the fact that she was a single mother leading a non-Christian life until she became born again at age thirty-two. She outlined the possible causes of lesbianism based on Nicolosi's book: a female disidentifies with her mother, the mother and infant do not properly bond, or a girl develops a heterosexual phobia due to sexual molestation. She also warned parents that lesbian daughters are different than gay sons because they are more apt to immerse themselves in feminist activism. Possible warning signs, they told the audience, include "an increased toughness," wearing all black, and having short hair. In her speeches, Starla Allen also maintains that women have "anger issues" and are drawn into lesbianism as they become involved with women's organizations. Despite some of her stereotypical assumptions, Terry Vratny exhorted parents to love their daughters unconditionally, even if they disagree with their homosexuality. After eleven years, the Vratnys have stopped trying to change their daughter, and Terry believes that her daughter's homosexuality is in God's hands. "Relinquish your daughter to the Lord," she told us.

Some ex-gay women take exception to the idea that their lesbian relationships were emotional attachments or a search for a mother figure. One woman who refuted this idea was a twenty-four-year-old named Arden. Arden had been a Queer Nation activist, had written for KQED (a National Public Radio affiliate), and had made headlines at age seventeen when she sued to divorce her mother and won. When she came out in high school, her mother had her kidnapped and committed to Rivendele, an institution for gay youth with behavioral problems, in Utah. After a dramatic escape, complete with barbed wire fences, dogs, and hospital ruses, Arden returned to San Francisco, where a lawyer at the National Center for Lesbian Rights took her case. After she won her freedom, two Jewish lesbians adopted her, and her life began revolving around gay activism. Years later, she met a Christian couple on a research trip, and through their influence, she gradually began to feel that Jesus was the Son of God and became a born-again Christian. She now works for Jews for Jesus and attends ex-gay conferences. Her leftist political views and background are unusual in the ex-gay movement, and she was more apt to criticize ex-gay theories about lesbians, especially their ideas of asexuality. She told me, "I definitely fit in a lot more with the guys at Exodus in terms of my sexual experience. I am definitely much more of a sex kind of person, not relationship focused." She continued, "I had a two-year relationship and I don't feel that it was codependent. I told that to Anita and she says I'm just in denial. I don't think so. They were healthy teenage lesbian relationships." Unlike other ex-gay men and women, Arden criticized the sexism within the ex-gay movement and often challenged many of its theories and assumptions—especially ideas about sexual abuse.

When the idea that homosexuality comes from bad relationships with parents isn't applicable to women, the ex-gay movement falls back on the idea that all lesbians are sexually abused. Starla Allen and Patricia Allan write, "Within Exodus circles we have consistently seen that at least eighty percent of the women coming for help have experienced sexual trauma."[85] At one New Hope conference, when Bob Davies, the former president of Exodus, cited this statistic, I asked where these numbers came from. No one could point to anything other than anecdotal evidence. While I listened to some horrific stories of abuse from both men and women, there was no acknowledgment that equal if not greater numbers of heterosexually identified men and women experienced sexual and physical abuse. Some of the stories I heard in public forums seemed to adopt an expansive definition of abuse. Anne Paulk, who completed the women's program at New Hope, testifies about her abuse in the book she coauthored with John Paulk, *Love Won Out.*[86] Anne recalls finding porn magazines in a fourteen-year-old neighbor's room and writes that the pornography triggered abuse by the same boy. The abusive incident involved the boy touching his genitals with a flashlight during a game of hide and seek: "I felt powerless and defenseless. I sensed there was nothing I could do to prevent such a sexual trespass from happening again."[87] The culture of ex-gay ministries involves constantly sifting through the past for crisis points and familial dysfunction as the causes of homosexuality. These become important devices within a larger testimonial narrative. Some people at the ministries relied on the idea of recovered memories to discover traumatic experiences from childhoods. When Bob Davies discussed the percentage of sexually abused women at the conference, one man stood up. He said, "People tell me that I've probably had sexual abuse in my past, and that's why I'm gay. Should I find that out? I don't remember anything."

Ex-gay theory presumes that through abuse a girl rejects her femininity and thus is drawn to homosexuality. Suzanne told me that her abuse taught her that it was safe to act and look like a boy. Jan explained, "If you're talking with the older people like me, I'd say a lot of them, the majority of them, sexual orientation has been shown to them in the form of rape or sexual molestation when they were very young." The ex-gay literature on lesbianism also suggests that relating to Jesus as a man will help women regain femininity and restore their trust in men. Allen and Allan write that their relationship with Jesus is like having a crush on someone: "It's exciting to discover that Jesus, who is male, is not like what you think men are like. God the Father nurtures us, like a hen gathering her chicks. Love of my soul, I will be with you forever."[88] Allen says that during her first year out of lesbianism, she spent the entire time alone with God, and she would never trade her relationship with him for any in the world. "Jesus is my reservoir of love that never runs out."

OVERBEARING MOTHERS AND ABSENT FATHERS

The role of family life and parents is central to how the ex-gay movement understands masculinity, femininity, and the root causes of homosexuality. Anita's role in the parents' ministry of New Hope is crucial in this larger context. She began the ministry for parents after marrying Frank and coming to work at the New Hope offices. She directs her book, *Someone I Love Is Gay,* at parents who feel they are to blame for their child's homosexuality. In the New Hope monthly newsletter, Anita pens a column, "Family Matters," that focuses on the parent-child relationship, and she counsels parents on the phone everyday. One of the first times I ever came into the New Hope offices, she was listening to a woman talk about her gay son. She rolled her eyes at me as she held the receiver between her cheek and shoulder even while she sounded compassionate and empathetic to the woman. Even though later she confided, "Some people just go on and on," she spent hours every day talking to parents with gay children. She was impatient with parents who refused to accept responsibility for their children. The woman she had spoken with when I walked in kept assuring Anita that although her son died of AIDS he was never gay, even though he had lived with his boyfriend. Anita said angrily, "How can she minister? She's trying to raise her son above the rest of us. She's in denial as far as I'm concerned." The idea of the "smother mother" that the ex-gay movement promotes has its origins in an earlier period, when mother bashing was common. Many of Anita's ideas about the role of parents and particularly mothers are reminiscent of the 1950s theory of "Momism." During the postwar period, when women were entering the workforce, anxiety about changing women's roles was channeled into the image of the domineering mother.[89] Philip Wylie's 1955 tract called "Momism" described mothers' pernicious influence as sapping the masculinity of boys. Even a letter from a mother of a gay son to other mothers in the *Mattachine Review* in 1957 echoed the Momism theory. "You may find that you have protected him too much in your own expression of mother love. It so often becomes 'smother love.' (Read Philip Wylie on Momism). You have probably not cut the apron strings sufficiently to allow him his own initiative in daily actions."[90]

Anita has a complicated and loving relationship with her own son, Randy, who is gay, HIV positive, and, at the time of my research, lived in the same apartment complex where New Hope hosts the residential program. Randy is friendly but avoids the New Hope men and has never yielded to either Frank or Anita's idea that he should change his sexuality. Anita raised him as a single mother in a Christian commune in Oregon, and they returned to Southern California when Randy was sixteen. Soon after, Anita discovered that he was gay after finding gay pornography in his room, and when she confronted him, he simply said, "Well, you know I'm gay, don't you?" She arranged to have him kidnapped by friends, who brought him to her brother's house in another state, because she believed that in an unfamiliar environment he might reconsider his homosexuality. This tactic failed miserably, and eventually they moved back to Southern California separately and had little contact until after Anita married Frank. They reconciled years later when Randy experienced financial difficulties and temporarily moved into the apartment that Anita and Frank shared in San Rafael.

Randy and Frank also have an unusually close relationship. When Frank and Anita vacation at the condominium they own in Mexico, Randy often accompanies them. Anita is proud of Randy's relationship with Frank: "I know he's talked to Frank about things that he won't talk to me about, which I just love. We do these vacations, and gosh, it's like a TV thing, the relationship between the three of us and how we get on."

She believes that in some bizarre way it is appropriate that a single mother with a gay son married a formerly gay man. "How would it be if I married some guy who sits in front of the TV watching football? How would he feel about my little gay son? And how would my son, if he were playing college football, feel about my ex-gay husband? Even though people say it's the weirdest match that I married Frank, in a way it's perfect. Truth is stranger than fiction." Anita's philosophy for parents with gay children is tolerance without acceptance. The difference, according to Anita, is that "I don't agree with you but I will engage with you anyway." While Anita is not progressive by any stretch, her experience has made her much more flexible than many other ex-gay ministry leaders. When Randy's long-term partner was dying of AIDS, Anita returned from Manila to nurse him and support Randy, and she is friendly to his new boyfriend but still sets certain boundaries. In her monthly column she addresses the contradictions of tolerance: "I feel it is always wrong to treat a gay couple as though they were married, and it is important that both know your stand on homosexuality. After your moral stand is clear, then you are free to love them. There are no easy cut and dried answers. I really like my son's partner and I try to show him that, but I constantly work at not treating them as a couple."[91]

Anita is particularly sensitive to Moberly's theories about overbearing mothers causing male homosexuality, and she initiated the ministry for parents because she felt there was too much emphasis on blaming mothers at New Hope. "There was a real negative thing about women and moms, and I changed that. Frank still has a negative view, and I don't let him get away with it." However, Anita still blames Randy's homosexuality on the fact that he did not have a father figure growing up in the commune, and she often berates herself for having been a single mother. Anita believes that parents have to acknowledge their role in causing homosexuality in their children and to try not to alienate them at the same time. The problem of a parents' ministry is that there is a delicate balance between not blaming parents and still basing an entire theory of homosexuality on parental modeling. "I don't want the parents to go away feeling that they're horrible people," Anita explained. "But I feel the only healing for parents is if they accept their responsibility—of what they've done. I can't tell them what they've done and haven't done. I can tell them my story because I did everything wrong and nobody can take that away from me."

She frequently shares anecdotes about her relationship with Randy in her newsletter column, and when she counsels parents she tells them to stop what she calls "stinkin' thinkin'," constantly wondering "what if" or "if only."[92] She writes that mothers can have healthy relationships with their sons by setting clear limits and not worrying about their children's relationship to God. She advises parents to confess their fears to God rather than to confront their children. Admitting that she feels responsible for Randy's childhood, Anita has also learned to cope with those feelings through her daily prayer and meditation. She writes that building a life beyond her son, finding hobbies and friends unrelated to homosexuality, and relinquishing control has transformed her relationship with Randy. "Over the years I've found that, as I've stopped trying to manipulate my son into spending time with me . . . he likes being with me more. The joy and peace in my life attracts him, and he sees Jesus through me. We're both more comfortable knowing where the boundaries are, and it's nice not feeling like a doormat! As I have grown closer to God I am able to trust Him to take care of Randy. Be kind to yourself and keep on moving forward."[93] She is also able to see the humor in her particular situation. Her car has a bumper sticker on the back with a picture of Jesus on one side and the devil on the other. Underneath it reads, "He loves me, he loves me not." When I commented on it, she replied, "It keeps Randy from borrowing my car."

Many ex-gays spent hours telling me about their families and childhoods in detail. New Hope stresses that part of therapy is to go back over childhood experiences and closely analyze familial relationships and dysfunctions. Some spoke resentfully about their families—like Hank, who responded to my question, "What was your family life like growing up?" with "It sucked." Many still placed the blame for homosexuality on their mothers for treating them as surrogate husbands. Drew's mother often complained about her husband to him, using him as a sounding board for her problems when he was only nine or ten years old. "In some ways, I see myself as being used, abused. I wasn't treated like any normal kid should be, where I had my own friends and my own life. I was always trying to keep her happy." Other men like Dwight refuse to blame their parents. "My dad was typically emotionally absent, but I think back in Scotland it would be quite strange for a father to express love in that way." Whereas all the men had an almost reverential regard for Frank, many seemed to feel antagonistic to Anita at times. Their sensitivity to Moberly's and Nicolosi's ideas about the prototypical overbearing and emasculating mother often made them resent Anita's no-nonsense style and the fact that she monitored access to Frank. Mothers often called asking for information about the program for their sons, and Drew and the other men in the office would refuse to send them information or they would refer them to Anita. They were suspicious of a mother who wanted to place her son in a program without his consent. Drew would not arrange any visits to New Hope or send out application materials unless he spoke to the man applying.

The men and women affiliated with New Hope interpret and make sense of NARTH's and Moberly's ideas about the causes of their homosexuality in their own lives by focusing on gender deficits and familial relationships. These wider ideas about reparative therapy are part of a much longer history, during which definitions of homosexuality have morphed and changed. Scientific expertise has shaped ideas about emotional dependencies and overbearing mothers, insisting that gender identity is central to homosexuality. Yet ex-gay men and women and gay activists have contested these ideas. The next chapter turns to how the therapeutic discourse of addiction and recovery provides another language for men and women in the ex-gay movement to conceptualize healing and sexual conversion.

CHAPTER 5

Testifying to Sexual Healing

As I was having dinner at New Hope one night, Frank inquired about my family. Did I suffer abuse, abandonment, and lack of a mother figure? Were my parents divorced? Did they drink? His line of questioning assumed that I would have a personal horror story to impart, which I would then share as my own narrative of self-healing. When I revealed no past abuse, codependency, or addiction, the men sitting around the table were flabbergasted. Frank said sympathetically, "It's too bad. You can't go to twelve-step groups for all your problems the way we can." At New Hope, everyone had coped with their own traumas in various recovery groups. Frank, Anita, and the men in the program proudly understood themselves as the weary survivors of battles with some kind of addiction, abuse, or syndrome. They believed that the only people who could cure an addiction were those, like themselves, recovering from its effects. "We are the ones who can testify to our own sexual healing," Frank told me. To them, personal experience was as important a credential as a professional degree, providing an essential measure of legitimacy. For born-again Christians, past lives of sin were a way to witness to others and to have authority. While we were discussing a prominent Christian ex-gay couple, Anita said that the woman was a virgin before she married. She implied that she envied the woman's pureness, but she also said, "That woman will never have an interesting testimony, and she'll never write a book like me."

The ex-gay movement draws heavily from the self-help and recovery movements' notion of the twelve steps to conceptualize healing homosexuality. In the "Steps Out" workbook and in classes and teachings, New Hope utilizes the language of healing to describe sexual and religious conversion as an ongoing process of recovery. Men and women affiliated with New Hope become conversant in a therapeutic language that is specific to the ex-gay movement, reinventing the language of sin and pathology as addiction. The term "sexual brokenness" describes their homosexuality or addiction. "Brokenness" signifies both a bodily and a religious state, so that healing is a reintegration of self. "Sexual sobriety" illuminates the process of recovery. Breaking the rules at New Hope, whether by smoking, wearing inappropriate clothes, "camping," or challenging leadership's authority, is "acting out." The response to acting out usually involves some kind of discipline, such as being held back in a phase, also called being "put on the level." When a man or woman has engaged in sex with someone or looked at pornography, they have had a "sexual fall." Men and women who leave the program unhealed have gone back to the "lifestyle."

The ex-gay therapeutic regimen of transformation defines homosexuality as not simply a sin, but as a sickness or addiction that is healed through personal effort in conjunction with a relationship with Jesus. New Hope's program manual reads, "Christ's capacity to touch and restore us at deep levels of shame and brokenness extends to all of us, regardless of the specifics of our issue."[1] Personal testimony is central to the ex-gay battle against a host of sexual addictions, and the movement insists that members publicly confess sexual lapses to one another in small accountability groups and in public forums. At New Hope, testimony blurs the distinction between the public and private, religious and therapeutic, making sexuality and sexual addiction part of a public discourse of confession and public intimacy. Part of accepting the twelve-step model of homosexuality as addiction is acknowledging that healing has no end. The ex-gay ministry, which functions as a support group, stands ready to renew a person's faith in recovery. Like evangelical Christianity, self-help is the ideology that salvation occurs through personal effort, sanctioned by the idea of grace. In this way, the ex-gay movement has reintegrated evangelicalism and therapy, enabling men and women to understand the process of religious and sexual conversion as a process of recovery. As Wendy Kaminer writes, "therapy is the door to redemption and faith is a door to recovery."[2]

SEXUAL PURITY

The ex-gay movement's adoption of recovery models overlaps with the vast numbers of twelve-step and self-help programs in existence throughout the United States. Frank founded Love in Action during a period in the 1970s when the concept of self-help, the idea of helping oneself to express one's feelings in the ordinary course of living, gained greater acceptance in American culture. Ellen Herman writes that after 1945, many Americans assimilated the idea of a healthy personality as the basis for a thriving democracy and as a strategy for the manufacture of normality into daily life.[3] By 1970 approximately twenty thousand psychiatrists were ministering to one million people on an outpatient basis.[4] Herman argues that during the 1960s and 1970s, the shift toward using therapy for exploring personality also drew from wider cultural trends. Feminist consciousness-raising groups and members of the gay-liberation movement counseled that self-actualization was necessary for human evolution and social change, advocating the idea that the personal was political.[5] Self-liberation as part of a wider political liberation was a matter of freeing one's emotions. Ideas about self-liberation and self-fulfillment meshed with evangelical religious precepts, like the focus on the individual's relationship with Jesus. As Wendy Simonds notes, "By the 1960s and 1970s, most evangelical spokespersons embraced modern psychology with great enthusiasm and only minor reservations. By then, the evangelical subculture was less a bulwark against than a variant of the therapeutic culture."[6]

The ideas of self-help and the primacy placed on feelings and self-expression in the 1970s blossomed into the recovery movements of the 1980s and 1990s.[7] Legions of specialized support and recovery groups burgeoned across the United States, allowing people to recover by sharing their most intimate stories of addiction.[8] This expansion was spurred on by the popularity of the television talk-show format, which exploited the entertainment value of performing addiction and dysfunction publicly. The twelve-step program emerged as the answer to alcoholism, drug use, overeating, gambling, and a variety of other addictions and "diseases." Practices once billed as bad habits and dilemmas became addictions, and syndromes like codependency gained currency in American culture. Marie Griffith writes, "The boom of twelve-step or recovery groups has often been treated as marking a kind of spiritual shift in American life, in which the boundaries between the public and the private have been repeatedly re-challenged and redrawn."[9]

Today there are over three million twelve-step and recovery pro-grams in the United States, and New Hope and other ex-gay ministries have appropriated many of their concepts, especially those of Alco-holics Anonymous (AA).[10] AA and the twelve-step model materialized out of the Oxford Group in the 1920s and 1930s, "a non-denomina-tional, theologically conservative, evangelically styled attempt to recap-ture the spirit and the impetus of what its members understood to be primitive Christianity."[11] The Oxford Group operated according to five basic assumptions, which became the foundation for AA's twelve steps: (1) men are sinners, (2) men can be changed, (3) confession is a prereq-uisite to change, (4) the changed soul has direct access to God, (5) those who have been changed must change others.[12] In the twelve steps, a "sin" is specified as being "powerless over alcohol" and having "char-acter defects." Alcoholics are not required to submit to Jesus, but instead they must turn their wills and lives "over to the care of God as we [understand] him."[13] In place of the Oxford Group's Bible, AA's pri-mary text is *The Big Book,* and confession becomes "a moral inventory." While an Oxford Group member experienced a spiritual conversion in stages or steps, an AA member recovers from alcoholism by following the twelve steps one by one, achieving a spiritual awakening as a by-product. New Hope borrows some principles from AA, but it eschews AA's more secular tone. Instead, New Hope's use of the twelve steps is a return to AA's evangelical roots in the Oxford Group.

AA had been in existence for thirty-five years in 1970. During the late 1970s and early 1980s, the ex-gay movement was feeling the rever-berations from its top leaders' public sexual falls and scandals.[14] Media reports claiming that men argued for change during daytime workshops while they had sex with each other at night during Exodus conferences had damaged the credibility of the ex-gay movement.[15] The scandals prompted Frank and other leaders to address the fact that religious con-version alone was insufficient to control the sexual desires and behaviors of men and women in ex-gay ministries. In 1983, after their annual con-ference, the board of Exodus held an impromptu meeting about the lack of sexual standards in the organization and the fact that most of the ex-gay leaders' counseling skills were based on their personal experience.[16] During this meeting, Frank introduced the concept of sexual purity, establishing it as a criterion for a person working in ex-gay ministry. He helped establish the testimony as the basis for a system of public accountability and confession in which he expected ex-gay men and women to testify about their struggles with pornography, masturbation, and an "undisciplined thought life." Local ex-gay programs like New Hope carefully categorized, named, and monitored a series of potential addictions in order to prevent men and women from having a "fall from grace." In naming homosexuality as one of many possible addictions, Frank normalized the idea of homosexuality as sin. He adopted ideas about sexual addiction and elements of the twelve-step process for the LIA residential program, and these concepts are still evident at New Hope. Frank tells the men that the first step toward "coming out of homosexuality" is to admit to yourself and to God, "I have a problem," in the same way that AA's first step is to admit, "We are powerless over alcohol."[17] Other steps include conceding, "We came to perceive that we had accepted a lie about ourselves, an illusion that had trapped us in a false identity" and "We learned to claim our true reality that as mankind, we are part of God's heterosexual creation, and that God calls us to rediscover that identity in Him through Jesus Christ."[18] The twelve-step focus also provides a specific way to monitor behavior and actions when submitting to Jesus is not sufficient.

Twelve-step and recovery groups, including the meetings themselves and the interactions within the group, have a premise that recovery requires a spiritual transformation, and many recovery groups are now geared toward specific religious constituencies. Frank emphasizes that although he believes in the process of recovery as central to healing from homosexuality, the men's Christian identities come first. He tells them, "Although today it is popular to identify yourself by your problem, this is not healthy or the way God intended us to identify ourselves. Our identity is Christian; this in itself is a full and complete identity; nothing more needs to be added."[19] At New Hope, healing from addiction, or "sexual and relational brokenness," involves recognizing:

- God's powerful love for us and how Jesus is central to our hope for wholeness
- The depth of our brokenness and our profound need for Him
- The power of the Cross to restore our souls, sexuality, and relationships[20]

Frank acknowledges that ex-gays are Christians with addictions and that any form of lust is a sin. However, he stresses taking on a Christian identity rather than an identity as an addict because he does not want the person and the addiction to become synonymous. "We can admit to an unmanageable problem [step one of AA] without having to take on the sinful identity."[21] Frank warns the men that people can grow into their labels. Rather than explaining, "I am Frank and I am a homosexual," the men in the program state, "I am Frank and I am dealing with homosexual tendencies" or "I struggle with homosexuality." They make a distinction between the binding nature of an identity versus an addiction that can be healed. Framing homosexuality as an addiction rather than a sin is a more palatable interpretation for ex-gay men and women. It is easier to define yourself as a person who suffers from a compulsive masturbation disorder than to believe you are simply condemned to hell. However, even though New Hope stresses that "our sin is not our identity," the adoption of the term "ex-gay" or "strugglers" nonetheless creates an identity defined around the problem of homosexuality as addiction. In twelve-step groups, members establish their identities as addictive and thereby gain fellowship into a wider community of others suffering from the same. By embracing the label "ex-gay," as most of the men at New Hope do, they also become part of the wider ex-gay community. The movement is able to contain all sinful sexual behaviors and feelings within their new identity. They are neither homosexual nor heterosexual but still Christian. Instead of a person who has used pornography, they are Christians and recovering porn addicts. Instead of homosexuals, they are ex-gays or strugglers.

The twelve-step concept is a familiar part of the lives of many men who arrive at New Hope. James, for example, had attended Alanon, AA, Sexaholics Anonymous, and Co-dependents Anonymous before arriving at New Hope. Eventually he felt that the sexual addiction model lacked a religious core that gave God responsibility for change. "In order to really recover, you need a personal relationship with God. God is the only person who can stand between you and a drink or acting out." Self-sufficiency is a sin in the ex-gay model of addiction and healing. Frank teaches that the men are not the masters of their fates, and they must acknowledge their dependence on God. Frank calls the inability to rely on God the "Sinatra syndrome." Rather than relying upon Jesus for healing, many men who are addicted to homosexuality insist on "doing it my way." Without turning to Jesus, any person struggling will always revert to his prior behaviors. "Freedom comes through surrendering to Jesus. If addiction stops us from facing the truth in our lives, then it can only be Jesus who knows the way out." Frank also believes that addictions are a form of idol worship, and that Satan has a direct interest in feeding addictions. Addiction is surrendering to anything other than Jesus, and Satan is the enemy who lures you from God and closer to harmful behaviors. For men and women at New Hope, Satan is directly responsible for addictive behavior. "Satan will reach us one way or another with a distortion of God's plan," according to Frank. "Many of our initial childhood sexual fantasies may have come directly from the evil one." The New Hope program teaches that compulsive addictions and behaviors are useful to Satan and that a man's urge to masturbate is often instigated by satanic suggestion. Some men also described their pornography addictions as satanic.

The "Steps Out" workbook is suffused with the language of submission. There is a section in the lessons on addiction where Frank writes that the ex-gay men are "bondservants." "We must love our Master and be willing to do anything to serve Him. This is a servant who has given up his rights to freedom. This is the attitude that will bring the healing we desire," he writes.[22] Journaling, a technique borrowed from the recovery movement, allows the men to record their feelings on a daily basis and provides another venue to hear God speak to them. The extremely emotional and personal relationships that ex-gays develop with Jesus are also a replacement for the lack of a sexual outlet in their lives. With restrictions on where they go, where they work, and whom they talk to, they focus almost compulsively on Jesus. Yet they believe that a person can never be addicted to or emotionally dependent on Jesus, so these relationships are sanctioned. The reliance on Jesus offers ex-gays not only the promise of salvation but also the assurance that they need not push themselves too hard or fret about their failures. Within the sexual addiction model, any individual whose life is in shambles can still have a relationship with Jesus, through submission and surrender.

ADDICTIONS AND SEXUAL FALLS

At the first of eight "Steps Out" classes about the idea of addiction, the workbook lesson presents the men with two scenarios. Option 1 involves going to a local men's room where they know a man will be available to service anyone sexually. The book asks: "Will you be there at three o'clock?" Option 2 involves going to the beach with an old friend who happens to be visiting that day. The book asks: "Will you choose to go to the beach?"[23] The lesson explains that those who choose the beach option are less addicted than those who forsake their friend to have anonymous sex. The men then take a quiz to determine whether they are addicted. They know they are if "they avoid interpersonal relationships and find solo activities pleasurable, their compulsive activities have a definite plan, they feel out of control, and they believe that if they are healed, their lives will be dull and without pleasure."[24] Hank describes his homosexuality: "Yes, I would say I was addicted in the sense that my behavior was uncontrollable in that it dominated me." After a lengthy discussion of these choices, men spend time sharing with each other and are permitted fifteen minutes to write in their journal page at the end of the lesson. At the next class, they discuss characteristics of addiction like obsession, anger, denial, boredom, paranoia, and self-degradation. Together they answer the questions: "Do you feel trapped by your addiction?" and "Are you in denial?" Responding to these questions is another part of assembling a public testimonial narrative.

Many ex-gays speak of their homosexuality as part of a wider problem of sexual addiction that includes pornography, masturbation, and any form of sex that occurs outside of marriage. The "Steps Out" workbook explains, "Homosexuality in itself may be a type of addiction, but usually homosexuality is broken down into a series of supporting addictions."[25] These addictions, including compulsive masturbation and "body-watching," "feed into" the main problem of homosexuality. Frank also writes and talks about the problems of pornography, masturbation, and lust primarily as male problems, often describing male homosexuals as sexual predators who cannot control their desire. Desert Stream in Anaheim, California, is an ex-gay ministry that treats homosexuality as part of a wider culture of sexual addiction. It has a twenty-lesson program called Living Waters, which is taught in a closed-group format over a thirty-week period and focuses solely on sexual addictions. Living Waters bills itself as particularly relevant for those struggling with homosexuality, sexual promiscuity or addiction, the effects of sexual abuse, codependency, self-hatred, or the inability to love others well.[26] It specifically runs groups for both straight and gay men and women in order to remove the stigma from homosexuality as the "worst of the worst" addictions. At one of their meetings in a church in San Diego, a truck driver admitted to cheating on his wife, a man spoke of struggling with homosexuality, and a woman talked about her codependent relationship. The facilitator reminded the group, "We are all broken in our ability to love others well." Living Waters foregrounds a relationship with God, and it centers its approach on the twelve-step model. Yet the Living Waters model regards homosexuality as one of a host of sins, while New Hope sees other addictions as stemming from homosexuality.

However, while the ex-gay movement conceptualizes homosexuality as part of a problem of sexual addiction, other twelve-step programs, like Sexual Compulsives Anonymous (SCA) and Sex and Love Addicts

Anonymous (SLAA), see homosexuality and sexual addiction as completely distinct. SCA and SLAA have substantial numbers of gay and lesbian members, and they do not view their own homosexuality as a problem that needs curing. In the course of their recovery process from different types of sexual addictions and compulsions, gay men and lesbians in these groups achieve healthy same-sex sexual and romantic relationships. Despite the fundamental difference in how they conceptualize homosexuality, those people entering ex-gay ministries and those entering these other twelve-step programs for recovery from sex addiction follow similar paths to achieve their results. However, unlike the ex-gay movement, sexual addiction recovery groups like SCA and SLAA do not place a central focus on Jesus or on the notion that only by becoming born again can one find healing.

SCA and SLAA also have large numbers of heterosexually identified men and women among their membership. These straight persons suffer from the same social and spiritual problems as do ex-gays and gay, lesbian, bisexual, or transgendered members of SCA and SLAA. Groups like Sexaholics Anonymous (SA) also directly confront problems of sexual addiction; they too have members who are heterosexual- or homosexual-identified, and they do not stress that a participant must overcome homosexuality in order to recover from sexual addiction. According to SA, a sexaholic is someone who "has taken him or herself out of the whole context of what is right or wrong. He or she has lost control, no longer has the power of choice and is not free to stop. Lust has become an addiction. Our situation is like that of the alcoholic who can no longer tolerate alcohol but is hooked. So it is with the sexaholic, or sex drunk, who can no longer tolerate lust but cannot stop."[27] Although some men in the New Hope program have attended these groups, the ex-gay movement does not recognize them officially because they lack an explicit religious component. Yet New Hope borrows many of the same ideas about the loss of sexual control and the need to control lust as part of the live-in program.

Despite the fact that the men at New Hope believe that ultimately they must place their faith in Jesus to conquer addictions, the New Hope program regulates their lives very closely in order to control potentially addictive behaviors. Accountability to the group and each other is a crucial part of this regulation. The men meet together as a large group at least twice a week as well as in smaller groups, where they dutifully relate any feelings of lust or sexual temptation they might have experienced. Every week they fill out an accountability report that they submit to their house leader, and they divulge any improprieties for group discussion. The sheet is an elaborate two-page questionnaire that asks everything from "Have you had a quiet time with God in prayer and Bible reading each day?" to "Have you looked at someone in a sexual way (cruise) or gone anywhere hoping to meet someone?" The questions begin on a more general level: "At any time did you compromise your integrity?" "Have you taken time to show compassion for others in need, or demonstrated a servant's heart?"

However, three-fourths of the questionnaire is devoted to possible behaviors related to same-sex attraction or sexual falls. The questions range from "Have you had sex with anyone?" "Have you looked at any personal ads, answered a personal ad, or placed a personal ad for yourself?" "Have you looked at, or do you have any pornography, fitness/ muscle magazines?" "Have you gone into a video store alone or looked at the adult video section?" "Have you masturbated, and is it compulsive?" Other questions ask about phone sex, entering public bathrooms without an "accountability partner," going to the beach alone, listening to music that reminds them of the past, leaving work early, using the Internet, opening a private voice mail account, and contacting friends in the gay lifestyle. At the end of this barrage of questions, just to cover the bases, the sheet even asks, "Is there anything else that has happened since your last accountability sheet that you should confess?" Frank designs the accountability sheets to stem men's addictive behaviors and provide them with structure, but they also have the unintended effect of inciting transgressive behavior. The sheets anticipate any possible form of behavioral transgression an ex-gay man might engage in, and even present men with ideas for off-limits behavior they may not have considered. At "Gayland" Curtis often expressed bewilderment at all the different activities that could get someone in trouble. The explicitly detailed prohibitions grant forbidden behavior more power precisely because those behaviors are prohibited, and by constantly focusing on what ex-gays are not supposed to do, the accountability sheets tempt them with what kinds of sexual behavior are possible but not allowed.

The year Brian participated in the New Hope program, seven out of eleven people left within the first two months. Brian and Drew stayed, but the other two who completed the program are now dating men. One of these men, Patrick, is living openly as a gay man in Norway, and he revealed that he fell in love with Brian during the program. After Hank, who was the house leader at the time, discovered Patrick's feelings, both

Brian and Patrick were "put on the level" for "acting out" in ways that would lead to a sexual fall. Hank forbade them to speak to or look at each other, sit on the same side of the table, or remain in the same room. Brian described Hank as "imposing martial law on our friendship." Hank described the relationship as an example of "sexual vampirism" that needed to be halted. Frank also uses the term "vampirism" to illustrate how men and women in same-sex relationships extract the vitality from each other and that same-sex relationships can never be healthy. The house discussed Patrick's feelings for Brian openly, calling it an emotional dependency, but even after they publicly confessed, Hank still felt he had to regulate and monitor their behavior.

The need for accountability and problems with addiction do not disappear once a man or woman has completed the New Hope program. Darren, who is now the father of four children, admitted that he still has to keep certain forms of sexual addiction at bay. He married a woman from Open Door Church and speaks openly about the fact that gay pornography is still a difficult and tempting area for him. After his wife "nailed him on it," catching him with pornography, he joined a support group at Open Door Church for men struggling with pornography. He met with them for a year and a half in a weekly accountability group, and he felt what he calls "the compulsion" gradually diminish. However, he conceded, "I still have to watch where my eyes go." Darren attributes his healing from pornographic addiction to God in addition to his support group. "I believe that I'm sitting in God's hands. I could never have the strength to stop pornography. I've just been held." Despite his assurance that God had been aiding his battle, he still had incidents of looking at pornographic material every few months, which he revealed to his wife. When she presented him with the ultimatum that she would leave him if he continued with his addiction, he determined to take more drastic measures. He told me that he visited every video shop in his town and nearby towns with a letter he composed. It read, "My name is Darren _____, and my wife is Trisha _____. Our phone number is_____. If you see me in here renting pornography please call my wife." "It was like cutting off my own arm," he explained. "That nixed it. I walked out of there, and knew I could never go back." Like Darren, many ex-gay men and women continue to struggle with sexual addictions even while they assert that it is God who directs their healing. At times, they require a more direct threat of abandonment or public humiliation in order to regulate their behavior.

NEW HOPE NIGHT

New Hope Night, the first time the ex-gay men testify in front of the other members at Church of the Open Door, is one of the most dramatic events of the year. With the antiquated disco ball whirling above us, Pastor Mike stands at the podium, speaking into a makeshift PA system with the Open Door band behind him. On this particular Sunday, there are three guest vocalists at the microphones. "God is good, amen, amen; God is good," Pastor Mike repeats. He tells the men from New Hope, "What I most appreciate is the courage and vulnerability in your lives, to be as transparent as you." The New Hope men have been preparing for this night for months by memorizing long passages from Romans. Abruptly, one at a time, they rise from their seats and begin reciting scripture as they stride toward the front of the church. Some have memorized longer passages and pronounce their verses in booming voices, while others appear noticeably uncomfortable, fearful that they will forget or flub the lines on their way to the stage. James recites, "For a sin shall not have dominion over you." When they all reach the front they proclaim in unison, "For the wages of sin are death and the gift of God is through eternal life." The band launches into a song: "Knowing you Jesus, there is no greater thing," and then they sing, "I will never be the same again, I will never return, I have closed the door." Each man approaches the microphone. Doug tells the congregation, "Thank you to a bunch of prayer warriors in Medford who never gave up on me," referring to his Pentecostal parents and their friends who prayed regularly for him during the years he lived as a gay man.

Mitch, a leader in training at New Hope in his late forties, gives a testimony. He talks about the years he lived a double life, participating in his church while having secret affairs with men. He relates how his church forced him to resign as a youth pastor when they discovered he was a homosexual, and he reached a crisis point.

> This is the part where I came to the place and I said, "God, either you let me go or you change my life, but I can't live in the middle anymore. I can't struggle with Christianity and how I believe the Bible teaches that homosexuality is wrong and still struggle with the feelings and the emotions and the attractions." Then I remember one night, I was walking to the adult bookstore to cruise. I really didn't want to, but I felt like I had no power over myself.
>
> I began to shake my fists. It was the middle of the night in downtown Charlotte. I was crying in the middle of the night in downtown Charlotte. I started screaming, "God, I hate you. I hate you. Get out of my life. I don't

want you anymore. You're sadistic. You don't care. You won't set me free. You won't let me act out. You just want me to suffer, and I'm not going to do this anymore." And that was right before the doors opened up for me to come to New Hope.

A week later, Mitch jumped in his car and drove out to California to attend New Hope, stopping in rest areas and cruising for sex along the way. He arrived at the ministry with piles of pornography on the backseat of his car. After reading the New Hope regulations and rules, he sheepishly mentioned his porn stash. That afternoon, Anita marched out to his car with gloves and a garbage bag and disposed of the contraband. Now he tells the congregation that he still fights the temptation to look at pornography, but he is well on his way to recovery. I had heard versions of Mitch's story from Drew and Mitch himself, but in this public retelling, the cross-country drive and the arrival were spun out for dramatic effect. However, within two weeks of testifying at New Hope Night, Mitch left the ministry after admitting to having gay pornography in his room. It was his second or third violation.

After Mitch's testimony, the congregation stands and claps. Pastor Mike asks the people in the audience to gather around the men and pray for them. "We encourage you to adopt some of these men into your lives this year. You are a big part of what happens in their lives. Come now, Holy Spirit, come, come, come, Lord, come. Come out of your seats and pray for these men." The men have bookmark-shaped prayer cards with their pictures, hometowns, and goals for the year in their pockets to pass out to members of the church. Ray's prayer for the year was, "That God shows me emotional healing and healing for my back." Evan's read, "To become the man God created me to be, deepening my relationships with Christ and becoming courageous and bold in my relationships with other men." James's said, "My heart aches to be filled with the grace and presence of God." The church members poured down the aisles to lay their hands on each man, kneeling and standing around them until the New Hope men were no longer visible in the crush. The service is designed as an introduction of the ex-gay men and their issues to the church. However, it also provides catharsis to the men at New Hope because it publicly enacts the fusion of the religious and sexual parts of their lives and symbolizes a departure from their previous experiences of secrecy and isolation, bringing their issues to the fore. Christian Smith writes, "The new evangelical churches know and accept their marginality in the culture and are growing precisely because they attend primarily to the therapeutic needs of individuals."[28] Open

Door and New Hope understand this idea, and as Curtis put it, "New Hope Night is like a giant therapy session."

Testimony in the charismatic evangelical tradition has always been a public process, a pronouncement intended for great crowds in churches or revivals. Preachers like Charles Finney and Billy Graham mesmerized crowds with their own born-again stories to convince the unsaved of the power of God in their lives. At New Hope, testimony is a form of therapy. Participants like Mitch speak publicly about the most secret and disturbing aspects of their lives as part of their healing, and New Hope expects ex-gays to talk about themselves in all kinds of forums. Ex-gay men and women express how Jesus has come into their lives, how they have become convinced of his presence, and how he has helped them transform their sexuality. By giving witness to the changes in their lives, they try to convince others that their only option is to disavow their sin of homosexual behavior and/or attraction. As Frank's story demonstrates, each testimony progresses to a crisis point that results in a born-again experience and the discovery of the relationship with God, finishing with participation in the ex-gay ministry and conversion. The most celebrated cases end with marriage or children.

Ex-gay testimonies also create a new form of self-revelation and identity formation centered on coming *out* of homosexuality. New Hope has an entire wall in its office with different shelves for every type of testimony: homosexual, lesbian, masturbation, pornography, transgender identity, parental, and even teenager. Every month, the Exodus newsletter has a testimony or story on the front cover. Most of them feature a ministry leader who has been out of the lifestyle for several years. The headline in March 2001 was "From Prostitute to Pastor: Mike Haley was once addicted to homosexuality. Today he is a fulfilled husband and father. How does he explain the change?"[29] Mike was one of the protesters at the APA conference in Chicago. His testimony contains a brief description of his life as a gay prostitute, his sexual relationships with other men, his experience of being saved by another ex-gay, and his eventually marriage to a woman. Other testimonies have a similar narrative structure but are geared to other issues. Barbara Swallow, a former lesbian, gives a testimony called "All Things Made New." The byline is "After being molested, I decided it wasn't safe being a girl. So I began to construct a new Barbara who wasn't female at all."[30] There are other testimonies by wives of men who are struggling, daughters of lesbians, and parents of gay children.

The testimonies often begin with a traumatic story about past lives of addiction and sin. In each of them, the person reaches a crisis point, and it is during that point that they find themselves either calling out to God or hearing God for the first time. Evan's moment of crisis occurred after he had already begun counseling with an ex-gay therapist. He became overwhelmed in his therapy sessions as he discussed his family and past. As a result, he told me:

> Two years ago I experienced a profound depression and I was suicidal. January of last year, I committed myself into a mental hospital because I was getting ready to buy a gun. And that was actually a good thing for me to do. My friends were very supportive. Even though I was confirming everybody's worst suspicions about how the ex-gay movement leads to suicide. But they brought in all these professors from my school trying to help me break through this. I would discuss Moberly with them, and they'd say, "Sounds cogent." I did one more semester, and part of me realized I needed a change, a place to heal, I need a place where I had community. I needed a place where I wasn't dealing in isolation with the whole ex-gay thing. So, I came and visited in November. New Hope was a much more open place than LIA, which was kind of scary. I needed a place where I could put my life back together, basically.

Diane's testimony illustrated the role her rejection from the church and the military played in leading her to an ex-gay program.

> I was going to New Renewal Church, and I was really close friends with a family in that church. I told them that I had struggled with the gay lifestyle, and after that, they totally disowned me, wouldn't talk to me, told me I was weird, and then the church, when I told them I was an alcoholic, the pastor told me, "No, it's lack of willpower."
>
> I got kicked out [of the military] for homosexual tendencies. I was trying to get a humanitarian discharge or reassignment back here to home because my drinking started increasing, and a lot of family problems started coming to the head. And I told my C.O. [commanding officer] about my brothers being in the lifestyle, and he asked me if I'd ever questioned my sexuality, and I said, "Yeah." And he said, "Have you ever had sex with women," and I said, "Yeah." So the air force kicked me out because of it. I got an honorable discharge, but I was kicked out for homosexual tendencies.

As the testimonies demonstrate, nothing is too private or painful to share, and it is those with the most unsettling tales who become the most sought-after speakers. Yet just as the idea of recovery directs people to focus exclusively on the self, to a certain extent, ex-gays lay claim to "brokenness" as a primary source of identity. The testimonial narrative of pain marks a person's entrance into the community of New Hope and signifies his or her new ex-gay identity in Jesus. But in some cases, ex-gays can only speak of themselves within this language of pain and brokenness. Doug says he has become weary of everyone in the program proclaiming their trauma. "We all have brokenness, but if you keep on using that as a crutch, then you're never going to move on. I think that's one of the big problems we have here. We get into this brokenness contest. I'm like, let's move on, people." In the program, the emphasis on group sharing often leads to what Dwight called "group hysteria." During many of the group meetings, one or two people would begin crying, and then suddenly everybody would be weeping. Although the men at New Hope felt that their confessions were fundamental to their healing, their focus on confession also fostered a sense of myopia. Many of them were too caught up in their own healing to envision their problems in a wider context or even to offer support to others. By focusing on individual stories of pain, the testimonies placed the blame on individual's choice rather than on the aspects of society that make it difficult to live as a gay man or woman. By making Jesus the only person who can transform a person, this process also removed any sense of agency from the individual, negating his potential power to transform the structures around him.

Testimony and accountability are integral to the New Hope program structure. Frank designs the weekly meetings so there is always time for testimonies from men in the house. He believes these testimonies, spoken publicly, help to enforce sexual purity. Yet other men thought that the frequency of men's confessions of "acting out" actually only incited more sexual falls. The more some people "acted out," the more others would follow. Doug also complained that often the same people would monopolize the group while others revealed nothing. Drew referred to these men as "high maintenance." However, there was rarely a time when someone did not have something to confess to the wider group, and instances of "acting out" happened frequently. At one point in the middle of the year, Curtis increasingly spoke of wanting to leave the ministry. One of the reasons involved Nick, his roommate, an older man who had recently left a long-term gay relationship. In their tiny bedroom, crammed with a bunk bed and two dressers, privacy was limited. However, it was a house rule that they could not take off their clothes in front of each other. Sometimes at night, as Curtis undressed, Nick would sit and watch him intently. At first, Curtis felt that this was harmless, since he was only taking off his shirt, and he admitted to enjoying the attention. Gradually, he became uncomfortable but was afraid to report Nick to the rest of the group. He warned Nick that what they were doing was wrong and that he would confess to leadership if it happened again. He later confided that he felt Nick was only waiting for the relationship to develop on a more sexual level.

After one more incident, Curtis confessed their bedroom ritual to the group. The revelation, while not unusual in the course of the year, provoked a three-hour house meeting. "We shared and apologized. Our actions affect everyone else. Everyone has a chance to say how they feel: 'This really hurt me, and this leads me more into temptation because if you're doing this, then it puts thoughts in my mind.'" Eventually, Curtis moved to the other side of the house, where he shared a room with a shy and unassuming man who was unlikely to make sexual advances. Compared to past incidents of men falling in love, this incident was minor, but it pointed to the necessity for constant group sharing and testimony in order to maintain a prohibition on any same-sex behaviors. At the same time, it had the contradictory affect of deliberately interposing illicit sexuality into an environment in which men are supposed to have chaste and masculine friendships. New Hope leaders fear instances of sexual falls precisely because of their potential domino effect on the other men in the program.

The sexual falls that occurred with Curtis and Nick and Brian and Patrick were part of the wider queer conversions men and women experience as ex-gays. While they attest to a new identity that stems from their relationship with Jesus, they still require the accountability structures of the group to control their behavior and desires. Sexual falls are an accepted part of their transformation. Healing their same-sex desires is a religious process, bolstered by the twelve-step elements of the ministry. Although their feelings may not change and their sexual falls continue, they feel transformed religiously. Addiction and recovery from homosexuality mirror the Christian ideas of sin and redemption. As with the idea of a sexual fall, the ex-gay movement believes that no matter how many sex acts you have committed, there is still the possibility of healing and grace if you publicly confess. Jesus extends grace to all people as long as they vow to stay with the ministry and maintain their faith. The individual who experiences a sexual fall can still become a new creation in Christ as long as his transgressive behavior does not continue to recur.

In order for the testimonial confessions to be effective in the program, the men have to adhere to a system of absolute truthfulness and openness. Little of a personal nature is felt to be off-limits for discussion, and whatever remains hidden is a potential source of shame, so confession is mandatory. The moral inventory for ex-gays must be thorough and shared with at least one other person. Private confessions or prayer are encouraged but not considered to have as much efficacy as a public confession. While recovering from homosexual addiction requires individual motivation and self-discipline, the group is extremely important at New Hope. According to Andy Comiskey, creator of the Living Waters program, "The only bridge that can connect the two parts of the struggler—pious Christian and detached addict—is confession to other people who mediate the reality of Christ's grace and truth."[31] Curtis explains, "I'm very honest, because if I'm lying about these things, I'm wasting my time and money here. If I'm going to come here, I might as well do it all the way." For this reason, when he had another instance of sexual temptation, Curtis made sure that Hank knew about it.

At the annual Exodus conference in 2000, Curtis developed a crush on a younger man he met who was part of a Christian youth group. Louis, according to Curtis, was everything he had always desired in a man, and Louis admitted to being attracted to Curtis as well. It was the fifth day of the conference, and we had run into each other on one of the pathways that snaked between the campus buildings. Curtis seemed drained and dull, and I was feeling the same. We headed into the campus bookstore, where we both immediately lunged for the magazine rack as a distraction from the half dozen workshops we had attended that day. I picked up the latest issue of *People* magazine, which one academic I know calls JPS, or Journal of Popular Studies, and Curtis grabbed *Young Miss*, with Enrique Iglesias on the cover. "I'm not attracted to Enrique, so it's okay if I look at this," he said defensively. For a minute, we flipped through the pages and bonded over our mutual exhaustion, and then Curtis confessed, "There is something weird going on." He had been spending hours with Louis every day, and they had prayed together once it became clear that there was mutual sexual attraction between them. Nothing had happened, but Curtis admitted that he wanted to kiss Louis so badly he could "barely stand it." However, Louis had consulted with his youth group leader, and he had decided not to have any more contact with Curtis. Curtis was waiting until he was back at New Hope to come clean to the other men in his accountability group, but he had already told Hank.

When he returned to the ministry, Curtis divulged the experience with Louis to the entire group of men. He confessed that he fantasized about Louis as his boyfriend all the time and that he was tempted to join an online chat forum he knew Louis was involved in. Sam reprimanded

Curtis for continuing to spend time with Louis even after he realized his reasons for wanting to do so were not "godly," but Drew admitted that similar situations happen all the time at the annual conference. A few weeks after that, Curtis brought in photographs from the conference that showed him in a group picture, standing next to Louis, their arms around each other. He told me that his crush had abated and that he had waited a few weeks to develop the pictures so his feelings would fade. Drew walked in as we were looking, and Curtis sheepishly pushed the picture aside, but Drew had seen it, and he rolled his eyes, saying, "Are you looking at Curtis's friends from the conference?" Later that day, I found Curtis alone at his desk, staring at the photo.

Frank writes that self-disclosure opens the way to healing because it creates shared, honest, and mutual vulnerability. Many men feel that the secrecy about their homosexuality and sexual addictions had been the most destructive force in their lives. Group sharing and confession mediates against the addictions for many men. Brian explains, "You see, the thing for me and for most of us is this secrecy, where it's all secret and you can never share. The aim is to bring our diseased attitudes and misdeeds to the light of others and God to be done with them. When it comes from such an attitude, sharing becomes a liberating and life-giving experience." The idea that someone would not confess was practically inconceivable. "What if Mitch had not told anyone about the porn magazines he was hiding in his room?" I once asked Drew. Drew looked dumbfounded. He had never even considered the possibility because the program is built on the premise of public disclosure. The compulsion and public pressure to confess is integral to the way New Hope functions.

In *The History of Sexuality,* Foucault argues that the West has become a confessing society. "One confesses one's crimes, one's sins, one's thoughts and desires, one's illnesses and troubles; one goes about telling, with the greatest precision, whatever is most difficult to tell; one admits to oneself, in pleasure and in pain, things it would be impossible to tell anyone else."[32] Foucault argues that defining sexuality as something sinful did not make it disappear but created a proliferation of discourse around sex, through "explicit articulation and endlessly accumulated detail."[33] A fixation with finding out the "truth" about sexuality arose, and sexuality did not exist unless someone confessed to participating in a sexual act. Confessions or public testimonies about sexual falls are part of the ritual of daily life at New Hope. Foucault writes that confession is a "ritual that unfolds within a power relationship, for one does not confess without the presence . . . of a partner who is not simply the interlocutor but the authority who requires the confession, prescribes and appreciates it, and intervenes in order to judge, punish, forgive, console, and reconcile."[34] New Hope requires that the person testifying do so in the most excruciating detail. "It is no longer a question of simply saying what was done—the sexual act—and how it was done," according to Foucault, "but of reconstructing, in and around the act, the thoughts that recapitulated it, the obsessions that accompanied it, the images, desires, modulations, and quality of the pleasure that animated it."[35] Confessions are not only redemptive but also help restore the confessor from a malady that is physical, mental, or spiritual. In the case of New Hope, confession heals homosexuality. New Hope is part of a wider public culture of intimacy in which ex-gay confessions of traumatized identity become part of a public testimonial discourse of conversion.

Even I was not immune from the pressure to confess and create a testimony that was intelligible to the ministry, even if it was not self-created. In May Drew asked if someone could write a feature on me for the monthly newsletter, which has a circulation of seven hundred, to explain what I was doing at New Hope. Dwight penned the final article, which accompanied a picture of me slouched at the computer. In it, he wrote that I was from New York City and that I had come to the ministry to conduct research for my dissertation. It included a paragraph asking people to contact the ministry office if they were interested in meeting with me to talk about their experiences in ex-gay ministries. It also explained that I had volunteered with the ministry and helped with their computer problems. The brief column appeared next to the article on the ex-gay protest at the APA annual conference in Chicago. Even though I asked them not to include any personal information about myself, the article served as a public disclosure. After it was published, I received many responses from people who wanted to be interviewed.

THERAPY IN ACTION

The models of self-help and developmental healing are implemented not only at ex-gay ministries, but also by individual therapists sympathetic to the ex-gay movement. The idea that Christians can counsel or minister to homosexuals has been around since the 1970s, when Anita Bryant Ministries and the Moody Bible Institute trained counselors.[36] Anita Bryant Ministries employed "the principle of conflict" to force the counselee to realize that his or her homosexual behavior was sinful and to create guilt and inner turmoil that would pave the way for an acceptance of Jesus Christ in his or her life.[37] Ex-gay therapists continue to use this form of pastoral counseling in individual or family therapy, focusing on problems of abuse or addiction. Ex-gay therapists combine self-help and recovery models as well reparative therapy techniques to counsel and minister to homosexual and lesbian patients. In addition to their focus on homosexuality as a developmental disorder, therapists also define homosexuality as an addiction. They use the small-group and confession approach in counseling, joining the psychological and self-help strands of the ex-gay movement.

Many men at New Hope criticized the program for placing too much emphasis on religion, and as a result, the New Hope program began to have a Christian counselor on the premises during certain days of the week to meet with men who wanted professional therapy. The counselor, Jim Boylson, a middle-aged man fulfilling his final credits toward his counseling credential, worked in the office Tuesdays and Thursdays. Boylson had been a Christian missionary to Southeast Asian refugees in San Francisco for years until he became interested in therapy for the ex-gay movement. He met Anita and Frank through a church friend, but before working at New Hope, he had never met a gay or ex-gay person in his life. Like the NARTH-affiliated therapists, he believed that family dynamics cause homosexuality and that men sexualize their desire to feel friendship or intimacy with other men. While he had not counseled any women, he did say that abuse was the key to lesbianism. He stressed that if a client chose to accept his or her homosexuality, he would not continue to work with that person because he cannot condone the gay lifestyle. Boylson's method for gradually healing ex-gay men and women consisted of confession in a therapeutic setting. He counseled six men from the program on a weekly basis, and by his account, he had helped them work through family trauma as well as become affirmed in their masculinity. He encouraged men to rehash early experiences in order to undo their "defensive detachment" to the same sex and affirm themselves as masculine. Boylson stressed the religious aspects of change as well, and he prayed with his counselees and recommended biblical scriptures for them to study. He told me that he understood Christianity and psychology as the same belief system simply because God created them both. Other Christian counselors use less traditional methods. Brian had been seeing Joe Dallas in Southern California before coming to New Hope. He told me that "With my counselor I would give him twenty bucks in an envelope, and if I could make it without doing anything [having a sexual fall] for a certain amount of time he would give me the money back. And if I didn't he would put the money in the offering at church. I just ended up losing a lot of money."

Richard Cohen is an ex-gay who is now married with three children. He is also a psychotherapist who founded the International Healing Foundation, an ex-gay-affiliated counseling organization. He combines the self-help healing and family development approaches in his slightly unorthodox counseling practice. The first step in healing is purchasing his book, *Coming Out Straight,* and watching the supplementary video. People can call him for an appointment only after they have bought the book, and then Cohen will design a personal healing plan for them, or they can use his twenty-one-step general plan. Through teleconferencing classes and his "Love/Sex/Intimacy" seminars, Cohen teaches the four stages of transitioning from homosexual to heterosexual. Part of this involves the notion of "touch therapy." At the 2000 annual Exodus conference, a few men at New Hope attended his men-only seminar, where they learned to overcome sexual attraction and experience intimacy through physical contact. During touch therapy, men stand pelvis to pelvis with their arms wrapped around each other to gain familiarity with touching another man in a nonsexual context. When someone asked what to do if they get an erection, Cohen urged the men to discuss it openly so they would not feel shame or embarrassment. Frank and other ministry leaders consider many of Cohen's techniques to be controversial. The premise that overt physical contact will help men heal their homosexuality is the absolute opposite of the rules and prohibitions of New Hope's program; Frank believes that Cohen's touch therapy provokes sexual falls and same-sex behavior. Cohen also offers individual and family healing sessions, where he works to "reconcile long standing issues, break down the walls of detachment and restore love between parents and children." For individuals, the healing involves "direct assistance to heal core wounds and fulfill unmet needs."[38]

By blurring the distinction between confession and testimony, the ex-gay movement transforms therapy, traditionally a private transaction between a patient and therapist, into a public process. Sharing as a form of self-help is always public, and people are expected to make their grief and pain visible. Bringing the intimate into public prominence is the vehicle for healing. For Christians, it is difficult to believe that God would create a gay person and then condemn homosexual behavior. It is a far more hopeful mode of thinking to believe that homosexuality is a learned behavior or addiction that can be cured through multiple methods. If so, then behavior can be unlearned. By combining the premises of therapy and religion, New Hope and the ex-gay movement can account for change on many levels and deflect criticism if one explanation seems inadequate.

Evan attended Cohen's touch therapy workshop, but he still felt that the developmental theories about his childhood and masculinity offered the most useful way to think about his homosexuality. However, in early September, when several men were visiting New Hope to decide whether to spend a year there, Evan found himself sexually attracted to a man named Jason. Over the weekend, they flirted and kissed. Evan waited a week, and then he realized he had to disclose the sexual fall to Hank, Sam, and Scott. Evan was normally cynical about aspects of the live-in program, and he was often in trouble for criticizing the Christian videos they watched or the way Pastor Mike discussed scripture. He had originally planned to depart after the year was finished, but the incident unsettled him, and he claimed that he still had a long way to go toward healing what he called his "relational deficits." He decided to remain another year to focus on sexual purity. Although Evan felt he could locate and explain the origins of his homosexuality through Moberly's theories, he believed that understanding the cause was not sufficient without a structure that helped him to regulate his behavior. New Hope offered rules and regulations in which it was mandatory to disclose and confess to mediate against sexual falls and improprieties. Even if he had more sexual falls, the structure was in place, and through public testimonies he would continue in his process of conversion.

CHAPTER 6

Love Won Out?

During the summer of 1998, full-page advertisements appeared simultaneously in the *New York Times*, the *Washington Post*, and other national newspapers.[1] One version featured Anne Paulk, her gleaming diamond wedding ring clearly visible. Underneath her picture the caption read, "wife, mother, former lesbian." The Center for Reclaiming America and a coalition of Christian Right groups conceived and paid for the ad as part of a larger media offensive against gay rights on the state and national levels.[2] Anne's testimony, as well as pictures of other men and women who had changed, was designed to illustrate that homosexuality is a choice and that people can become married heterosexuals through accepting the tenets of the Christian faith, applying therapeutic principles, and living communally in ex-gay programs.

John Paulk, Anne's husband, was also visible in these ads. A former drag queen named Candi, John met Anne at New Hope in the early 1990s while both were completing the residential program. John and Anne became prominent Exodus spokespeople who were catapulted into the national spotlight when *Newsweek* placed them on its cover shortly after the ads appeared.[3] John describes the beginning of his journey out of homosexuality: "Tons of makeup, jewelry and a blonde wig couldn't hide the pain. There was a beautiful woman staring back at me in the mirror. But that woman was me—John Paulk, a man."[4] He wrote, "I opened my up my closet and I looked at all the dresses, wigs, high heels, makeup and jewelry I had accumulated over the past three years.

It suddenly hit me. Somehow I knew I didn't need Candi anymore. I realized that 'crown of jewels' I wore left me feeling empty and alone. So I said goodbye to her, put everything in a cardboard box and threw it into a dumpster."[5] At the time of the ads, John Paulk was a homosexuality and gender specialist working in the public policy division at Focus on the Family, a conservative Christian organization headed by James Dobson. Anne was writing a book about ex-gay women while serving on the Exodus board of directors (a post that John used to occupy). He and Anne now have three children. With the help of Mike Haley, another New Hope Ministry graduate, John Paulk organized Focus on the Family–sponsored ex-gay conferences throughout the country. John Paulk and Haley have designed the Love Won Out conferences to reach conservative Christians and churches with the message that homosexuals can change.

In early 2005, a new set of ads featuring Alan Chambers, the president of Exodus, with his wife, Leslie, appeared in the *Cincinnati Examiner*. The advertisement was part of a series that Exodus was releasing in various media markets throughout the year. However, the ad, featuring Alan's testimony, directly addressed the issue of gay marriage. The title above Alan and Leslie reads, "I Questioned Homosexuality. By finding my way out of a gay identity, I found the love of my life in the process. Gay marriage would only have blinded me to such an incredible joy." The text reads, "My name is Alan Chambers, and I lived for nine years with a homosexual orientation. Today I'm married to Leslie, and we're beginning a family with our first child this year." He writes, "I grew up with the secret shame of being sexually molested by an older man," and this lead to his homosexual feelings at age ten.

> I never imagined my marriage partner could *ever be a woman*. I just assumed that if I ever "got married," it would be with a man. Like so many of the gay men I came to know, I was starved for genuine male love and affirmation. But after years of searching, I realized that acceptance in the gay community always wore the same tired nametag called "sex," and every sexual encounter with a man only emptied more of me than it filled.
>
> And so the questions began.
>
> In all honesty, my search for answers was difficult. . . . Changing old responses and patterns, then finding security on the deepest level, takes time. *But, it was totally worth the journey!*
>
> Here's the truth. *If I had a gay marriage option ten years ago, I'd never have dealt with the root issues of my homosexual behavior.* I'd probably be in and out of half a dozen "marital" relationships. And I'd never know the complete peace I now have about my past. Leslie is not my diploma

for "healing," nor is she a prop that shows how I've abandoned a sexual identity. She is my perfect complement and completes me in ways no male relationships can ever do . . . physically or emotionally.

I'm living proof that change *is* possible.[6]

Chambers's polished testimony has all the elements of ex-gay ideas about homosexuality: sexual abuse, a "gay community" focused only on sex, a gay identity versus homosexual behavior, and the contention that his marriage is real rather than a diploma or prop. Unlike the ad campaign featuring Anne and John Paulk, this ad explicitly poses an argument against gay marriage. Instead of claiming that gay marriage is wrong for biblical reasons, the ad proclaims that making gay marriage legal will prevent gay men and women from realizing "the root issues" of their homosexual behavior and that they are truly heterosexual.

Since the early 1990s, organizations of the Christian Right have taken their cue from people like the Paulks and Alan Chambers, utilizing their stories of sexual conversion to move from a politics of condemnation of homosexuality to one of compassion. Anti-gay legislation is no longer supported simply by anti-gay rhetoric but through the message that there is hope for healing. Christian Right activism now directly relies upon the personal testimonies of ex-gays to oppose any local, state, or national attempts to secure rights for gay people in the realm of marriage, gay-positive school curricula, partner benefits, and adoption policy. Using the testimonies of ex-gay men and women, the Christian Right promotes wider anti-gay activism cloaked in the rhetoric of choice, change, and compassion. Ex-gay testimonies are politically important not just for use in opposing civil rights, but also in framing the process of identity construction and the legitimacy of a particular identity. The ad campaigns and organizations of the Christian Right have been successful because they use ex-gay testimonies to provide an alternative narrative to being gay.

Even Jerry Falwell has joined the bandwagon. On National Coming Out of Homosexuality Day, October 11, 1999, Falwell reversed his stance of a dozen years that homosexuality is the scourge of Christianity and told the audience and gay protesters in an unusually conciliatory manner, "Homosexuality is not more sinful than heterosexual promiscuity."[7] Falwell's much-publicized meeting with Mel White of Soulforce in October 1999 and other gay and lesbian clergy members was another attempt to create a more compassionate and inclusive image for the Christian Right.[8] Yet Falwell cancelled his meal with White at the last

minute in order to avoid alienating his constituents. At the annual
Exodus conference in North Carolina in July 2005, Falwell was the
headline speaker.

The use of ex-gay testimonies as a political strategy also reveals the
contradictions around changing sexuality, the ex-gay movement, and
gay rights. Christian Right organizations draw on ex-gay stories to contend that anything other than heterosexual, monogamous sexuality is
invalid and that gay people do not merit political or civil rights. However, most men and women in ex-gay ministries do not experience the
clear-cut change that Alan Chambers advocates. Their lives do not end
in marriage but become a continual process of having sexual falls, recom-
mitting to Christ, being celibate, participating in ex-gay ministries, and
so on. Their queer conversions attest to the fact that change is a process
of sexual and religious conversion and that their identities are constantly
in a state of flux. The Christian Right's anti-gay agenda cannot account
for the queer conversions of men and women because its political stance
requires that men and women actually become heterosexual.

Despite the overt politicization of Exodus since Alan Chambers
became president in 2001, men and women have their own political
ideas about change and conversion that often conflict with the Exodus
leadership and other Christian Right organizations. The idea of queer
conversions also denotes the ambivalent stance of the ex-gay movement
to the politics of the Christian Right. Many men and women at New
Hope, who are not public figures, expressed that the idea of change was
misrepresented by the ad campaign. Their experiences in ex-gay programs do not necessarily translate into public personas or public activism
like that of John and Anne Paulk, Mike Haley, and Alan Chambers.
Nor do their politics neatly fit into the gay rights/anti–gay rights political dichotomy. The queer conversions that men and women at New
Hope undergo refute the wider politics of the Christian Right, and at
times conflict erupted when ex-gays strove to remain separate from the
agendas of ex-gay leaders and Christian Right organizations.

SELLING OUT SOME OF THE GRAYNESS

Not all leaders and men and women who join ministries would support
Alan Chambers's proclamations about gay marriage. Most men at New
Hope balk at the label "anti-gay." In conversations, they often opposed
any legislative efforts against gay civil rights, and they frequently spoke
of their own identification with gay men and women, even as they

rejected that label for themselves. The ad campaigns relied on the claim that people have changed from homosexual to heterosexual, but most men and women at New Hope experienced change as a more fraught, fluid, and uncertain process. They readily conceded that change is a process that involves identity, behavior, and desires and believed that their own conversions are primarily religious. As a result, their beliefs about gay rights and the ability to change often conflicted with the public activism of the Christian Right. They assert that they have a right to change their sexuality and participate in ministries, but they also feel their stories should not be appropriated by larger organizations to promulgate a message that they feel is misleading and false.

Brian believes that anti-gay laws like those that Focus on the Family promotes are anathema to a Christian agenda. He is strongly opposed to the legislative and public policy agendas of the organization. "What I don't like is what I sense is the whole idea that we're going to make you do something, the whole idea that we're going to make it uncomfortable for you socially if you choose to be gay in this society—to the point of taking away your rights or even throwing you in jail. Anything along those lines I believe is repulsive." Unlike John Paulk or Alan Chambers, Brian has elected to make his struggle a more private issue. Since completing the program in 1997, he has had sexual falls with other men, but for him, trying to change is the only path he can follow and still remain true to his faith. He is the first to admit that the idea of change is a process and that some men and women never change their desires even if they control their outward behavior. Arden, who became a Jew for Jesus after years as a member of Queer Nation, also had a more complicated political relationship to the agenda of Exodus and Focus on the Family. She recalled how she protested the annual Exodus conference at Point Loma in 1994 as a member of the Lesbian Avengers. She and others interrupted an ex-gay session bare chested and began singing "Amazing Gays." She was an attendee at the same conference in 2000. "If I look at my political views, they have not changed that much. I'm not a Republican. I'm not speaking out against gay rights. Equal rights to housing and employment, I'm not against that. I feel really pressured to be anti-choice and hold onto all these conservative views about all these things. I haven't changed completely my opinions about it. I'm in a stage of not knowing." She was still caught between her previous affiliations with activist groups and the explicit activism of Exodus. More and more women and men like Arden and Brian are worried that an organization they view as a means to change their sexuality has increasingly drawn them into association with the Christian Right. Not all the men in the New Hope program believe in the conspiratorial idea of a radical homosexual agenda. In fact, many find themselves more sympathetic to gay rights than to the Christian Right. Curtis said once, "With this whole issue, because you've been ridiculed and mocked and bashed, that's why the pride thing comes in and why gay activists are so in your face because there's so much anger and bitterness. Their motives come from such a hurt. My whole life was like that."

What the ad campaign finally brought to light was the shaky and often tenuous association between the ex-gay movement and more influential organizations like Focus on the Family. Although often lumped into the rest of the religious Right, Frank and other members of the ex-gay movement had for years sought to gain legitimacy or even a hearing with James Dobson and had been repeatedly ignored. Dobson and other leaders treated Frank and the ex-gays who had "come out of homosexuality" as a bit of an embarrassment. As emissaries from New Hope like Haley and Paulk joined Focus on the Family, it became politically expedient to use the message of change to revamp its anti-gay agenda. This time, instead of outright condemnation, Dobson could showcase John Paulk as proof that people could change into heterosexuals through Christian love.

The complicity of the ex-gay movement in the 1998 ad campaign emerged from the history of its exclusion by other Christian Right organizations. Because of a desire for validity and publicity, Frank and the president of Exodus at the time, Bob Davies, agreed to allow the Center for Reclaiming America (CRA) to utilize their stories. Suddenly, after years of being shunned, the ex-gays were at the center of a wider Christian coalition. Brian, who was vehemently opposed to the participation of New Hope and the ex-gay movement in the CRA campaign, explains, "The impression that I got . . . was that they were willing to sell out on some of that grayness in order to get some national recognition from these organizations that they've been wanting to get for a long time—some validation. Because Exodus has had trouble, Focus didn't want to touch it for years. It's a weird issue in general even for Christians so they were willing to sell out. It was almost like a deal, that's what I saw." Frank's motivations were less political; rather, he sought to finally garner the publicity he felt the media had denied him for years. "We have been ignored by the church and the culture for twenty-five years. . . . The media, in particular, has had a conspiracy of silence about the presence of ex-gays." Whereas Frank and Bob saw churches as their main target,

Alan Chambers, as the new president of Exodus, saw policy and politics as Exodus's arena of struggle.

After the people from the CRA requested testimonies and pictures, Frank didn't hear from them again until the ads were published. No one had asked their opinion about the advertisements' texts or messages. Janet Folger, the architect of the ads, appeared on *Nightline* and *ABC Evening News* in 1998, but the ministries themselves were largely forgotten by the larger Christian organizations. When prominent gay organizations like the National Gay and Lesbian Task Force and the Human Rights Campaign responded to the ads with outrage, the New Hope office and Exodus headquarters received the brunt of the phone calls and protests. Gay rights groups had sporadically staged protests at New Hope since its inception in 1973. In 1991 the Lesbian Avengers, of which Arden was then a member, even dumped a box of crickets in the Love in Action office, forcing the workers to call 911. This time, however, they were unprepared to handle the deluge of calls. Frank and the rest of the men at the office wound up devoting themselves entirely to dealing with the media, and in the process having disagreements with the rest of the CRA coalition. When Frank or Drew explained that change is a complicated process that doesn't work for some people and is often more religious than sexual, Janet Folger chastised them for contradicting the message of the ads.

After some of the men at New Hope read the ads, many were appalled that the CRA had used ex-gay testimonies to argue against money for AIDS research and other civil rights issues. "I got very upset." Brian remembers. "I said to Frank, 'If you want to do advertising, do your own. They are using ministries to promote their agenda.'" Many, like Brian, felt that the entire premise of the ads and the anti-gay agenda of the coalition that created them was misleading. None of these men felt they had really changed. James said, "It was too plastic. It wasn't enough. It made it sound like, 'Ta da, just walk through our program and it will all be changed.' I felt like it wasn't completely honest and it smelled of Christian cheesiness." Another man named Ethan told Frank, "You're playing in the Republicans' backyard, and you're giving them exactly what they want. And you're making yourself look like a fool." After Brian watched a debate on *Nightline* with Janet Folger of the CRA and Andrew Sullivan, it confirmed his feeling that he was a pawn in a larger political game. "They used [the testimonies] as if to say, 'We now have a way for you to change, and if you don't we will pass laws against you,'" he told me. "Janet Folger went as far as to refuse to deny that her organization would not defend legislation for the incarceration of homosexuals. In other words, they supported the state's rights to choose to throw people into prison for homosexual behavior. So that didn't sit well with me, and I started to become angry that something I was a part of was going public with a message that I wasn't in agreement with."

Soon after the televised debate, Brian and Hank had an argument that created a rift in the New Hope program. Hank told the men that he believed states should pass laws to incarcerate homosexuals, and that homosexuality should be illegal. Brian furiously stormed out of the meeting and left the ministry for a few hours. The conversation made him question whether he wanted to remain a part of New Hope at all. "Suddenly my whole worldview was turned upside down, thinking that maybe everyone believed that in the church. What was I part of? It was a very hard time for me." He spoke to Frank about the issue, and Frank's comments, while not going as far as Hank's, did not reassure him. He questioned many of the men in the program, but he was frustrated that even though they claimed to disagree with Hank, they were afraid to speak out. For a few weeks, he avoided the classes and meetings while he decided what course of action to take. Although he ultimately decided to stay and eventually came to an uneasy truce with Hank, there was no resolution to the issue. To vent some of his frustration and anger, he wrote an essay on why he thought the Bible would oppose legislation for the incarceration of homosexuals. In early 2005, when Brian learned that Jerry Falwell would be a speaker at the annual Exodus conference, he wrote a letter to Alan Chambers in protest.

SAVING AMERICA FROM COMMUNISM, 1960–1975

The emergence of the "hope for healing" and "change is possible" strategy dates to the 1990s, but early Christian Right organizations maintained the same obsession with homosexuality. Christian Right discourse about homosexuality has shifted between "homosexuality as communism," a backlash against feminism and gay liberation, and the idea of "special rights" and the "promotion of homosexuality." In the 1960s, Billy James Hargis, head of the Christian Crusade (CC), was often quoted as saying that homosexuality and communism went hand in hand. The CC, which lasted from 1948 until 1974, chose communism as one of its foremost targets, but Hargis and other members of his organization eventually addressed issues of sex education, the sexual revolution, and homosexuality as issues of national security. Hargis's CC linked secular humanism to communism, which would destroy the Christian family. These fears came to focus on homosexual threats to youth as the CC grew.

Founded in 1948 in Tulsa, Oklahoma, by Hargis, a pugnacious fundamentalist pastor, the CC expanded to include a youth program called Summit Ministries, the American Christian College, and the David Livingstone Foundation.[9] Eventually, the CC had a membership of five hundred thousand, and Hargis appeared on over five hundred radio stations nationally.[10] To become a member or set up a local chapter, an applicant was required to sign a pledge stating, "I believe in Jesus Christ and the constitution of the United States of America."[11] From the outset, the organization's message conflated national security with Christianity, heterosexuality, and moral conservatism. "Christian Crusade is America's largest organization devoted exclusively to exposing and fighting the evils of Godless communism."[12] In one pamphlet Hargis wrote, "Unless the religious, moral and traditionalist forces of America can hold the line against this trend toward Satan and Satanism, America as we know it, will perish; and we will be engulfed in a monolithic Marxist society where freedom of religion is denied as it is behind the Iron Curtain today."[13] With fiery and inflammatory rhetoric, Hargis railed against communism in many guises: sex education, the civil rights movement, and homosexuality.[14] According to Hargis, the very future of the nation was at stake.

By the mid-1960s, Hargis had declared that the focus of the CC would be internal moral problems within the United States.[15] "Today's youth are caught up in a satanic, immoral and Godless sex revolution," he wrote.[16] From as early as 1964, Hargis devoted his letters to the issue of homosexuality. He was especially incensed that the National Council for Churches was "accepting homosexual perversion as legal and normal."[17] Hargis viewed homosexuality as a direct threat to the safety of youth: "One of the first rules of the Communist revolution is to corrupt the morals of the youth primarily by illicit sex or a breakdown in the moral code."[18] His preoccupation with youth resulted in the creation of a youth ministry and American Christian College to function as the educational arm of the CC.[19] "Our greatest concern today should be the growing influence of communism and communist ideas among college and high school age youth."[20] In 1964 the Christian Crusade purchased a hotel in Manitou Springs, Colorado, where they hosted Summit Ministries for youth, "to train young people during the summer months to be leaders in the fight for God and country."[21] High school students attended classes and seminars at Summit during the summer, and some later entered the CC-sponsored American Christian College upon graduation. Hargis designed the youth ministry and college to counter the leftist organizations that were prevalent on college campuses during the same period. "No youngster, after his or her Summit training, is liable to swallow the bait thrown by liberal or Marxist professors in a college classroom."[22] Hargis's youth choir, All American Kids, was also part of this effort. Throughout the late 1960s and early 1970s, Hargis toured with this choir, staging "musical extravaganzas in major cities across America."[23]

Despite his heated anti-homosexual rhetoric, Hargis, like many other preachers before and after, had been committing the very sins he railed against in his sermons. In October 1974, Hargis abruptly wrote in his weekly newsletter that he was taking a leave of absence from the CC. He cited fatigue and the need to recuperate from an illness as the rationale. In 1976, *Time* magazine broke the story and detailed allegations that Hargis was having sex with high school boys who were part of his All American Kids Choir.[24] Five students revealed to David Noebel, the dean of Summit Ministries and second in charge to Hargis, that Hargis invited them to his farm in the Ozarks where they had sex. Hargis justified the relationships by citing the friendship between David and Jonathan in the Old Testament. Hargis had also conducted a wedding ceremony for one of these students, and during the honeymoon the bride and groom both confessed that they each had had sex with Hargis. Hargis avoided responsibility for his behavior, citing "genes and chromosomes," and then later claimed that he had been attacked and defamed by "liberal newspapers."[25] David Noebel became head of the American Christian College and Summit Ministries, which are now funded by Focus on the Family, and after a prolonged struggle with Hargis, Noebel eventually separated from the CC entirely in 1976.[26] After the scandal, the CC lost clout and money, and Hargis faded into ignominy. He sent desperate fundraising letters that included denunciations of the media and Noebel, his former protégé. "I need you to stand by me. If you lay this letter down and forget it, Billy James Hargis' ministry will suffer as never before."[27]

Hargis, who died in November 2004, was one of a long line of fundamentalist preachers, starting with Billy Sunday in the early twentieth century. However, he was one of the first to effectively combine fundamentalist rhetoric with an explicit political agenda that connected anti-communism and family values, and he was not the last to lose his ministry in scandal. His connections with political figures like George Wallace and the John Birch Society established a precedent for later Christian Right organizations that would flourish from the 1970s to the 1990s. Hargis also laid the groundwork for connecting anti-gay politics and anti–sex education programs with the moral state of the nation. The link between sexuality, the family, and the future of the country was an important theme that Concerned Women for America, Anita Bryant, and Focus on the Family would reiterate in the 1970s. Hargis's rhetoric about homosexuality was also bolstered by the growth of the New Right during the 1960s and 1970s. With the creation of the New Right, a political movement was born that incorporated economic libertarians, conservative fundamentalists, and evangelicals.[28] In the 1970s, other politically oriented Christian organizations joined the political coalition loosely defined as the New Right.[29] As a result, the success and influence of Christian conservatives in the spheres of public policy and popular opinion improved dramatically. The CC marked the beginning of what would become a three-decade-long shifting constellation of Christian political groups and institutions.

FROM BIBLE BELIEVERS TO CHRISTIAN RIGHT ACTIVISTS

When George Gallup Jr. polled Americans about their faith and religious beliefs in the mid-1970s, he found that over one-third described themselves as "born again," meaning "a turning point in your life when you committed yourself to Jesus Christ."[30] Roughly, fifty million adult Americans agreed that "the Bible is the actual Word of God and is to be taken literally, word for word."[31] *Time* magazine dubbed 1976 the year of the evangelical, and Jimmy Carter's religious beliefs as president made headlines. Although hard-line fundamentalists like Hargis and Carl McIntire had ventured into the world of cold war politics, few rank-and-file conservative Christians had followed them. At the same time, conservative religious organizations were the first to recognize and exploit the power of televangelism, and McIntire, the "Radio Fundamentalist," and others gained expertise in using the airwaves as a proselytizing medium. In the 1970s, New Right entrepreneurs and professional organizers like Paul Weyrich, Richard Viguerie, and Howard Phillips saw the opportunity to carry out a conservative revolution and party realignment. Through radio, fundraising techniques, and direct-mail initiatives, they corralled the latent conservative Christian voting block into politics and mobilized a transdenominational Christian Right constituency. By 1979 conservative Christians had established the Moral Majority, Christian Voice, and the Religious Roundtable.

Jerry Falwell's rhetorical strategy of naming his group the Moral Majority in 1979 served to capture the diffuse experiences and beliefs of conservative Christians under one umbrella. Susan Harding writes, "In two short words, Falwell marked the majority status of theological conservatives among Protestants, elided it with majority status among all Americans, and claimed the right to reintegrate culturally disenfranchised fundamentalists into national public life."[32] Falwell replaced the idea of a silent majority—Christians with moral values who did not enter into public and political debate—with that of a vocal and public moral majority. The category "moral majority" was deliberately combative and drew distinct battle lines. It signified that the majority, comprised of conservative Christians, had values that were in conflict with secular society. Falwell, who had previously eschewed involvement in political causes, underwent a political conversion. He asserted that religious conservatives—Protestants, Catholics, and Jews—had a new moral imperative to organize a movement to fight communism abroad and feminist and gay rights reforms at home.

Falwell required a strategy to convince this constituency to organize politically and to justify fundamentalist religious involvement in the public realm rather than separation from it. Part of his tactic was to prove that something radically new had happened during the preceding twenty years. Falwell argued that progressive social movements had irrevocably altered American culture beyond recognition. He told followers that these forces were encroaching upon both the state and world of the church. Therefore, he warned fundamentalists that if they wanted to defend their traditional world, they should act jointly to reverse historical trends before it was too late.[33] Opposition to feminism, gay liberation, the Equal Rights Amendment (ERA), and the sexual revolution politicized a generation of Christian activists and provided a set of symbolic moral issues to unite them. It also furnished them with a common enemy, and it enabled Falwell to claim that Christians were besieged and assailed by the wider secular culture.

Most important, Falwell reframed political issues such as the ERA, pornography, abortion, homosexuality, creationism, public school curricula, television sex, and violence as moral issues. By using religiously inflected language, he united primarily white conservative Protestants from different theological and denominational backgrounds around distinct symbols like moral decay and secular humanism. Falwell fused public activism and Bible-believing Protestantism, and the moniker the Religious Right became the rubric that enabled these organizations to work in coalitions. These symbolic issues renewed a shared language and an expanded definition of what it meant to be a Christian. Instead of quarreling over theological debates, what counted was that the person realized he or she was a sinner, asked Jesus to forgive him or her, and accepted Jesus into his or her heart as a personal savior. Instead of denominational differences, what mattered was shared opposition to abortion, homosexuality, sex education, and the separation of church and state.

Theorists of the Christian Right have argued that cultural accommodation has led to the secularization of Christian Right groups. This work asserts that as conservative Protestantism moved into the mainstream of American society, Protestants sacrificed their theology and religious principles to secular political objectives, such as trying to shape the legislative agenda of the Republican Party and insert morality into politics.[34] Yet organizations of the Christian Right bridged the divide between churches and politics, creating religious-political para-church organizations where people could become involved in anything from local school issues to national elections. Some of these early organizations and leading figures included the Christian Crusade, Pat Robertson of the Christian Coalition, Jimmy Swaggart and Jim Bakker, Charles Swindoll of the Evangelical Free Church, James Kennedy of Coral Ridge Ministries, Bill Bright of Campus Crusade for Christ, Demos Shakarian of Full Gospel Business Men's Fellowship, Beverly LaHaye of Concerned Women for America, Tim LaHaye, politician (and future author of the best-selling Left Behind series), Louis Sheldon of the Traditional Values Coalition, Phyllis Schlafly of the Eagle Forum, James Dobson of Focus on the Family, and Gary Bauer of the Family Research Council, now run by Tony Perkins.

Although the activism of these Christian Right groups was religiously inflected, the groups did not always share tactical or ideological goals. But the Christian Right leaders created a common vision and justification for public activism in several ways. They specified a time to which their constituencies could trace the origins of the threatening changes in American society; they identified culprits like feminists, gays, and secular humanists; and they delineated the consequences of the actions of these groups: a permissive society, the abandonment of moral standards, and the proliferation of alternative lifestyles. They also provided a concrete and ambitious overarching goal: to establish a coalition of morally active citizens who were pro-life, pro-family, pro-morality, and pro-American. The language itself enabled them to portray their political work as a countermobilization to an attack from without and to convey a sense of embattlement.

FORGING FAMILY VALUES

In 1979 Senator Paul Laxalt of Nevada introduced the Family Protection Act in the U.S. Senate. The purpose of the act was to "counteract disruptive federal intervention into family life in the United States, and to encourage restoration of family unity, parental authority and a climate of traditional morality."[35] Its provisions included thirty-seven parts related to education, welfare, taxation, and domestic relations. Laxalt requested that the Senate deny federal funds to schools whose textbooks "belittle traditional women's roles in society" and prohibit legal service funds for gay rights litigation.[36] The act did not pass, but it embodied the sentiments of many conservative Christians at the time.

In the 1970s, as movements like feminism and gay liberation asserted themselves in the public realm, the challenges they posed to gender roles, the organization of the family, and traditional sexuality undermined the Christian idea of a white, heterosexual, family-oriented citizenry. As more women entered the workforce than ever before, organizations like Concerned Women for America (CWA) reemphasized the centrality of women's traditional roles.[37] Even as the need for two family wage earners rose with the recession and job losses of the 1970s, making the nuclear family in which only men worked less economically viable, organizations like CWA emphasized that women should stay home. The fluid notions of sexual identity espoused by lesbian feminists and gay liberationists, who argued to varying degrees that sexuality was a choice and that it changed over a lifetime, were also deeply threatening to Christian ideas about sexuality.

Conservative Christian organizations strategically located the causes for the economic downturn in radical feminism, homosexuality, unattached men, cultural liberalism, and the counterculture. By defining themselves as "pro-family," these organizations set the terms of debate, pitting themselves against "deviant" identities like homosexuality and single motherhood. Family values became something "we" all stood for, and the Christian Right explained how "they" undermined it. The concept of family values invoked a mythical idea of the nuclear family that conservatives insisted the feminist and gay rights movements of the

1960s and 1970s were intent on destroying. David Noebel, Billy James Hargis's former protégé, also wrote in answer to the question, "What sort of lifestyle do American women want?" in the Summit Ministries newsletter, "According to a Gallup poll, 74% chose marriage with children as the most interesting and satisfying life for themselves. Only 7% preferred to remain single, free, and occupied with a full-time career."[38]

The emergence of family values Christian activism meshed well with the theology of many nondenominational and evangelical Christians. Reformed evangelical theology upholds the idea that America is God's chosen nation. Therefore, to be effective Christians, people must strive to create America "in God's image." In the theology of evangelical Christianity, the family has always been the vehicle through which Christians lead a godly life. Historians have argued that some Christians view women as the members of the family most likely to receive the word of God and that women represent their families in church.[39] Many conservative Christians believe that the heterosexual nuclear family is divinely mandated. This theological and political imperative became more pronounced in the 1970s when groups like CWA, led by Beverly LaHaye, and Focus on the Family, led by James Dobson, mobilized Christians on the grassroots level through direct-mail and letter-writing campaigns. The ERA united Christian organizations around the twin "menaces" of feminism and homosexuality. Beverly LaHaye wrote that the ERA would desegregate prisons and other public facilities like universities and place women at risk. She also argued that the "ERA will require you to acknowledge homosexuality as an acceptable lifestyle."[40]

LaHaye's rationale for launching CWA was that God ordained her to bring biblical principles into public policy in opposition to feminists' viewpoints: "As I was traveling around and speaking with my husband in our family seminars, I became aware that the feminist movement was dominating the attention of the press. I was particularly upset when these feminists stated that they spoke for all American women."[41] LaHaye's husband, Tim LaHaye, was a prominent member of the Christian Right and a cosponsor of the Moral Majority. They met at Bob Jones University, and by 1980 Tim LaHaye had organized the Council for National Policy, a vehicle for conservative religious leaders, politicians, and businesspeople to come together to share and implement their ideas. In 1984 he formed the American Coalition for Traditional Values and began training seminars for conservative religious leaders.[42] Beverly LaHaye's decision to become the head of what is now a five-hundred-thousand-member organization stemmed from her existing political connections as much as her opposition to feminism. The basis of LaHaye's opposition to the ERA was that it supposedly denigrated women's traditional roles in the home. However, as a woman who worked and was rarely at home, LaHaye seemed to contradict her own rhetoric. To address this inconsistency, LaHaye signed her newsletters "author, lecturer, mother and pastor's wife."

In answer to an interviewer's question, "What movements in America do you feel are the greatest threat to the family and moral principles?" LaHaye unequivocally stated: the National Organization for Women.[43] In an article reminiscent of the anti-communist rhetoric of Billy James Hargis, LaHaye wrote, "You may not wish to get involved in the battle against feminism/humanism/Marxism. But these anti-God forces leave you no choice. You are involved already and your freedoms are in serious jeopardy at this very moment."[44] However, unlike the anti-communist vitriol of Hargis, CWA situated itself as pro-family, pro-children, and pro-women. "We're against these social evils because we're for the right to life for every human being, we're for the traditional family, and we're for normal, God-created heterosexual relationships."[45] LaHaye believed that sex between men and women was acceptable as long as it was contained within marriage. In 1974 the LaHayes cowrote a sex manual for evangelical Christians called *The Act of Marriage: The Beauty of Sexual Love*.[46] Rhetorically, CWA forged an imagined community of like-minded Christian women who were striving to align America with conservative Christian values.

Although CWA did not have contact with members of the ex-gay movement until the 1990s, LaHaye highlighted the idea of conversion from feminism to Christianity by gathering testimonies of former feminists who renounced their prior political involvement in feminism or gay rights. One article in the CWA newsletter read, "Ex-Feminists Are Finding Truth." The testimonials enabled CWA to demonstrate the fallacy of feminism by showing that a feminist identity was a delusion. LaHaye portrayed feminists as miserable and angry, fleeing "the false promises and deceit" of feminism. "We can help to liberate these women from their bondage to the empty philosophies of humanism and feminism."[47] LaHaye conceived of feminism, like homosexuality, as harmful to women and a condition that could be overcome through repentance and adherence to a conservative Christian worldview. The use of testimonies was an early strategy of these organizations that became the basis of the hope for healing message.

Leaders like Beverly LaHaye and James Dobson began to understand the appeal of anti-gay propaganda as a means to organize and mobilize conservative Christian constituents and raise money. Their organizations viewed sexuality as only acceptable within heterosexual marriage. The ex-gay movement was largely peripheral to these coalitions of conservative Christians. The idea that men and women were actively trying to convert themselves from homosexuality had not yet become a politically expedient tool. Although anti-gay politics were a major part of the Christian Right's campaigns, the idea that people could transform themselves from homosexual to heterosexual seemed to mirror the notions of sexual fluidity espoused by gay liberation, and as a result, Exodus had little contact with Focus or CWA throughout the 1970s. Anita Bryant was one of the only figures from the 1970s who supported counseling and ministry for homosexuals.[48]

Frank and other ex-gay leaders were more interested in working within churches than creating coalitions with Christian Right organizations during the 1970s, but this would change in the 1990s. The ex-gay movement had conceptualized homosexuality as a moral and religious issue, mirroring Falwell's views. This framing reversed the 1970s adage that the personal was political and privatized homosexuality as an issue of personal religious faith that was based on individuals' rights to seek change. It was a maneuver which enabled Exodus leaders to dodge accusations that they were a political organization or movement. These charges would be more difficult to avoid as the ex-gay movement developed a more explicit political agenda and overt alliances with groups like Focus on the Family.

In 1976 Anita Bryant, a singer and spokeswoman for Florida orange juice, led the first religious initiative against gay rights in Dade County, Florida. Her campaign opposed the Dade County commissioners' decision to prohibit discrimination against gay men and lesbians in housing, public accommodation, and employment.[49] Bryant promoted a successful referendum to repeal the commissioners' vote, and her organization gained strength and notoriety. She inspired state senator John Briggs, who had worked with Bryant in Miami, to sponsor the Defend Our Children Initiative in California as part of the general election ballot in November 1978. The Briggs amendment would have banned homosexual teachers from public schools, but it was defeated by a wide margin. These two national events emboldened Christian organizations and spurred more anti-gay organizing. Reverend Louis Sheldon, who is head of the Anaheim, California, based Traditional Values Coalition (TVC), was executive director of California Defend Our Children at the time. Although the initiative failed, Sheldon remained active in anti-gay organizing. When Bryant's campaign ended in 1979, hampered by a lack of political organization and her own divorce, other groups like Focus on the Family and CWA arose to take the campaign's place.[50] That same year, David Noebel published *The Homosexual Revolution*, which he dedicated to Anita Bryant. He wrote, "Homosexuality is rapidly becoming one of America's most serious social problems."[51] In it, he discussed the threat that homosexuality posed to youth as part of a larger theme of child endangerment, which remains a key myth of the Christian Right anti-gay agenda and a frequent justification for groups that promote anti-gay legislation.

"THE PROMOTION OF HOMOSEXUALITY" AND "SPECIAL RIGHTS"

In 1998 Steve Schwalm, a family policy analyst for the Family Research Council, wrote, "The reason for the focus on homosexuality is not because it is worse than other sexual sins, but because this behavior has an aggressive lobby of activists trying to influence public policy and ultimately redefine the family."[52] Schwalm expressed the sentiments of the major players in the Christian Right: Focus on the Family, CWA, TVC, and the American Family Association. Their anti-gay political campaigns became more sophisticated at the national and local levels because of coalition building and the coordination of political resources. Much of their anti-gay work occurred on the state and city level, and in most cases this was made to look like a grassroots effort instead of one guided by national organizations.[53] In the late 1980s and early 1990s, the promotion of school curriculum reform to reflect a greater acceptance of gay men and lesbians and the passage of gay rights ordinances, bills, and initiatives in state legislatures galvanized these organizations into action.

In addition to using the rubric of "family values," these groups argued that gay men and lesbians were demanding "special rights" or "special protections." The slogan "no special rights" came to epitomize their opposition to gay rights. It fostered the idea that gay people were demanding more than their share of rights, or seeking political and cultural dominance over heterosexuals. It also implied a militancy and threat to the family on the part of gay activists. In his public pronouncements, Louis Sheldon of the TVC argued that gay activists were promoting homosexuality and arguing for the right to engage in a perversion. "We don't believe in using taxpayer dollars to advocate and promote homosexuality."[54] As part of a wider media strategy, Jeremiah Films produced the film *Gay Rights, Special Rights* in coordination with the TVC to demonstrate that gay groups sought cultural dominance in schools, media, and politics.[55]

Two prominent theorists of the anti-gay agenda of the 1990s were Paul Cameron, director of the Family Research Institute, and former congressman William Dannemeyer of California. In his book *Shadow in the Land,* Dannemeyer luridly described homosexuality as a perversion and argued that homosexuals were demanding the right to participate in perversion—what he called "the right to sodomize."[56] "From what source do we derive them the 'right to sodomize'? Certainly not from the Constitution of the United States. . . . So it is not a 'civil right'—that is, a right derived from our government or its Constitution. Not yet."[57] By defining homosexuality as a perversion and a set of behaviors, Dannemeyer was able to conflate the "right to perversity," or "the right to sodomize," with civil rights. His rhetoric disavowed a gay identity, making sexual behavior constitutive of identity.

Dannemeyer believed his goal was to expose "the truth of the perversion" the American public had been lulled into accepting as a right. In opposition to liberal gay rights rhetoric that argued that homosexuals should have minority status, Dannemeyer attempted to counteract the idea of a public critical mass that would establish the status of minority. He made a private/public distinction between acceptable, gay, private same-sex behavior and public gay activism. Part of this political strategy was to draw on anti-gay rhetoric for the protection of children. "We must not allow our children to be the victims of an unnatural appetite that has become obsessive in our society."[58] Dannemeyer's utmost fear was that society would accept homosexuality as a legitimate identity. His contention that homosexuals were demanding rights to engage in perversion was a crucial strategy for opposing their citizenship and civil rights claims.

The strategy of defining homosexuality as a perversion continued in the 1980s and early 1990s. In October 1989 Reverend Lou Sheldon led the West Coast Symposium on Homosexuality and Public Policy Implications in Orange County, California, with Dannemeyer as a headline speaker. Based on the success of the meeting, Sheldon organized a conference in Washington, D.C., in January 1990 as a national summit meeting on homosexuality. In 1986 and 1988 he endorsed California's anti-gay initiatives sponsored by Lyndon LaRouche that sought to require quarantine for people with AIDS. In his newsletter, Sheldon asserted that the main vehicle the gay movement was using to "overhaul" straight America was state and federal statutes granting homosexuals minority status. For Sheldon, the ramifications of having homosexuality as a minority status would include "teaching the viability of homosexuality in schools through rainbow curriculum, gay pride month in schools, forcing the boy scouts to have homosexual scoutmasters, and the elimination of sodomy laws in twenty-three states."[59] In keeping with this activism, the TVC lobbied against a domestic partners bill granting marital benefits and status to gay couples in California in 1994. He wrote:

> This bill is one of the worst anti-family pieces of legislation that we have seen in many years. It strikes at the very core of the family—the concept of man and woman recognized by God in the holy state of matrimony. AB2810 redefines the family. It goes beyond being pro-homosexual and tears at monogamous, heterosexual marriage. Women should be opposed to the legislation because there is no protection for them. Men will leave these relationships and look for new ones when disagreements occur. Women will simply be abandoned.[60]

Sheldon combined many of the tactics of the anti-gay Christian Right by arguing that it was a threat to the family and children, a perversion, a demand for special rights, and harmful to women by releasing men from their duties as husbands and fathers.

Focus on the Family marked the shift from the rhetoric of "no special rights" and "the promotion of homosexuality and perversion" to a "hope for healing" and "change is possible" message.[61] Led by James Dobson since 1977, Focus on the Family is a conservative Christian conglomerate with daily radio broadcasts; over sixteen publications geared toward youth, parents, teachers, physicians, and church leaders; overseas missionary organizations; and other media ventures. Dobson sends a monthly letter to everyone on his mailing list in which he outlines his thoughts on current political controversies. He has been crucial in furthering the agenda of the anti-gay movement because of the financial and media resources of his organization.[62] Like Beverly LaHaye, Dobson professes that his objective for starting his organization was to react against the excesses of the 1970s. "The decade of the 1970s may well be remembered as the decade of the war against the family. Traditional biblical values for the home were bombarded by educators, authors and sociologists. Television programs portraying 'alternate lifestyles' condoned adultery, divorce, teenage sex and homosexuality. And society seemed to acquiesce. . . . Homosexuality marched across America with 'gay pride marches.'"[63]

By 1988 Focus was publishing articles such as "There Is Hope for the Homosexual," in which Dobson argued that homosexuals could learn to control their attitudes and behavior even if they never lost the desire for the same-sex.[64] However, the rhetoric of "no special rights" and "the promotion of perversion" continued to dominate Focus's publications. John Eldredge and Brad Hayton, spokespeople for Focus, wrote, "Homosexuals already have the same rights as other Americans. They want special privileges. . . . Homosexuals are not like other minorities. Race, nation of origin and gender are innate, immutable and do not necessarily affect one's lifestyle or moral behavior."[65] In another article entitled "Gay Aggression," Eldredge detailed how homosexuals "vigorously promote their agenda in schools, media, the courts, the military, medicine—and on the streets."[66] Eldredge emphasized that homosexuality was a lifestyle of perversion rather than an identity group and even compared it to bestiality. "There are people in our society who find sexual satisfaction from engaging in intercourse with animals—bestiality. . . . Would anyone suggest that these groups deserve special protection because they happen to follow bizarre sexual practices?"[67] When John Paulk began working at Focus in 1994, the polemic of these articles abated. Focus on the Family adopted the ex-gay testimony of change and transformation to make their anti-gay agenda less overt and more palatable to a conservative Christian agenda.

Today Dobson refers the millions of readers and listeners of his newsletters and radio show who have questions about their sexuality to Exodus and NARTH. More than anyone, Dobson has created increased visibility for the ex-gay movement and presented it to a Christian audience through the Focus-sponsored Love Won Out conferences that feature ex-gay speakers. Dobson is also effective because he combines the intimate persona of a therapist or friend with Christian activism. In his newsletters and radio broadcasts, he discusses childrearing, marriage, relationships, and personal finances. In a tone of benevolence and familiarity, he speaks to people's discontent in ways that enable them to trust him. In one audiotape, "What Wives Wish Their Husbands Knew about Women," he discusses the need for husbands to communicate and for wives to cultivate friendships with other women for emotional sustenance.[68] Those who have learned to trust and follow his advice on these issues are ripe for his messages about homosexuality and other political issues.

In his other publications like *Citizen Magazine,* a monthly publication about issues affecting the family, the rhetoric is more explicitly anti-gay and it includes legislative updates and suggestions for action. In one issue he writes: "Homosexuality has become the cause du jour of those who seek to undermine the family. Though homosexuals comprise only 2–3 percent of the population, they exert incredible influence over the political arena. Abetted by a pro-homosexual news and entertainment media, the radical gay activists' assault on morality has reached a fever pitch."[69] He then goes on to tell readers that homosexuals achieved "a form of gay marriage in Vermont and are pushing for recognition of same-sex unions in the other 49 states."[70] He urges them to write their representatives and get involved on the state level. In the past, his newsletters also endorsed anti-gay ballot initiatives like Amendment 2 in Colorado.[71]

Ex-gay developmental theories about homosexuality have shaped Dobson's thinking about the origins and cure for homosexuality. In his Father's Day newsletter in June 2002, Dobson devoted eight pages to how father-son relationships are the key to preventing homosexuality. He iterated that homosexuality is a disorder that is not genetic, "There is no such thing as a gay child or a gay teen. But left untreated, studies show these boys [boys with a poor relationship to their fathers] have a seventy-five percent chance of becoming homosexual or bisexual."[72] Exhorting readers to note signs of effeminacy in their sons, Dobson told readers, "The truth is, Dad is more important than Mom. Mothers make boys. Fathers make men."[73] He warned readers that children who lacked fathers were more likely to develop homosexuality and that fathers must become more involved in their son's lives. He also advised parents to send their children to an ex-gay therapist if they exhibit signs of homosexuality at a young age. At the end of his letter, he provided referrals and dates for the Love Won Out conferences sponsored by Focus and Exodus.

Organizations like Focus, CWA, TVC, Campus Crusade for Christ, Promise Keepers, and others now regularly cite ex-gay testimonies as proof of change and refer callers and clients to Exodus International. Rather than harping on "special rights" or the "promotion of perversion," these organizations have incorporated the message of healing and change. John Eldredge declared in a speech to members of Colorado for Family Values in 1994, "We must never attempt, we must never appear to be attempting to rob anyone of their rights, of their constitutional rights. We must be shrewd to build a consensus for our position by appealing to shared values and concerns, issues of fairness and justice."[74] Even though these organizations would discover, if they read them closely, that ex-gay testimonies are not always evidence of definitive change, they draw on them to make their anti-gay political agendas appear to be a question of Christian morality, compassion, and fairness.

HOPE FOR HEALING

National Coming Out of Homosexuality Day is one of the ways that the political arm of the Christian Right links up with the ex-gay movement as part of the wider strategy of hope for healing. The ex-gay testimonies are a counternarrative to the notion of coming out, and they enable Christian organizations to oppose the argument that homosexuality is an innate identity and sexual orientation is genetic. Don Wildmon, president of the American Family Association (AFA), summarized the importance of a partnership with the ex-gay movement.[75] "The homosexual rights movement in America is bringing us to a very significant crossroads. Indifference or neutrality toward the homosexual rights movement will result in society's destruction by allowing civil order to be redefined and by plummeting ourselves, our children, and grandchildren into an age of godlessness. A national 'Coming out of homosexuality day' provides us a means whereby to dispel the lies of the homosexual rights crowd who say they are born that way and cannot change."[76] Just as the Family Research Council now provides support to the organization Parents and Friends of Ex-Gays, the AFA has been instrumental in linking ex-gay ministries with the public National Coming Out of Homosexuality Day events. Reverend Sheldon of TVC and John Eldredge are regularly featured speakers.

On October 11, 1999, the AFA sponsored a Coming Out of Homosexuality Day in San Francisco in an auditorium in the middle of Golden Gate Park. Michael Johnston, an HIV-positive ex-gay man who was head of Kerusso Ministries in Newport News, Virginia, was the featured speaker.[77] Jerry Falwell was initially part of the lineup, but he cancelled at the last minute, choosing to address the audience through a live telecast. Almost two-thirds of the forty people in the room were activists from Act Up San Francisco, a pro-gay AIDS activist organization, and the atmosphere was tense. Stephen Crampton from the AFA nervously told the audience, "We have a message we wish to share. We want to be heard. There is help in Jesus's love." To justify why they were holding the event on the anniversary of Matthew Shepard's death, Michael Johnston explained, "This is not a hateful message, it is a message of hope, a compassionate message. If we hated homosexuals, we would ignore you; we do this because we care for you." He continued, "We stand against a social and political agenda that affirms the homosexual lifestyle. It is detrimental to family and society and the homosexual himself. It's not easy for me. I've had AIDS since 1996."

After his testimony, Johnston's mother, a slightly bewildered-looking elderly woman, spoke in support of him. She told the audience that it would have been easy to accept Johnston's homosexuality, but instead she told the truth, that it made her want to commit suicide. A member of the audience yelled, "Remember Matthew Shepard's mother." Next Yvette Cantu, a policy analyst at the Family Research Council in Washington, D.C., testified about her six years as a lesbian. She reminisced about how she searched for acceptance and meaning through lesbian relationships and that she went to gay pride events and fought with Christians. When it came time for Falwell's telecast, the audience grew restless, and before Falwell had finished speaking, an Act Up activist hurled a pie in Michael Johnston's face. The police barged in, and four officers, each holding a leg or an arm of the pie thrower, hauled the activist outside as the rest of the speakers vanished. Events like National Coming Out of Homosexuality Day create media spectacles that perform and publicize ex-gay identity. On their press release, the AFA even used the pie incident to describe the "hostility of the gay community to the idea of hope and change."[78] Stephen Crampton, the only speaker who lingered after the event, seemed pleased by the media attention. Crampton believed that Christian organizations like the AFA have to be involved in the political realm, something he thinks Exodus eschews. As he turned to go, Crampton abruptly changed the subject, asking if I knew who was from Tupelo, Mississippi, the headquarters of the AFA. When I replied "Elvis," it was the only time he smiled the entire day.

The ex-gay movement particularly highlights testimonies from those people who were politically active as gay men and women before becoming Christians. Six months later, I sat in the audience as Amy Tracy, an ex-gay woman, spoke as part of New Hope and Open Door Church's annual Pro-Life Night event. Tracy testified about becoming born again, leaving her lesbian partner, and changing her political views. Tracy, a former communications director for the National Organization of Women, was a recent convert to Christianity and widely proclaimed as an ex-gay success story who was working for Focus on the Family.[79]

She began her testimony with a description of her pro-choice activism defending women's health centers. This was her first pro-life rally, she tentatively revealed to the audience. In her testimony, she explained that her father did not affirm her once she was no longer successful in sports, and as a result she was drawn to the lesbian faculty at a women's college. Despite her relationship and career, "My soul was never satisfied." After joining a Calvary Fellowship church, "I learned it was possible to have a personal relationship with Jesus Christ, and that by placing my life in his hands he would change me from the inside out." She recalled that she felt her "hardened shell melting away and innocence and youth beginning to return." As a nod to her activist past, Amy testified that "Christians involved in influencing policy need to constantly remind themselves that there are human beings behind the issues." Her personal experience stood as the ultimate testament to the possibility of conversion for ex-gays.

People like John Paulk, Mike Haley, and Amy Tracy have chosen to make their ex-gay identities the public vehicle of their activism, and they collaborate with James Dobson and the vast financial and media resources of Focus to speak of compassion in the service of anti-gay activism. Since 2001, members of New Hope and other ex-gay ministries have been attending the Focus-sponsored Love Won Out conferences around the country, where they set up booths in order to advertise the residential program. Love Won Out conferences reach conservative Christians in churches and political organizations who would never attend an Exodus conference and who may have never considered the issue of homosexuality. The goal is to establish referral networks between the churches and ex-gay ministries and to help churches create their own ex-gay support groups.

The ex-gay movement has transformed the political strategy of Focus on the Family. In his monthly newsletter to Focus members, Dobson invokes an anti-gay message and the Christian ideas of love and acceptance: "Never in the history of this ministry have we insulted or ridiculed homosexuals or anyone else for that matter. . . . We believe every human being is precious to God and is entitled to acceptance and respect. There is great suffering among homosexuals, and it is our desire to show compassion and concern for those caught in the lifestyle."[80] In another issue of the same newsletter, John Paulk writes, "As the church, we must continue to speak out boldly against the radical homosexual agenda while we minister to those who are trapped in the lifestyle. Some Christians see an inherent conflict between exhibiting compassion and speaking the truth in love. But it is compassionate to warn about the dangers of homosexuality."[81] Anti-gay policy decisions are repackaged in the rhetoric of healing with the stories of people in ministries like New Hope as "evidence." The "hope for healing" message also neatly aligns itself with the "love the sinner, hate the sin" message of evangelical Christianity.

In addition to promoting the message that change is possible, the ex-gay movement and Focus still speak of a militant gay community in the same way that Billy James Hargis did in the early 1970s. Frank reiterates the idea that ex-gays are embattled, "We're on the outside of the circle looking in at the world, everyone seems to be against us. A small band of people are holding to the truth; we do feel marginalized and persecuted. We were asleep and they took over."[82] Ex-gay leaders frame their activism as a necessity against a growing and amorphous gay movement that has provoked and pushed them until their only option is to fight back. Being on the defensive enables them to disclaim responsibility for a long history of Christian organizations that actively lobbied against gay rights. Ex-gay movement members disengage themselves from this past by arguing that their activism is only a reaction to a supposedly militant gay community. Janet Folger, the head of the CRA, claims she created the ad campaign featuring the Paulks and Alan Chambers because she felt Christians were ridiculed by pop culture. Folger argues that gay people are "not advocating tolerance. If that were the case, they'd live and let live. Instead, they do things like demand that the Boy Scouts change their position by accepting homosexuality. It's basically forcing people to embrace their behavior."[83]

Activists like John Paulk only reinforce the message to Christian supporters that the "gay community" or "radical gay activists" are gaining in numbers, force, and strength. In a talk at the 2000 annual Exodus conference in San Diego, Paulk capitalized on this fear of a gay takeover. Describing a publication called "Overhauling Straight America," he told the audience that in it gay activists outline how they will wrest control of the press and film industry. He warns that gay men and women are now visible on television as psychologically sound characters. "What," he asked the five hundred or more men and women at the conference, "has Exodus been doing to counteract all this?" Paulk exhorts men and women to "engage our culture and communicate with conservative Christians. People need to become visible in a culture where they believe we can't change." Paulk's speech employed the same kind of testimonial approach of many ex-gays. He confessed that at his first

Exodus conference thirteen years earlier, he refused to leave his dorm room without bronzer on his face. In contrast to the long, romantic walks he took at night with another man at this first conference, he now pushes a stroller with his young son in it. In reference to the 1998 ad campaign, Paulk told the audience, "God is calling us into unfamiliar territory. We have to love our culture enough to exhort a nation to repent in the face of a gay agenda which would like to destroy us."[84]

No one is more invested in political activism than Joe Dallas, a prominent Exodus spokesman who also works as an ex-gay therapist. He counseled Brian and other men at New Hope. Dallas was the former president of Exodus and has written several books, including *A Strong Delusion: Confronting the "Gay Christian" Movement* and *Desires in Conflict: Answering the Struggle for Sexual Identity*. Formerly a member of the Metropolitan Community Church, Dallas believes that the ex-gay movement must take a stand on social issues. He has the appearance of a robust, middle-aged, high school physical education teacher, and his speeches are unusually truculent. To him, the movement has a "prophetic mandate to provide healing and to impact the culture and articulate a standard and uphold that standard." At an Exodus workshop, he told the audience that Christians may choose political involvement as one of many options. He passed around a handout with an overview of the gay-related political issues they currently faced: marriage, adoption, public education, hate crimes legislation, the banning of gays from private associations like the Boy Scouts, and gays in the military. Dallas quoted Martin Luther King Jr. to show that the state necessitated the operative influence of the church: "The church must be reminded that it is neither the master of the state nor is it the servant of the state. Rather it is the conscience of the state. The voice of the church is not a law, but in some cases we will fight to make it so." Yet Dallas, despite his public proclamations, is a complicated figure. He explained that after participating in a march against anti-gay violence, he told the Christians around him that it is important to have regard for the people you oppose, and he openly criticized his ex-gay friends who gloated after the Boy Scouts made its decision to ban homosexuals.

Dallas also supports the ex-gay strategy of defining homosexuality as child endangerment. An age-old tactic, this has been particularly effective in galvanizing Christians to oppose sex education campaigns and to lobby to eliminate gay-positive curriculum and books from schools. Mike Haley has spearheaded this campaign in his position as manager of the Homosexuality and Gender Department for Focus on the Family's

Public Policy Division. At an Exodus workshop called Why Is What They're Teaching So Dangerous? he highlighted pro-gay books like *Heather Has Two Mommies* as a threat to children. "To those of you who are parents, I say, 'Be aware!' Your children are being inundated with inaccurate—but enticing—messages about homosexuality. Television, movies, music, and an increasing number of public schools constantly reinforce the idea that 'gay is good.'"[85]

The It's Elementary curriculum, which includes books for children that portray homosexuality as normal, and California's Project 10, which provides educational services to gay and lesbian youth, are of particular concern to Haley.[86] Louis Sheldon led the opposition to Project 10 through his coalition Stop Homosexual Advocacy in Public Education in the 1990s, and now Haley has joined him. Haley believes that these programs give children and high school students the idea that being gay is normal. Not even *The Lion King* escapes his critique because it features the voice of Elton John. In addition, Haley rails against school curricula that undermine parents' moral authority and their ability to decide what a child could and should learn about homosexuality. During his talk, Haley held up a large, glossy photograph of the singer George Michael, who was arrested by police in 1998 for engaging in "lewd behavior" in a public restroom. When he told us, "Our country is fighting to make sex in public restrooms legal," members of the audience gasped. His strategy of fear and overstatement is effective. As he spoke, people in the audience carefully copied the names of the book titles he mentioned in order to demand that their local libraries not stock them.

Since 2001 Exodus and Focus on the Family have also made a concerted effort to target their resources and materials toward youth as the next wave of ex-gay ministry. Since climbing out of debt, Exodus has created an entirely separate Web site called Exodus Youth with testimonies, a question-and-answer forum, and links to Refuge, the Love in Action–sponsored ex-gay ministry for teenagers age thirteen to eighteen, which John Smid opened in 2002. Exodus has also developed *The Map,* an interactive CD-ROM developed by Jason Thompson of the Portland Ministry. *The Map* is hip and youth oriented, with pulsing techno music that plays every time you switch to another section of the program. In "Journey to Freedom," a car zooms down a highway. There is a question-and-answer area where Mike Haley, with a brand-new goatee, and Christine Sneeringer from the femininity workshop sit on swivel stools in a diner, ready to answer high school–age kids' questions about homosexuality. To the question, "Is homosexuality the worst sin of all?" Haley says, "There are spiritual, physical, and emotional consequences of homosexuality. Spiritual is the worst because our sin separates us from God. With the physical there is the risk of AIDS and disease, and the emotional means you are unable to relate to someone of your same sex on a platonic level."[87]

Other questions include, "What are the consequences of homosexuality? Is homosexuality genetic? Can you be gay and Christian?" In answer to the question, "How do you overcome same-sex attraction?" the CD-ROM tells the teenagers, "Be honest with yourself. Admit that you are wrong. Choose God's way, not your own. Repent. Now you're on the journey." The final part of *The Map* takes place in a movie theater. Six teenagers are sitting in chairs, and the user can click on one of them to hear their story. Seth, an overweight teen in a hockey shirt, tells viewers, "I was looking for love and acceptance that I should have gotten from my father. I wanted to be one of the guys. I started looking on the Internet." As he speaks, the screen flashes to a danger sign, and then to a picture of a computer screen with shadowy images of men with a sign on the Web site that reads "Join Us." Seth tells viewers that he met his boyfriend on the Internet, and *The Map* warns teens against "homosexual recruitment." The idea behind *The Map* is to provide an alternative to the online gay and lesbian networks and chat rooms, which have enabled isolated gay youth to come out of the closet and find community. *The Map* tells questioning and confused youth that their same-sex feelings are not an identity but a condition, and it directs them to ex-gay ministries and resources.

THE RIGHT TO CHANGE

Leaders like John Paulk and Mike Haley link their activism to a lineage of struggle beginning with the civil rights movement. To them, being ex-gay is a matter of exercising their right to change. They appropriate the language of civil rights to argue for minority status for Christians and ex-gays. Frank and others are intent on disproving the validity of a gay identity and are quick to pit gay people against what they feel are other legitimate minority groups. Frank argues, "As homosexuals saw other minorities gain social significance, they were tempted with the idea of getting on the minority band-wagon. . . . In the last thirty years, they have brainwashed almost the entire population of the United States into believing that their condition is unchangeable and is equally acceptable as heterosexuality."[88] Joe Dallas, Frank, and others strongly argue that members of the gay movement pay lip service to celebrating diversity but want to censor ex-gays' message of change. Their argument against the gay rights movement is that if gay people can be out and visible, then ex-gays should be able to publicly promote their message, too. While the ex-gay movement refutes the validity of a gay identity or community, it also lays claim to the status of an identity group in order to argue for members' own rights. For example, James Dobson compares civil rights activists with anti-abortion activists. "Police brutality against non-violent civil rights protestors in the 1960s shocked the nation, but the media and Congress have ignored . . . abuses against Operation Rescue."[89] He argues that not to accord anti-abortion activists the same treatment as other protesters is "to destroy the most prized achievement of the civil rights movement—the recognition of rights of everyone."[90] Dobson and others in the Christian Right use the civil rights movement to argue for the same rights that they are unwilling to accord to gay men and lesbians.

The civil rights approach was most apparent at a speech given by Michael Lumberger, the head of Dunamis Ministries in Pittsburgh and one of the only African American leaders at the annual Exodus conference in San Diego in 2000. Verging on tears, he invoked the history of slavery, saying that Martin Luther King referred to African Americans as a chosen people and talked about a holy nation. "African Americans found freedom because they refused to give up."[91] He declared that gay activists stole the song, "We Shall Overcome" from the civil rights movement and that it did not apply to them. Instead, he told the crowd that it should be the anthem for ex-gays struggling to overcome homosexuality. "In the atmosphere of the Exodus conference it is a prophecy." As Lumberger spoke, he kept repeating, "We shall overcome," and then he began uttering the words to the song, "Deep in my heart, I do believe, we shall overcome some day. He didn't bring you this far to leave you." Within minutes, Lumberger had the entire auditorium, close to seven hundred people, on their feet, hands clasped across the aisles, singing "We Shall Overcome."

The men at New Hope also view their participation in an ex-gay ministry as a right, even if they acknowledge that the process is more fluid than Focus on the Family or Mike Haley proclaims. They consider change as a process of religious conversion that affects their identities but not necessarily their desires or behaviors. Drew defended his position this way:

I'm all on for these gay guys doing what they like and everything else, but I have a right to believe what I believe and not go that way. Why not let people who want to, change. It's not like we're going out there preaching in the Castro, saying, you must come. We have guys phoning up here and they're desperate and suicidal and there's tons of organizations out there that are helping people who are gay. Is it wrong for me to not want to accept the gay lifestyle? Must I do it because everybody else says I have to do it?

Drew believes that his participation in New Hope is a personal choice that does not translate to the political realm. Arden also complains, "Other people have said I'm such a traitor. They spout out all this stuff about being tolerant and loving and how the straight community rejects us, and they go ahead and reject me. I haven't done anything to reject them. I have not spoken out against gay rights." Men and women like Drew and Arden are living as ex-gays with lingering same-sex desire and attraction, firmly believing they are on a godly path, but the ad campaign showed them that the decision to change sexual identity can never be divorced from the realm of politics. Matt, a thirty-three-year-old program member from Georgia whose father was a Pentecostal preacher, felt that the ads were "sneaky and manipulative." Ultimately, he believed that people would become aware that the message was false. "There's a verse in the bible that says, 'What is hidden in darkness will be brought out into the light.' And that is so true about Exodus. The ads did not say, 'It may be a long process; you may always have these sexual feelings for other men.' They never mentioned that."

CRA and Focus were soon to learn this in an extremely public way. In September of 2001, two men who worked for the Human Rights Campaign recognized John Paulk in a gay bar in Washington, D.C., called Mr. P's.[92] Even Paulk—husband, father, and former drag queen—could not escape the fact that although behavior and identity change, desire and attraction do not. Paulk initially tried to flee the bar when he realized who was speaking with him, and then he denied that he knew it was a gay bar in the first place, protesting that he was only looking for a place to use the bathroom. What was common within ex-gay ministry programs became a national scandal. As soon as the story broke, Anita found me in the office and explained her side of what happened. She had known John for years through the New Hope program and later as a comember of the Exodus board of directors. More than his going to a gay bar, she confessed, what was particularly hurtful and galling was that Paulk initially lied to the Exodus board, claiming that he didn't realize Mr. P's was a gay bar. He only broke down and admitted the truth when photographs of him fleeing the bar surfaced in the press. Anita added, "I'm not gay, but I think you would know it was a gay bar." According to Anita, the problem Exodus now faced was whether to chastise him publicly. By doing so, she felt they ended up siding with the gay press and media. Instead, as a compromise, Exodus required Paulk to temporarily resign from the board of directors. She could have put another positive spin on the situation to protect Paulk, but she did not, even though she realized Paulk's story would once again damage the credibility of the movement.

Weeks later, Paulk and his wife, Anne, appeared on the Focus on the Family radio broadcast with James Dobson.[93] Dobson had not fired Paulk, but he wanted to get the whole scandal out in the open. At New Hope, we all gathered around to listen. I had been sharing articles about the incident with Drew, Curtis, Dwight, and Anita, and we had been discussing it incessantly. I knew the scandal had demoralized many men, especially because it was not long after the Exodus conference, and it forced many to question what they were doing. After Nick, Curtis's former roommate, decided to leave New Hope because the Paulk controversy discouraged him, Curtis's response was, "You can't put your faith in man. If you do, you'll always be disappointed. I was committed to Jesus before I was committed to change. Without Jesus this would be impossible. You have to put your faith in him." On the air, Dobson was stern but forgiving. He reprimanded Paulk but showed support as long as Paulk continued to disavow the gay lifestyle. Paulk told Dobson and the millions of Christians listening that he was curious about the bar because he allegedly had not been in one for fifteen years. He justified his failure to immediately come clean because he had panicked that he would lose his job and family. Still, Paulk maintained, even his decision to enter the bar could not be blamed on his own volition. Satan had been working in his life, he said, and gay activists were calling and threatening to ruin him. This is what drew him into the bar.

When it was over, Anita and everyone at New Hope seemed resigned. After all, this was not the first time a member of the ex-gay movement had experienced a public sexual fall, and variations of Paulk's experience happened frequently at New Hope. However, Anita was upbeat about the fact that Dobson had supported Paulk publicly. "It couldn't have been easy to stand with him on this issue in front of his entire radio audience." Ten years ago Dobson would have kicked Paulk out and that would have been the end of it. She felt the Love Won Out campaign had transformed Dobson's perspective from that of a homophobe to someone with a bit more compassion. In the end, even Dobson realized the fallacy of his own anti-gay activism; some people may purport to change, but they never really do entirely. This was just another battle they had to endure. Eventually, Anita and the others believed, they would overcome.

Conclusion

Walking in a Dark Room

In early December, at the end of the program year, Anita and Frank invited me to attend the New Hope graduation ceremony at a restaurant in downtown San Rafael. This would be the final event before the men returned to the Lord's Land for the culmination of their year together. The restaurant had provided its private banquet hall, which was undergoing renovations, and Drew lit giant rotund candles as a festive gesture in the dim and windowless room. As we were waiting in the living room to drive over from the New Hope apartments, Curtis bemoaned certain men's excessive use of cologne, and he had convinced Drew that candles might overpower the scent. Curtis may have been feeling a bit defensive. He had been visiting all the local tanning salons, taking advantage of their free first session, so he could depart California with a tan, and his burnt, orange-colored face had generated quite a few jokes. When I had first arrived, Curtis was not perched at the office window in his usual place; he was getting a manicure. "Yep, he's always off tanning and getting a manicure these days," Hank said, shaking his head.

At the banquet, Frank, Anita, Hank, Sam, and Scott sat in the middle of the horseshoe-shaped table with the rest of us fanned out on either side. I was farther toward the end, near Doug, James, and Curtis, the only woman there aside from Anita. Mounds of food arrived in three courses, and the mood was surprisingly somber as the men ate intently, cautious not to spill on carefully ironed and cleaned shirts and ties. As we ate, Curtis turned to me and said, "Did you ever think you'd be here?

For this?" After dinner, the men were less subdued as we watched a twenty-minute slide show of high and low points from the year. The four wheels of slides showed them climbing Half Dome in Yosemite (including Scott's painstaking ascent), a visit to a doughnut factory and a naval base, and camping trips in various wilderness locales. The men could barely restrain their raucous commentary as the slides flashed by. The overnight where they encountered the Bay Area gay and lesbian hiking club elicited many laughs. When Evan appeared in a hot tub with a sagging chest and a grumpy look, the ribbing was brutal. Another showed Curtis and Jack dressed in pants and caps they had purchased at the naval base, prompting several "Hey, sailor" jokes, much to the delight of everyone present. When an extremely unflattering photograph of Curtis in the hospital after his overdose with an IV and a puffy face surfaced, the men laughed just as much. To a slide of Frank and Evan looking away from each other, Anita commented, "Not connecting."

There were many pictures of Paul, who had been dead for only a few months. One of them showed Paul and Ray beaming proudly next to the flowering garden they had created on the New Hope porch. Interspersed with pictures of field trips and freeze frames of off-guard moments were snapshots of the men who had not made it through the program. When their faces appeared, the room fell silent. Seven people had left: Tim, barely remembered, had disappeared in February; Mitch was caught with pornography and was now living in the community house; Jack had returned to North Dakota; and only weeks before the banquet, George, a former Mormon, had absconded as well. It was definitely more than the ministry would have preferred, and Anita hastened to explain the defections: "You were there for one of our bad years."

After the slide show, Frank shuffled to the front of the room. A month earlier he had been diagnosed with cancer and just weeks before had undergone an operation to remove the malignancy. Although his doctors warned that his recovery would be long and difficult, he was back in the whirl of New Hope in a few weeks, teaching classes, attending events, and counseling. He looked frail as he told them, "We've had more than the usual amount of grief this year, but the pictures reminded me that we've also had a lot of joy. I appreciate all of you, and even though this is my calling, nothing is more important than seeing you graduate from the program. No matter where you go, this will always be home." Next, he thanked Hank, Scott, and Sam for their work as house leaders and officially designated Sam and Hank as assistant directors for the following year. After almost five years, Scott would return to his hometown in Nebraska. Frank's health problems had forced him to acknowledge that his tenure as director would not last forever, and if he were unable to continue the work at New Hope, Hank and Sam would take over.

Finally, the moment of graduation arrived. Hank, making a rare appearance in a jacket, tie, and shoes, stood at the front of the room and called the names of each man to receive their diplomas. In calligraphy, the certificates read, "This certifies that _____ has successfully completed the 2000 Steps Out program." Curtis whispered, "When I first read the New Hope literature before applying to the program, I thought there were 2000 steps I needed to complete in order to leave homosexuality. Thank God that's not the case." Each man came forward, grasped his certificate, and shook Hank's hand, pausing so that Drew could snap his picture. Even though the moment was supposed to be celebratory and everyone appeared exuberant, I knew that there were men who were still struggling and frustrated with their progress just as there were those who would take a second year and move on to leadership training. The program had ended but the process of conversion had not.

Critics of the ex-gay movement assert that no one changes their sexual desires, and the New Hope men would have readily agreed. To them, change is a process of conversion and belonging that is uncertain, fraught with relapses and some temporary successes. For many, years after doing a program, change remains simply a leap of faith or a belief that they are doing what God wants for them. Much more than immediate change, the men and women undergo a process of religious and sexual conversion bolstered by relationships forged in the program. The idea that change may occur but not in the form expected is borne out by the queer conversions of men and women at the ministry. Even the term "ex-gay" signifies that only some form of change is possible. Frank writes, "We recognize that it is an artificial label and it is a humiliation to all of us. But it is our witness to the world, in terms that the world can understand. It proclaims that change is possible. It is a light, shining in the darkness of deception."[1] Like the symbolism within the New Hope lighthouse logo, the promise of change beckoned from the distant future, but there was no certainty about the outcome. Bob Davies, the president of Exodus for twenty-two years, explained, "We know behind closed doors that change is possible, but change is rarely complete. I know many men who are totally transformed compared to twenty years ago, but that doesn't mean that they never have a thought or a memory or a temptation or a struggle. It means that the struggle has diminished significantly. It means that for all of us, redemption is still incomplete."[2]

In the wake of the Exodus ad campaign, more ex-gay leaders have begun to make this claim. Sonia Balcer, an ex-gay woman who cofounded Justice and Respect, now presents a workshop at Exodus conferences called So What If My Attractions Don't Change? Jeremy Marks, a former ministry leader, has moved toward a new way of conceptualizing change in the ex-gay movement. "We definitely want to be separated from the ex-gay label and be more focused on supporting Christians who are gay. . . . It is possible I am on to something important to Exodus. They are facing the possibility that we could have been wrong. The potential is a major paradigm shift after 25 years."[3] What Marks has declared publicly, many others admit in private forums. Drew explained, "You do not come for one year to New Hope and leave here a heterosexual, because it's just too short a time. I've certainly seen lots of guys and their behavior has totally changed and all that, but as far as their psyche and that type of thing, I don't think that many people leave here as heterosexual at all. I definitely don't. I don't say that as a negative because I don't believe the ministry expects people to be that way." No one at the New Hope banquet would have admitted to feeling heterosexual or having sexual feelings for the opposite sex. Their notion of change was a matter of faith and maintaining a relationship with Jesus and each other.

When Frank describes the change process he uses the term "non-practicing homosexual syndrome" to describe an ex-gay person who is simply operating under denial and repression. "What ex-gay ministries are not offering is a lifestyle of repression and denial. Perhaps the most dismal ex-gay existence is to simply become a non-practicing homosexual. This is a life lived without growth or hope."[4] However, he claims that ex-gay ministries offer precisely the opposite of denial. They offer faith and religious belonging. Yet behavioral control and learning to deny desires is still central to how many men and women eventually cope with same-sex attractions on the way to other religious and identity transformations. Darren confesses that denial is a huge part of his life. He related how two gay men in his office told another coworker that they believed Darren was in denial. "At first that really made me angry, and then I thought you know what? That's the greatest compliment. You bet I'm in denial. The Bible says deny yourself, pick up your Cross, and follow me. What a compliment that they would think I was denying something. Denying immorality, denying the direction my life was going. Let me deny more if I can deny more."

Identity, desire, and behavior were always shifting for most of the men and women at New Hope, and many felt that desires would never change. Laura told me that her sexual feelings still lingered decades after completing the LIA program.

> The most primary thing that has to change is your heart and your mind. What kinds of things do you desire, and why do you think about those things, and why do you desire those things. I'm at the point in my healing where I haven't acted out with a woman in, my goodness, fifteen years, but in my thoughts I've had on occasion a fantasy of acting out. In my heart I've felt close to her and drawn to her and wanted to be near to her. There are different levels of healing. You have to push yourself. And that's what I think; the ones who are going to push themselves to get through the pain are the ones who are going to have the most healing. Because it's hard, it's really hard; it's not an easy thing to change.

She continued, "I do not think it's possible, for me, for Laura. I do not think there will ever be a day until I am either cremated or ten feet under when I will not have an occasional thought about a woman. I don't think that is possible. I don't think it's ever going to all be over." Suzanne is one of the few people who swore she was a "fully heterosexual person." "I am one of the fortunate ones who has none of the sexual attractions," she professed. "God has restored me so much that it's hard to relate to now. When I listen to the gals talk about their struggles, I have to think really hard, What was this like?"

For Frank and others, becoming a new creation with a relationship to God is central to avoiding the nonpracticing homosexual syndrome. Even if they still deny sexual attractions, they have an anchor in their new religious identity. Frank writes about the need for a deep or inner religious healing of the "wounds that caused homosexuality. If these roots are left untouched, they will grow once again, what is repressed will emerge and will lead to stumbling."[5] They experience a sense of faith that is not easily quantifiable by the standards of the secular world. "Our problem with identity has been solved. We have a new firm identity with Christ that nothing can shake," writes Frank.[6] Ex-gays claim the critics of the movement who attest that change does not work because desires remain are missing the point. Drew told me:

> I am learning in ever greater degrees that my life must be based on the truth revealed in God's word—not cultural values or popular opinion. I have friends who have stopped pursuing healing because they say they haven't changed and so they assume change is impossible. If I haven't achieved the level of healing I had hoped for, that doesn't make scripture

any less true. God's word is true whether or not I experience healing in this life, and it is his standard that I must continue to strive for.

Men and women like Drew who go through ex-gay ministries are supposed to measure change, conversion, or transformation by comparing their present situation to their past, and the key to "wholeness" revolves around faith and a relationship with Jesus. Many feel that the secular world only measures change in terms of desire, behavior, or attraction, whereas ex-gays measure it in relationship to a more ephemeral sense of faith and relationship with God. "We are whole when we depend only on Christ, not any longer on outward circumstances," Frank explains. "We cannot expect the world to measure our change accurately. But those who have been changed will gladly testify that God never abandons us to sin, but stands ready to rescue all who call out to Him."[7]

Those who declare they have conquered sexual attraction are not immune to having sexual falls, which are part of the process of healing and conversion. Of his first year at New Hope, Hank told me, "By the end of my program year, I could honestly say I was no longer attracted to men. I can still say that. There is an attraction—this weekend I saw a guy and he was just gorgeous, good body, good hair and a moustache—I've always liked the moustache. And I asked myself, 'Do you want to have sex with him?' and I said, 'No.'" Yet he still made a distinction between desire and behavior, thought and action. Despite Hank's sexual fall the previous year, Frank would view someone like Hank as a "liberated celibate"—the answer to the nonpracticing homosexual syndrome. Frank writes, "Much has already happened, we have been saved, we have been changed. The prison door has been unlocked, we have only to push the door open and begin to live as a LIBERATED PERSON."[8] Hank is an example of someone who has no desire to marry but remains in a leadership position at New Hope. He believes that celibacy is a gift from God and that it is possible to lead a contented single life because as a single person, he can give himself entirely to "the work of the Lord." Whatever happens, Hank believes his life is in Jesus's hands. "And I'm very much at peace with life and my position in it because I know this is what I'm supposed to be doing." For Hank, marriage is not the idealized utopia that the ex-gay movement portrays it to be. Instead, his sense of belonging at New Hope sustains him.

After the banquet graduation ceremony, I had planned to thank the ministry for their help with my research, rehearsing in my head what I might say. Instead, Anita preempted me, "We've never allowed an outsider into the program, but this year we've let someone come in." The men all made an "ooooohhhhh" sound. Anita continued, "And we want to thank her for all her work. She's been a good friend to us." She motioned for me to stand by her at the front of the room, and she presented me with a bright blue pashmina shawl that the men had picked out, in what Curtis explained was one of my "flattering colors." Embarrassed, I stammered that I was thankful that they had taken a chance and allowed me to do this research. I told them I wished them the best on whatever path they chose. "We can't wait to read your thesis," Doug heckled from the audience. That night, I drove Curtis, Drew, and two men who had arrived in September as part of the preprogram back to the ministry. In the car, speaking like a program veteran, Curtis turned to face the newcomers in the backseat. "There were days in the office I was going to lose it, and having Tanya and Drew to vent to saved me." Drew, in an uncharacteristically emotional moment, said to me, "There was a reason you came to the program this particular year. It all just seemed to make sense that we got along so well in the office." Curtis nodded in agreement. Squashed in the car with everyone, I found myself caught up in the moment, too.

The following Thursday I headed to New Hope for one of the last times I would see the group of men together before their departure. As I took the freeway exit and waited as I had countless times before for the light to change, I felt a jolt as someone bumped the back of my car. I glanced in the rear view mirror, but the sun was glaring, so the driver behind me was not visible. It happened again, my car lurched, and I turned around to glare while the person in the car seemed to gesticulate frantically. When I entered New Hope's street and blew through a yellow light, the car followed. As I stopped in front of New Hope, I realized Curtis was driving Sam's car, which lacked a functioning horn. He emerged laughing, "You gave me the look of death back there." "I was about to flip you off," I said. Meanwhile, Sam came down from the apartments to retrieve his keys from Curtis. When he saw my car's Massachusetts license plate, he bent down and pretended to kiss it. He missed his home state. I told Sam I almost did not recognize Curtis because he had dyed his hair brown and had been tanning so assiduously. When we got upstairs to the office, Curtis announced to Drew and me, "I'm going to look hot tomorrow." Tomorrow was the long-awaited lunch and shopping excursion in San Francisco.

Curtis left the offices, and I handed Drew and Dwight cards that I had picked out for them. Drew would be around, but Dwight was returning to Scotland in a few days. Dwight's card had an intricately drawn picture of a compass that read, "Good luck in your new path." "Are the compass directions supposed to be pointing to gay or straight?" he joked. When Dwight went in his office to continue working, Drew and I discussed my plans with Curtis the next day. Curtis had been anticipating the day for so long that even I was nervous about it. I admitted to feeling a bit like a chaperone, and Drew seemed amused. "You should be a house leader," he said sardonically. I popped my head into Frank's office, and he spun around in his chair, saying "Hi" in his bright, cheerful way, which always surprised me. "What are your plans now that the year is over? Will you stay in California?" Before I could answer, he said, "Well, just make sure Curtis gets back here in time for the Lord's Land." The men were returning for a final retreat experience as a cap to the yearlong program. When I returned to the other room, Drew had departed. It was one of the only times I had ever been alone in the office. Everyone was concerned about security since Anita had found a copy of *Hustler* magazine in the women's bathroom a few weeks earlier. I took the key out of the hiding place on the side table, stepped outside, locked the door, and shoved it back underneath.

The next day, Curtis and a new program member, Danny, drove into San Francisco, where they met me at a café near my apartment. Danny headed off to see his family, and Curtis and I drank coffee before setting off for the Castro. As we walked, Curtis commented on how many people were holding hands, and suddenly I found myself noticing the gay men in my local coffee shop and on the streets in a way I usually did not. Every rainbow flag hanging from a house elicited a comment from Curtis, and when we entered a bookstore to buy a calendar, Curtis was mesmerized by the posters and calendars of men. "I really couldn't be here by myself," he admitted. Everything related to what Frank called the "gay lifestyle" had been prohibited for so long that Curtis seemed to be on sensory overload, recognizing each item that would be considered contraband at New Hope. Usually confident and the center of attention at New Hope, he was in unfamiliar territory and seemed a bit uncertain, asking me if I thought he was attractive and what he should buy in the stores. It was a relief when we emerged from the Muni into a swarm of preholiday shoppers. As we entered Macy's, he proclaimed, "This is what I love." He tried on a dozen things, none of which seemed to fit his specifications. Frank had given him a $100 gift certificate card, and he was determined not to waste it. After Macy's, we went to meet one of my oldest friends for lunch, whose car I had been borrowing all year. After we had chatted awhile, he asked her, "What do you honestly think of the whole ex-gay thing?" She looked worried about what to say but finally responded carefully, "I think the whole religious aspect is interesting." "Good answer," I laughed. Curtis told her he wanted to be married with children in three years. "Why?" she replied. "What makes you think marriage is the end all be all?" Later, Curtis and I went to more stores, and in Old Navy, with its labyrinthine aisles of clothes and multiple levels, we were separated. I strode from floor to floor searching for him for twenty minutes. In a bit of a panic, I imagined calling Drew and saying I had lost Curtis, and he would not be coming to the Lord's Land after all. I finally bumped into him in the long, snaking checkout line, and I held his giant Macy's bag while he purchased a T-shirt. It had suddenly become late, and we had to race to catch the bus to Marin. It was about to pull out as we arrived, and Curtis scampered on board, saying, "Thanks. This was all I'd hoped for." It was the last time I would see him for three years.

Curtis's time at New Hope and after demonstrates the instability of the process of conversion. At first, Curtis adopted the community living he learned at New Hope and applied it to his own life. He lived with a gay friend and hoped that through his example the friend would become interested in a relationship with Jesus. Whether he converted his roommate, however, was unimportant: "I'd rather he was a gay Christian rather than just gay, but he's still my friend." Once a week they would talk about their lives and bring up any issues bothering them. Even when he was working at a Canadian ex-gay ministry, every now and then, Curtis would tell me about having a "boyfriend day." However, in one of our last conversations at New Hope, he still believed that his relationship with Jesus was ultimately the most vital part of his life:

> Heterosexuality isn't the goal; giving our hearts and being obedient to God is the goal whether you're straight or gay. That's why I need to stay by him because my life is going to be a big fat loser mess if I don't. Extra-strength and glory to those people who can live without God because I can't. I tried and I was miserable. The way I see things, life is hard, and either I can do it on my own or I can do it with Jesus. Regardless, it's going to be hard. Being a Christian isn't easy, but [by] being a Christian I always have someone to turn to when I need help, to go to, and I know that I'm changing, and I'm getting somewhere, as slow as the process may be.

Six months after leaving New Hope, Curtis had a string of relationships with men. Eventually, he stopped dating men and began to work part time at a local ex-gay ministry and part time at a hair salon. Even though he had relished his sexual experiences, he was plagued by his family's disapproval and a sense that he was not "right with God." He briefly dated a woman he met through ministry-related work, telling me he was sure she was the one he would marry, but eventually they broke it off. Finally, he decided to leave his small town and move to a large city, where he obtained a coveted job at an upscale hair salon.

When I attended a conference there, we met for dinner. I had not seen him since his visit to New York over a year earlier, but I knew he was dating men, identifying himself as gay, living with two gay roommates, and even marching in the city's gay pride parade. A few months earlier, he had angrily written an email to a conservative Christian group that opposed gay marriage, and he forwarded it to me.

> HELLO . . . what is the statistic now? 50–60% of marriage (1 man 1 woman) ends in divorce. Can we blame the gays for this? It sounds to me that you seem to have an issue about pointing the finger to someone else's problem to cover up your own. What is that called? Oh yes, blame shifting.
>
> It is time to start taking responsibility for your actions and stop playing on the ignorant people of this country. I am very sad about how hateful our society still is.
>
> I think that the heterosexual community needs to take a good look at themselves, their spouses and their children before accusing the gay community of threatening marriage and family.

During dinner, he recounted that he reached a point a year earlier where he could not continue struggling and hoping for a sexual conversion. "I had tried and tried. How much did I have to suffer? Nothing was changing." The decision to move away from the orbit of his small town and family had been instrumental in the process of coming out. This time he was not a sixteen-year-old boy coming out as "someone who wanted to change"; he was a twenty-six-year-old man who embraced his gay identity. He was not bitter about the year he spent at New Hope, only incredulous that he had never been anywhere before he entered the program. "New Hope taught me how to think, how to look inside myself," he said. Although he no longer attended church, he spoke wistfully of his relationship with Jesus, explaining that he still felt nagging doubts that being a gay man meant he would always be separate from God. He spoke of how having an intimate and personal relationship with Jesus had made the process of coming out as a gay man wrenching. "Catholicism is conservative, too, but it's a much easier relationship with God because it's so rules based, and it's easier to break rules. Everyone does it." He continued, "Being a Christian like I am is about personal relationships; it's so intimate, so being gay feels more like a betrayal of a personal trust with Jesus. It's more heartbreaking." We walked back toward my hotel before he set off to meet friends. As we departed, he added, "God is still speaking to me, is still working on me. I feel that."

Many of the men who formed the core of New Hope from 1999 to 2002 have scattered to other parts of the country. Brian returned to Southern California, where he volunteered for an evangelical mega-church while he finished his master's degree. He had also attempted to date a woman from church, which amounted to a chaste courtship of occasional dinners and group outings. It eventually fizzled. After some disillusionment with the church's ideas about homosexuality, he stopped attending. When he was accepted into a PhD program, he left me a message: "Now I'm going to join you in the world of PhDs. Can you get a job here, too?" Sam decided not to accept the assistant directorship of New Hope and instead returned home to Massachusetts. Evan was living in California and counseling troubled teenagers. Drew stayed on at New Hope for several years as office manager even as his close group of friends dispersed. In 2003 he returned home to Denmark after more than three years of not seeing his family. Two weeks later, he moved to Africa to work with Open Door's missionary program. Like anyone's, the lives of the men and women at New Hope are in a constant process of conversion and reinvention, often eluding any definitive conclusions about change. They will continue to evolve even after I have tried to contain them within the narrative of this book. I could have ended with Curtis's heterosexual dating attempts or his life as a gay man, but neither fully reveals the multiple ways he lives and envisions his identities. Curtis has defined our phone calls as a "never-ending conversation," while Brian and I rarely talk about New Hope. "I'm through with Exodus and the ex-gay movement," he says. "I don't want to think of myself that way."

When Brian visited New York a few years after the program, I met him for brunch, and we wandered around the city, catching up. He admitted feeling depressed by some of the practices of his former church and abruptly asked, "What would you think if I were to give up this struggle? If I admitted that I was wrong, there is no God, there's no reason to have faith? Because even though I know God is there, some-times I just can't take it. What if I threw it all in?" It reminded me of a time a few years before when he boarded a bus to San Francisco and wandered around the Castro for hours alone. He was frustrated with how little his sexual desires had changed, and he felt that if this was what God wanted him to do, he would have married a woman by now. "Imagine telling all your friends and your family that you'd become a Christian, born again and everything. Imagine what they'd do," he said. "Well, that's what it's like for me telling everyone in my life that I'd given up. Imagine giving up your friends and your family."

At that time he described himself as waiting in limbo—uncomfortable with being gay but feeling like his attraction to men had not even faded.

> Where I'm at today is that I'm still attracted to men. I still desire. I still have days when all I'd like to do is go find an anonymous encounter, get drunk, and forget the world. The idea of a gay relationship doesn't appeal to me, not just cognitively, in my heart I don't long for it.
>
> To be honest with you, I've never heard of one person who's ever said that that [complete heterosexuality] is where they've come to. I don't expect it to. But some people say that we can change. To me, what's more important is—are you willing to submit your life, to become something that is higher than your animal impulses, your desires?

Regardless of his frustration, Brian couldn't let go of the idea that God supported what he was doing. He called his faith in God "walking in a dark room."

> I love God—very deeply. When you give up something as deep as your sexuality there's always the doubt inside you that you're doing something impossible. Maybe they're right. Maybe you can't change. You start to worry that maybe what you're doing is crazy. So in other words, in order to go forward, you have to walk in faith in a dark room without seeing things clearly for the sake of one thing, and that is that you love God.

Since that conversation, we have traded emails and phone calls. We argued about the war in Iraq, and after the 2004 presidential election, he sent the infamous red state/blue state map, writing, "I also hope you have no plans for expatriation. Please don't hate the conservatives too much. Or, at least spare a place in your heart for me! I certainly hope we never have a theocracy in America. That would be disastrous." Brian was unique in his own conservative Christian community and among the New Hope men because he was willing to interrogate his own political and religious belief system. Unlike almost anyone I knew, he could also admit when he was wrong. A few months later, he wrote, "I need to say that many of your concerns in the past about the war in Iraq have proven to be true. I have been wanting to acknowledge that with you for some time. While I still think Michael Moore is an idiot, I do think that many of my own suppositions are much less solid, and I have to say that you told me so on many points." He was teaching college courses as he worked toward his degree, and he had begun seriously dating a woman he met through his new church, with whom he could be completely honest about his past. His emails often included pictures of them together, and early in 2004, I received an invitation to their wedding.

Before he left for Africa, Drew called to tell me that the New Hope program was ending, if not for good, then definitely for the time being. The number of applicants had dwindled, and most of the men that were applying had serious mental health issues. The program simply did not have enough people to continue. When I spoke to Hank, he said it had been extremely hard on everyone, and they had been forced to give up some of their office space and consolidate into two rooms. On the phone he sighed, "This is what God wants us to do. It's hard. This is the last house, the last banquet. But God is faithful; he knows what he's doing." Later he said, "Sometimes I wonder if we did something wrong and God is punishing us. But God uses our mistakes to bring good out of it." Frank and Hank had decided that if they could not run the program in California, they would focus on establishing international ex-gay programs. Their goal was to visit other ex-gay ministries abroad and provide leadership training, cycling the leadership from New Hope into these programs to help build up leadership over a period of several months. They had chosen the fledgling ministry in Ecuador as one of their targets, but first Frank, Hank, and Anita headed to Manila to check on the progress of Bagong Pag-Asa. The support group there had suffered because the ministry leader, Rene Gomez, was now part of Exodus's lecture circuit.

The fact that Love in Action in Memphis was "going gangbusters," according to Hank, and turning people away from its program particularly stung. LIA had changed its rules to accommodate people for a thirty- or ninety-day intensive program instead of a year-long one, and the program members did not have to work, clean, or cook as a condition of participation. "They don't have to do anything, which is very appealing," Hank explained. He went out of his way to say he was not criticizing LIA, only that it represented a different model. "It's not who we are. We need to be true to our vision. I'm uncomfortable with the idea that after thirty days you are changed or that ninety days is enough." He differentiated New Hope from LIA by saying, "We're a relationship program. I was one of the people that thought we shouldn't do it that way [adopt the LIA model], and I wonder about that. But for us to go to a twelve-step model like LIA, it wasn't what our core values are— LIA is like drug rehab. God was saying we have to stick with our core values."

New Hope relies on the idea of Jesus working in the men's lives and on the sense of belonging they gain from being a part of New Hope rather than a program of addiction treatment or recovery. "The thing that attracted me to New Hope is God—it was God, it was core, it was because you want to serve God. Anything else would be a compromise. It is unique to us," Hank continued. Unlike the LIA program, the flexibility of New Hope allowed Hank, Brian, Curtis, and Evan to rebel and question the program, to have sexual falls, to argue with leadership, to go barefoot or bleach their hair, and to let a stranger conduct ethnographic research. Love in Action is extremely secretive, and it may also be thriving precisely because of the clinical and therapeutic nature of its program. LIA uses psychological tests to screen applicants, has psychiatrists on staff, and employs counseling as a mandatory and integral part of the program, while counseling is elective at New Hope. Its church sponsor is also larger and wealthier than Open Door. For a person considering investing time and money to attend an ex-gay ministry, LIA appears more professional, from its slick newsletter to the familiarity of the twelve-step structure of its program. Although Frank and program members follow the "Steps Out" workbook, at New Hope, there are no definitive steps out of homosexuality, and although there are rules and regulations, there are always exceptions to them.

New Hope understands conversion through the multiple discourses of addiction, developmental theories, biblical scripture, and religious faith. Sexual and religious conversion is also part of a process of belonging built through relationships with each other and immersion in the daily life of the program. While the Christian Right speaks with assurance that men and women can become heterosexual, using testimonies as proof of healing, men and women in ex-gay ministries know that walking in a dark room means that hope for sexual and religious transformation is at best a leap of faith. Rather than concrete evidence that change happens, ex-gays retain the belief that change is possible. It is that possibility which keeps some of them stumbling forward despite sexual falls, statistics, and public scandals. If they place their faith in someone like John Paulk, they will always be disappointed, and so they place their expectations, faith, and hope in Jesus, who is immune to temptations and doubts. The Christian Right's absolutist definition of homosexuality—as a threat to marriage, a developmental condition, or a sin-to-be-overcome—has dominated debates over gay rights and citizenship. At the same time, the liberal political position that status or protection should be based on genetic immutability is equally limiting. The lives of ex-gay men and women demonstrate that sexual and religious identities are never static or permanent. This idea must become a part of the larger public discussion about sexual rights in order to imagine a world in which everyone is entitled to the full benefits of citizenship. Ex-gays' process of walking in a dark room forces us to re-envision spaces of belonging and politics that are not predicated on the idea that Christianity and homosexuality are incompatible, but on a recognition of the diverse array of sexual identities, practices, and arrangements. This recognition might have enabled the sixteen-year-old Curtis to come out to his church and family as proud and gay rather than someone who is "gay and wants to change."

Acknowledgments

Many people contributed to the creation of this book. My first debt is to Frank and Anita Worthen, who extended their trust and cooperation to me. I thank them for their willingness to debate, share information, and permit a stranger to be part of their ministry. My deepest appreciation also goes to the numerous men and women who spent hours answering my questions in interviews and other informal conversations. Father John Harvey and Dr. Ralph Blair also patiently contributed their perspectives on the ex-gay movement. I am especially grateful to "Brian," "Curtis," "Drew," and "Hank," who have each taught me in different ways that it is possible to find commonalities across the gulfs of religion and politics.

This study, which began as a dissertation, benefited from a great deal of support from both individuals and institutions. Research assistance from a Sexuality Research fellowship at the Social Science Research Council under Diane DiMauro enabled me to complete the fieldwork. An American fellowship from the American Association of University Women and a Dean's Dissertation fellowship from New York University were crucial at the dissertation stage. Rebecca Shulte, Lin Frederickson, and James Helyar at the Wilcox Collection of Contemporary Political Movements in the Kenneth Spencer Research Library at the University of Kansas made archival research a pleasure. Laird Wilcox, the impetus behind that vast collection, offered crucial advice at an early stage. David Kessler at the Bancroft Library at University of California,

Berkeley, entrusted me with access to the Sara Diamond Collection before it was publicly available. A Mellon postdoctoral fellowship in the Humanities in the Religion Department at Barnard College furnished the time and space to revise this book.

Carole Vance first suggested the ex-gay movement as a research topic, and she offered important initial feedback. Faye Ginsburg taught me to theorize ethnography and deepened my understanding of how people live and experience religion, sexuality, and politics in everyday life. Diane Winston's expertise in American religion inside and outside the academy expanded my knowledge of evangelicalism in America. Early on, Andrew Ross and Lisa Duggan advised me to think of my research as a political intervention, and their work serves as models of politically engaged scholarship. Lisa Duggan has been advisor, editor, and reader extraordinaire since I first became interested in conservative politics. This book is vastly better because of her expertise and suggestions. I am also grateful to a number of scholars who have read portions of this project and helped me to think about sexuality, religion, and politics in conversations and correspondence: Alison Redick, Micki McElya, Omri Elisha, Julie Sze, Betsy Esch, Andrea McArdle, Adria Imada, Barbara Abrash, Angela Zito, Heather Hendershot, Tal Halpern, Maggie Fishman, Melissa Checker, Susan Sered, Gayle Rubin, Minoo Moallem, Ann Pellegrini, Elizabeth Castelli, Erin Runions, Janet Jakobsen, Rebecca Young, Randy Balmer, Jack Hawley, Peter Savastano, and R. Marie Griffith. Students in my courses on right-wing politics, especially Jill Pasquarella and Jimmie Venturi, enthusiastically debated many of the ideas in the book. My colleagues in the Department of Comparative Studies at Ohio State University have been supportive of this project: Brian Rotman, Hugh Urban, Tim Choy, Luz Calvo, Nina Ha, Maurice Stevens, Barry Shank, Lesley Ferris, Julia Watson, Debra Moddelmog, and David Horn. Special thanks to Reed Malcolm, Kalicia Pivirotto, and to the anonymous reviewers for the University of California Press, who offered invaluable feedback on the manuscript. Jimmée Greco and Jacqueline Volin did a superb job editing and shepherding this project through the final stages.

In the end, friends and family sustained me. Kim Gilmore and I survived the long journey together, and this project would have been inconceivable without her unwavering friendship and intellectual savvy. Thanks to Sandra, David, George, Amy, Adam, and Sabrina Marsh, Riek Vandernoen, Annemarie, Jim, James, Tom, and John Quigley for reminding me that there is life beyond academia. I am extraordinarily fortunate for the friendship of Cathy Harris, Maisie Weissman, Abigail Crain, Shireen Deboo, Isabel Lee, Sobha Shukla, Beth Trimarco, Sujung Kim, Andrea Saenz, and Rena Rosenwasser. My gratitude toward my parents, Robert and Susan Erzen, and my brother, Alex Erzen, who have remained unfailingly supportive and patient, is immeasurable. Finally, Bill Quigley's unswerving faith, his combination of optimism and mordant humor, and his willingness to read chapters multiple times made all the difference. A dedication does not seem sufficient for the article from the *Onion* and everything after.

Notes

INTRODUCTION

1. I have changed the names and identifying details of the men and women at New Hope and other ministries to protect their anonymity. Throughout the book, I refer to public figures and organizations such as ex-gay ministry leaders, Christian activists, and ex-gay ministries by their actual names. Unless otherwise indicated, all quoted material is taken from fieldnotes I collected from 1999 to 2005.

2. The other residential ex-gay programs are Love in Action in Memphis, Tennessee; Freedom at Last Ministries in Wichita, Kansas; Higher Ground Ministries in Billings, Montana; and Pastoral Counseling and Restoration Ministries, Inc., in Woodstock, Georgia.

3. See Faye Ginsburg, *Contested Lives: The Abortion Debate in an American Community* (Berkeley: University of California Press, 1989); Susan Harding, *The Book of Jerry Falwell: Fundamentalist Language and Politics* (Princeton: Princeton University Press, 2001); Kathleen Blee, *Women of the Klan: Racism and Gender in the 1920s* (Berkeley: University of California Press, 1991); Meredith Burlein, *Lift High the Cross: Where White Supremacy and the Christian Right Converge* (Durham, NC: Duke University Press, 2002).

4. Susan Harding's experience listening to a preacher witness to her is exemplary of this dynamic. See Harding, *The Book of Jerry Falwell*.

5. This is from Tanya Luhrmann's comments on the panel "Gospel Ethnography: Predicaments of Fieldwork in the Cultures of Evangelical Protestantism" (American Anthropological Association meeting, Washington, D.C., December 1, 2001).

6. Michael Moffat, "Ethnographic Writing about American Culture," *Annual Review of Anthropology* 21 (1992): 211.

7. Seymour Martin Lipset, *The Politics of Unreason: Right Wing Movements in Political Perspective* (New York: Harper & Row, 1970); Daniel Bell,

The Radical Right: The New American Right, rev. and expanded (New York: Books for Libraries/Arno Press, 1979); David Bennett, *The Party of Fear: From Nativist Movements to the New Right in American History* (New York: Vintage, 1995); Catherine McNicol Stock, *Rural Radicals: From Bacon's Rebellion to the Oklahoma City Bombing* (New York: Penguin, 1997).

8. Mark A. Shibley, *Resurgent Evangelicalism in the United States: Mapping Cultural Change since 1970* (Columbia: University of South Carolina Press, 1996); Michael Lienesch, *Redeeming America: Piety and Politics in the New Christian Right* (Chapel Hill: University of North Carolina Press, 1993); Steve Bruce, *The Rise and Fall of the New Christian Right* (Oxford, England: Clarendon Press, 1988).

9. Jerome L. Himmelstein, *To the Right: The Transformation of American Conservatism* (Berkeley: University of California Press, 1990).

10. Clyde Wilcox, *God's Warriors: The Christian Right in Twentieth-Century America* (Baltimore: The Johns Hopkins University Press, 1992).

11. See Ginsburg, *Contested Lives,* and R. Marie Griffith, *God's Daughters: Evangelical Women and the Power of Submission* (Berkeley: University of California Press, 1997). In their work on pro-life women and evangelical women, Ginsburg and Griffith explicate the link between evangelical narratives of conversion and life stories.

12. Queer theory is an evolving field that has influenced other academic disciplines, but some of its most prominent thinkers base their work on the writing of Michel Foucault, specifically his work in the three volumes of *The History of Sexuality,* trans. Robert Hurley (New York: Vintage Books, 1988–1990). A representative but not exhaustive list of writing in the field of queer theory includes Judith Butler, *Gender Trouble: Feminism and the Subversion of Identity* (New York and London: Routledge, 1990), *Bodies That Matter: On the Discursive Limits of "Sex"* (New York: Routledge, 1993), and *The Psychic Life of Power: Theories in Subjection* (Stanford, CA: Stanford University Press, 1990); Lauren Berlant and Elizabeth Freeman, "Queer Nationality," in *Fear of a Queer Planet: Queer Politics and Social Theory,* ed. Michael Warner (Minneapolis: University of Minnesota Press, 1993); David L. Eng and Alice Y. Horn, eds., *Q & A: Queer in Asian America* (Philadelphia: Temple University Press, 1998).

13. Andrew Sullivan makes this argument in *Virtually Normal: An Argument about Homosexuality* (New York: Vintage Books, 1996).

14. Here I refer to the study on the hypothalamus conducted by LeVay in which he argues that there are biological signs of sexual difference. His study shows a purported difference in the size of the clusters of neurons called instial nuclei of the anterior hypothalamus (INAH) in men and women. See Simon LeVay, *The Sexual Brain* (Cambridge: MIT Press, 1993). Hamer's study was designed to find a gay gene based on studies of inheritance and twins. See Dean Hamer and Peter Copeland, *The Science of Desire: The Search for the Gay Gene and the Biology of Behavior* (New York: Simon and Schuster, 1994).

15. In her ethnography of an organization that prepares meals for people with AIDS-related illnesses, Courtney Bender argues that secular activities like cooking are invested with religious meaning and symbolism and provide a way

for individuals to understand their own spiritual lives. See Courtney Bender, *Heaven's Kitchen: Living Religion at God's Love We Deliver* (Chicago: University of Chicago Press, 2003).

16. Susan Harding also writes about the ways that the secular academy has represented fundamentalism as an "internally orientalized" other that does not warrant the same careful analysis applied to other forms of identity. See "Representing Fundamentalism: The Problem of the Repugnant Cultural Other," *Social Research* 58, no. 2 (Summer 1991): 373–93.

17. Faye Ginsburg, "The Case of Mistaken Identity: Problems in Representing Women on the Right," in *When They Read What We Write,* ed. Brettell, 164.

18. "'Have You Ever Prayed to St. Jude?' Reflections on Fieldwork in Catholic Chicago," in *Reimagining Denominationalism: Interpretive Essays,* edited by Robert Bruce Mullin and Russell E. Richey (New York: Oxford University Press, 1994), 135.

1. STEPS OUT OF HOMOSEXUALITY

1. This account is taken from interviews with Frank Worthen, as well as from materials he has published with his own testimony.

2. There are no biblical origins for the sinner's prayer, nor is this specific prayer mentioned in the Bible. The modern usage of the sinner's prayer originated in the nineteenth century and was popularized by the experience-oriented evangelistic style of Charles Finney. There are hundreds of versions. However, the sinner's prayer is the hallmark of conversion for many conservative Christian denominations, whose adherents recite some version of the prayer, repenting for their past sins and professing their belief in Jesus as their savior.

3. For a historical perspective on Pentecostalism and the Assemblies of God church, see Grant Wacker, *Heaven Below: Early Pentecostals and American Culture* (Cambridge: Harvard University Press, 2001).

4. James T. Richardson, Mary W. Stewart, and Robert B. Simmonds, *Organized Miracles* (New Brunswick, NJ: Transaction, 1979); Richard Quebedeaux, *The New Charismatics: The Origins, Development, and Significance of Neo-Pentecostalism* (Garden City, NJ: Doubleday and Co., 1976); Ronald M. Enroth, Edward E. Ericson Jr., and C. Breckinridge Peters, *The Jesus People: Old-Time Religion in the Age of Aquarius* (Grand Rapids, MI: Eerdmans, 1972); Jorstad Erling, *That New Time Religion: The Jesus Revival in America* (Minneapolis: Augsburg Publishing House, 1972).

5. For a detailed discussion on the history and current practices of Calvary Chapel and the Vineyard Fellowship, see Donald Miller, *Reinventing American Protestantism: Christianity in the New Millennium* (Berkeley: University of California Press, 1997).

6. See Nancy Ammerman, "Bowling Together: Congregations and the American Civic Order" (lecture transcript, Hartford Seminary, Hartford, CT, February 26, 1996).

7. See Stephen Warner, "The Place of the Congregation in the American Religious Configuration," in *American Congregations,* vol. 2, edited by J.P. Wind

and J. W. Lewis (Chicago: University of Chicago Press, 1994), and Roger Finke and Rodney Starke, *The Churching of America, 1776–1990: Winners and Losers in Our Religious Economy* (New Brunswick, NJ: Rutgers University Press, 1992).

8. Miller, *Reinventing American Protestantism*.

9. Kent Philpott, *The Third Sex? Six Homosexuals Tell Their Stories* (Plainfield, NJ: Logos Publishers, 1975), 172–73.

10. Ibid., 198–99.

11. As quoted in Kent Philpott, *The Gay Theology* (Plainfield, NJ: Logos Publishers, 1977), 145.

12. As quoted in ibid., 170.

13. Ibid., 181–82.

14. For an informative discussion of the role of conservative Christianity in Orange County, California, and the early history of Melodyland Church, see Lisa McGirr, *Suburban Warriors: The Origins of the New American Right* (Princeton: Princeton University Press, 2001).

15. Michael Bussee, interview, *One Nation under God,* documentary by Teodoro Maniaci and Francine M. Rzenick (New York: First Run Features, 1990).

16. Ibid.

17. As quoted in Bob Davies, "The History of Exodus International," in *The Crisis of Homosexuality,* ed. J. Isamu Yamamoto (Los Angeles: Victor Books, 1990), 19.

18. Ibid., 34.

19. John Gill, "What Is Exodus?" *San Francisco Examiner,* June 24, 1977.

20. Bussee, interview.

21. Ibid.

22. "Ex-Gay Ministry Founders Recant," "Keeping in Touch," the Universal Fellowship of Metropolitan Community Churches, May 1990.

23. Davies, "The History of Exodus International," 18.

24. Bussee, interview.

25. Frank Worthen, "Ministry in a Foreign Land," New Hope publication, p. 3.

26. Exodus International Fact Sheet and Referral List.

27. See Andrea Smith, "Devil's in the Details," *Colorlines* magazine, Spring 2002.

28. Alan Chambers, "From Alan's Desk," www.exodusnorthamerica.com, September 2003.

29. Alan Chambers, "Update North America," Exodus newsletter, http://exodus.to, September 2003.

30. Ibid.

31. Ibid.

32. Evangelical Council for Financial Accountability, www.ecfa.org.

33. Courage mission statement, 1981, http://couragerc.net/TheFiveGoals.html.

34. The contemporary American version of apocalypticism is based on the writings of John Nelson Darby. His thirty-two volumes of collected writings describe a view of history called dispensationalism, which segments God's relationship to humanity into periods of time during which humans are subject to

different divine laws and criteria for salvation. According to Darby, the current dispensation began with the Crucifixion; the next will begin with the Rapture of the Saved, leading to a seven-year period during which the Antichrist will rule the earth; followed by Armageddon and the Last Judgment. Darby wrote that this was the literal truth of Revelation. Darby's dispensationalism was adopted by the fundamentalist C. I. Scofield's First Reference Bible and is one of many readings of Revelation among those Christians who believe in biblical inerrancy. This idea has been popularized in the twelve-volume Left Behind series by Tim LaHaye and Jerry Jenkins.

35. JONAH mission statement, www.jonahweb.org.

36. Ibid.

37. Ibid.

38. Arthur Goldberg, "*Trembling before God* Critiques Orthodox Jewish View of Sexuality," letter to the *Jerusalem Post,* May 4, 2002.

39. Worthen, "Ministry in a Foreign Land," 6.

40. Alex Williams, "Gay Teenager Stirs a Storm," *New York Times,* July 17, 2005.

2. NEW CREATIONS

1. Frank Worthen, "Overview of the New Hope Program," in "Steps Out" 2000 residential program workbook, first quarter, p. 1. The "Steps Out" workbook is an unpublished book of lessons produced by New Hope and available only to New Hope members. There are four workbooks composed of separate lessons; each lesson has its own title, and each begins at page 1. The book is used as the basis of classes during the residential program year. This source was provided to me by Frank Worthen during my fieldwork.

2. Ibid.

3. I use the term "Christian" because that is how people at New Hope and in the ex-gay movement describe themselves. I also use the terms "Bible believers" "saved," and "born-again Christians" to refer to their brand of postdenominational Christianity. Some will define themselves as fundamentalist when their other options are to call themselves mainline, liberal, or other.

4. Frank Worthen, "Church Involvement," in "Steps Out" 2002 New Hope Ministry program manual, 4. The "Steps Out" manual is an unpublished program manual produced by New Hope and available only to New Hope members. It contains the rules, regulations, and basic information about the residential program, and it is updated each year. This source was provided to me by Frank Worthen during my fieldwork.

5. Ibid., 11.

6. See Paul Boyer, *When Time Shall Be No More: Prophecy Belief in Modern American Culture* (Cambridge: Harvard University Press, 1992); Melani McAlister, *Epic Encounters: Culture, Media, and U.S. Interests in the Middle East, 1945–2000* (Berkeley: University of California Press, 2001); Melani McAlister, "An Empire of Their Own," *The Nation,* September 22, 2003.

7. Robert Wuthnow, *The Restructuring of American Religion* (Princeton: Princeton University Press, 1988), 35.

8. Miller, *Reinventing American Protestantism,* 11.

9. Stephen Prothero, *American Jesus: How the Son of God Became a National Icon* (New York: Farrar, Straus and Giroux, 2003), 48.

10. Nathan Hatch, *The Democratization of American Christianity* (New Haven: Yale University Press, 1989); Christine Heyrman, *Southern Cross: The Beginnings of the Bible Belt* (New York: Alfred A. Knopf, 1997); R. Laurence Moore, *Religious Outsiders and the Making of America* (New York: Oxford University Press, 1986); Whitney Cross, *The Burned-over District: The Social and Intellectual History of Enthusiastic Religion in Western New York, 1800–1850* (Ithaca, NY: Cornell University Press, 1950).

11. For a history of evangelicalism in the United States, see Randy Balmer, *Blessed Assurance: A History of Evangelicalism in America* (Boston: Beacon Press, 1999). Also, see Christian Smith, *American Evangelicalism: Embattled and Thriving* (Chicago: University of Chicago Press, 1998).

12. "Statement of Faith and Purpose," Church of the Open Door, http://opendoorsanrafael.net

13. Ferenc Szasz Morton, *The Divided Mind of Protestant America, 1880–1930* (Tuscaloosa: University of Alabama Press, 1982); Ernest R. Sandeen, *The Roots of Fundamentalism: British and American Millenarianism, 1800–1930* (Chicago: University of Chicago Press, 1970).

14. See José Casanova, "Evangelical Protestantism: From Civil Religion to Fundamentalist Sect to New Christian Right," chap. 6 of *Public Religions in the Modern World* (Chicago: University of Chicago Press, 1994), 135–66.

15. Ibid., 142.

16. Nancy Tatom Ammerman, *Bible Believers: Fundamentalists in the Modern World* (New Brunswick, NJ: Rutgers University Press, 1987), 21.

17. For a discussion on the media representations of the Scopes Trial, see Susan Harding, *The Book of Jerry Falwell. Inherit the Wind,* the play, was produced on Broadway in 1955 by Jerome Lawrence and Robert E. Lee. The United Artists 1960 version of *Inherit the Wind* was written by Nathan E. Douglas and Harold Jacob Smith. Even though these were fictionalized versions of the trial, they became the way most Americans came to understand the Scopes Trial. The conception of fundamentalism as anti-modern was symbolized by the song "Give Me That Old-Time Religion."

18. Recent work disputes the claim that the Scopes Trial represented a melodrama that resulted in the resounding victory of modernity over fundamentalism and argues that fundamentalists had conflicting and contradictory stances on theories of evolution and the trial itself. See Edward J. Larson, *Summer for the Gods: The Scopes Trial and America's Continuing Debate over Science and Religion* (New York: Basic Books, 1997). George Marsden has argued that the fundamentalist controversy of the 1920s was not a rural-urban or Southern-Northern conflict, but one that took place primarily within northern Presbyterian and Baptist denominations in New York, Philadelphia, and Chicago. Despite the movement's association with anti-modernism, Marsden argues that since 1925, fundamentalists like J. Frank Norris, Carl McIntire, John R. Rice, Bob Jones Sr., Bob Jones Jr., and even Jerry Falwell in his earlier years involved themselves in politics and social issues to the same extent as leaders in other

denominations. See George Marsden, *Fundamentalism and American Culture: The Shaping of Twentieth-Century Evangelicalism, 1870–1925* (New York: Oxford University Press, 1980).

19. Joel Carpenter, *Revive Us Again: The Reawakening of American Fundamentalism* (New York: Oxford University Press, 1997).

20. These included the publishing and radio enterprises of the Moody Bible Institute, Fuller Theological Seminary, Charles Fuller's *Old Fashioned Revival Hour* on radio, and student organizations like Youth for Christ and Inter-Varsity.

21. In this story, the men of Sodom demand to "know" Lot's male guests, and many have interpreted the verses to mean that God destroys Sodom because of the men's desire to commit homosexual rape. However, biblical scholars on both sides of the gay issue have debated whether the sin of Sodom was one of homosexuality or mere inhospitality. Ronald W. Graham, "Homosexuality: A Look at the Scriptures," *The Disciple*, March 19, 1978. However, the idea that Sodom was destroyed for the sin of homosexuality is based on uncertain translation, and Ezekiel 16:49–50 provides other reasons for God's judgment. See *Evangelical Dictionary of Theology*, 2nd ed., ed. Walter A. Elwell (Grand Rapids, MI: Baker Book House Company, 2001), s.v. "Homosexuality."

22. Frank Worthen, "Did God Say?" chap. 2 in *Helping People Step Out of Homosexuality: A Handbook for Pastors, Counselors, Lay Workers*, rev. ed. (San Rafael, CA: New Hope Ministries, 1995), 28.

23. John Boswell, *Christianity, Social Tolerance and Homosexuality: Gay People in Western Europe from the Beginning of the Christian Era to the Fourteenth Century* (Chicago: University of Chicago Press, 1980), 92.

24. For discussion of the emergence of homosexuality as an identity, see David Halperin, "Is There a History of Sexuality?" in *The Lesbian and Gay Studies Reader*, ed. Henry Abelove, Michele A. Barale, and Dwight Halperin (New York: Routledge, 1993); George Chauncy, *Gay New York: Gender, Urban Culture and the Making of the Gay Male World, 1890–1940* (New York: Basic Books, 1995); Lisa Duggan, *Sapphic Slashers: Sex, Violence, and American Modernity* (Durham, NC: Duke University Press, 2000); Jonathon Ned Katz, *The Invention of Heterosexuality* (New York: Plume Books, 1996).

25. Marvin Ellison, *Same-Sex Marriage? A Christian Ethical Analysis* (Cleveland: Pilgrim Press, 2004), 3.

26. Ibid., 5.

27. Jon Barrett, "The Lost Brother: A Special Investigative Report," *The Advocate*, November 24, 1998.

28. Frank Worthen, "Retreat," in "Steps Out" 2000 residential program workbook, first quarter, 1.

29. Dawne Moon, *God, Sex and Politics: Homosexuality and Everyday Theologies* (Chicago: University of Chicago Press, 2004), 204.

30. Frank Worthen, "Overview of the New Hope Program," in "Steps Out" 2000 residential program workbook, first quarter, 9.

31. For a fascinating and detailed cultural history of the meaning of Jesus in American culture, American Protestantism, and other religious traditions, see Prothero, *American Jesus*.

32. Worthen, "Purity/Holiness," in "Steps Out," second quarter, meeting twenty-eight, 5.

33. Ibid.

34. R. Marie Griffith, *God's Daughters: Evangelical Women and the Power of Submission* (Berkeley: University of California Press, 1997).

35. Anita Worthen, "How to Phone Counsel," New Hope memo, 1998.

36. Worthen, "Image of God," in "Steps Out," third quarter, meeting fifty-eight, 4.

37. Ibid.

38. New Hope Ministry, introduction to "Steps Out."

39. Freedom in Christ mission statement, www.freedominchrist-sf.org/ministry.htm.

40. Ibid.

41. Some examples of recent groups include Affirmation (www.umaffirm.org), Dignity USA (www.dignityusa.org), Lutherans Concerned (www.lcna.org), More Light Presbyterians (www.mlp.org), Soulforce Inc. (www.soulforce.org), United Church of Christ (www.ucc.org/index4.html).

42. See Edward R. Gray and Scott L. Thumma, *Gay Religion: Innovation and Tradition in Spiritual Practice* (Walnut Creek, CA: Altamira Press, 2005).

43. Ralph Blair, "The Best of Both Words: A Brief History of Evangelicals Concerned, Inc." (New York: Evangelicals Concerned, Inc., 2000), 5.

44. Ibid., 8. The consultants for the Homosexual Community Counseling Center included Kinsey Report coauthor Wardell E. Pomeroy, Virginia E. Johnson (of Masters and Johnson fame), psychologist Evelyn Hooker, Troy Perry (founder of the Metropolitan Community Church), and Barbara Gittings, founder of Daughters of Bilitis.

45. Blair, ibid., 11.

46. Ibid.

47. Ibid., 12.

48. Don Frye, "Insights," *The E Cable of Evangelicals Concerned,* Winter 2000, p. 5.

49. Ralph Blair, "The Real Changes Taking Place," *Open Hands* 2, no. 2 (Fall 1986).

50. Blair, "Best of Both Words," 5.

51. See www.indegayforum.org.

52. MCC official Web site, www.mccchurch.org/.

53. Melissa Wilcox, *Coming Out in Christianity: Religion, Identity and Community* (Bloomington: Indiana University Press, 2003), 149.

54. Ibid., 77.

55. Barbara Dozetos, "UK Ex-Gay Leader Claims Conversion Therapy Futile," www.gay.com, accessed January 29, 2001.

56. Quoted in "Record," newsletter of Evangelicals Concerned, Spring 2002, 1.

57. From www.justice-respect.org/.

58. Tom Cole, "Gays and Exgays: Sharing the Pain of the Past," Justice and Respect Web site, www.justice-respect.org/, accessed November 22, 1999.

3. A REFUGE FROM THE WORLD

1. Frank Worthen, "The Gay Image," in "Steps Out" 2002 New Hope Ministry program manual, 10.

2. Kathy Rudy, *Sex and the Church: Gender, Homosexuality, and the Transformation of Christian Ethics* (Boston: Beacon Press, 1997), 72.

3. Ibid., 75.

4. Frank Worthen, "Steps Out Program," in "Steps Out" 2002 New Hope Ministry program manual, 3.

5. Ibid., 3.

6. Scholarship on homosociality has also emphasized that changes in the meanings of manhood intersected with the shift from entrepreneurial capitalism to organized and efficient corporate capitalism in the late nineteenth century. In the mid- to late 1800s as men entered the all-male world of corporate capitalism and bureaucracies from previous ways of life in farming and working in the home, women's influence over child raising, education, and the churches dramatically increased. Masculinity became something that men could possess that would differentiate them from women, and it came to signify all that was not feminine: aggressiveness, physical force, and unhidden sexuality. See Anthony Rotundo, *American Manhood: Transformations in Masculinity from the Revolution to the Modern Era* (New York: Basic Books, 1993); J. A. Mangan and James Walvin, eds., *Manliness and Morality: Middle-Class Masculinity in Britain and America, 1800–1940* (New York: St. Martin's Press, 1987); and David Gilmore, *Manhood in the Making: Cultural Concepts of Masculinity* (New Haven: Yale University Press, 1990).

7. Luther Gulick, "The Alleged Effeminization of Our American Boys," *American Physical Education Review* 10 (September 1905): 61.

8. See Donna Haraway, "Teddy Bear Patriarchy: Taxidermy in the Garden of Eden, New York City, 1908–1936," in chap. 3 of *Primate Visions: Gender, Race and Nature in the World of Modern Science* (New York: Routledge, 1990), and Gerald F. Roberts, "The Strenuous Life: The Cult of Manliness in the ERA of Theodore Roosevelt" (PhD diss., Michigan State University, 1970). Roosevelt's cult of strenuous masculinity associated masculine strength with the western plains and the life of the frontier. Men in fraternal organizations such as the Order of Red Men utilized and mimicked Native American rituals as part of a masculine primitive ethos. Scouting, fraternal orders, and male supper clubs gained in popularity during the late nineteenth and early twentieth centuries. Strenuous exercise and team sports also became crucial to the development of manhood through homosocial worlds. The Boys Brigade, a precursor to the Boy Scouts, was aimed at young boys who were expected to surrender their personal goals to those of the group in deference of a heroic leader. Scouting was designed to protect boys from the femininizing influence of their mothers and teachers. See Mark C. Carnes, "Middle-Class Men and the Solace of Fraternal Ritual," chap. 2 of *Meanings for Manhood: Constructions of Masculinity in Victorian America,* ed. Mark C. Carnes and Clyde Griffen (Chicago: Chicago University Press, 1990), 37–53; Jeffrey P. Hantover, "The Boy Scouts

and the Validation of Masculinity," *Journal of Social Issues* 34, no. 1 (1978): 184–95; Michael Kimmel, "Men's Responses to Feminism at the Turn of the Century," *Gender and Society* 1, no. 3 (September 1987): 261–83; Clyde Griffen, "Reconstructing Masculinity from the Evangelical Revival to the Waning of Progressivism: A Speculative Synthesis," in *Meanings for Manhood: Constructions of Masculinity in Victorian America Chicago,* ed. Mark C. Carnes and Clyde Griffen (Chicago: University of Chicago Press, 1990), 183–204.

9. Worthen, "Discipline/Dismissal," in "Steps Out" 2002, 8–9.

10. Worthen, "Television, Movies, and Videos," in "Steps Out" 2002, 7.

11. New Hope Ministry, application form, 2000.

12. Ibid.

13. Ibid.

14. S. R. Hathaway and J. C. McKinley and the MMPI Restandardization Committee at the University of Minnesota Press: James N. Butcher, Grant Dahlstrom, John R. Graham, and Auke Tellegen, *Minnesota Multiphasic Personality Inventory* (Minneapolis: University of Minnesota, 1989).

15. Drew, personal correspondence to applicant, September 11, 2000.

16. Worthen, "Submission to Leadership," in "Steps Out" 2002 New Hope Ministry program manual, 10.

17. Worthen, "Personal Responsibility and Attitude," in "Steps Out" 2002, 5.

18. Ibid., 13.

19. Ibid.

20. Worthen, "Dress Code," in "Steps Out" 2002, 9.

21. Ibid.

22. Worthen, "The Gay Image," in "Steps Out" 2002, 10.

23. Worthen, "The Four Components of Homosexuality," in "Steps Out," second quarter, meeting thirty-four, 6.

24. Alan Medinger, *Growth into Manhood: Resuming the Journey* (Colorado Springs, CO: Shaw WaterBrook Press, 2000), 5.

25. Ibid., 84–85.

26. Ibid., 91.

27. Alan Medinger, "Healing for the Homosexual: What Does It Mean?" *Regeneration News,* June 1991, p. 3.

28. Leanne Payne, *Crisis in Masculinity* (Grand Rapids, MI: Hamewith Books, 1995), 82.

29. Ibid., 20.

30. Ibid., 37.

31. In the years 1890–1920, the cultural phenomenon of muscular Christianity transformed Jesus into a muscular, working-class carpenter without the feminizing qualities that had been ascribed to him. It provided a rationale for men to take back control of churches, which they believed had suffered under too much feminine influence. Jesus was recast as the first heroic artisan.

Revivalist preachers like Billy Sunday and Dwight Moody, the Men and Religion Forward movement, as well as the popular press were grappling with similar anxieties about the feminization of the American home, schools, and churches and racist, xenophobic fears of working-class immigrants wresting control of politics from white, middle-class men at the turn of the century. Middle-class men's response and the masculinization of the church were symptoms of a fear that women controlled churches and schools. See Gail Bederman, "'The Women Have Had Charge of the Church Work Long Enough': The Men and Religion Forward Movement of 1911–1912 and the Masculinization of Middle-Class Protestantism," *American Quarterly* 41 (September 1989): 432–65; Thomas Hughes, *The Manliness of Christ* (Boston: Houghton Mifflin, 1879).

32. Worthen, "What's Good in the Book: *Crisis in Masculinity*," in "Steps Out," third quarter, meeting sixty-two, 4.

33. Worthen, "Questions for the Book: *Crisis in Masculinity*," in "Steps Out," third quarter, meeting sixty-one, 3.

34. Worthen, "What's Good in the Book: *Crisis in Masculinity*," in "Steps Out," third quarter, meeting sixty-two, 3.

35. Ibid., 4.

36. Ibid.

37. Worthen, "Interview with a Straight Man," in "Steps Out," fourth quarter, meeting sixty-six, 3.

38. Alan Medinger uses this phrase in *Growth into Manhood* as part of what helps men find their core heterosexual and masculine identities.

39. Medinger, *Growth into Manhood*, 8.

40. Steven G. Sarosy, Terry Clark Cook, J. Gerramy Quarto, and Lester B. Brown, *Gay Men and Aging*, Garland Studies on the Elderly in America (New York: Garland Publishing, 1997).

41. Worthen, "Lifestyle," in "Steps Out," second quarter, meeting thirty-four, 3.

42. Frank Worthen, "The Gay Lifestyle," New Hope pamphlet.

43. Worthen, "Marriage," in "Steps Out," fourth quarter, meeting seventy-one, 9.

44. Ibid., 5.

45. Medinger, *Growth into Manhood*, 202.

46. Ibid., 200.

47. Ibid., 205.

48. Ibid., 206.

49. Ibid.

50. Worthen, "The Four Components of Homosexuality," in "Steps Out," second quarter, meeting thirty-three, 8.

51. Worthen, "Marriage," in "Steps Out," fourth quarter, meeting seventy-one, 6.

52. Ibid., 11.

53. Medinger, *Growth into Manhood*, 218.

54. Ibid., 217.

55. Intimate Issues, www.intimateissues.com, accessed August 17, 2005.

56. Frank Worthen, "The Future of an Ex-Gay Person," New Hope pamphlet, p. 11.

57. Andy Comiskey, keynote address, Exodus annual conference (August 26, 2000).

4. ARRESTED DEVELOPMENT

1. American Psychiatric Association position statement, www.psych.org, March 2000. The statement was approved by the board in March 2000 and by the general assembly in May 2000. Other professional organizations that oppose reparative therapy include the American Academy of Pediatrics, the American Medical Association, the American Psychological Association, the American Counseling Association, and the National Association of Social Workers.

2. Frank Worthen, New Hope Ministry newsletter, June 2000, p. 1.

3. Robert L. Spitzer, "Can Some Gay Men and Lesbians Change Their Sexual Orientation? 200 Participants Reporting a Change from Homosexual to Heterosexual Orientation," presentation at the American Psychiatric Association annual convention, New Orleans, May 9, 2001. Subsequently published in *Archives of Sexual Behavior* 32, no. 5 (October 2003): 403–17.

4. Ibid.

5. Ariel Shidlo and Michael Schroeder, "Changing Sexual Orientation: A Consumers' Report," *Professional Psychology: Research and Practice* 33, no. 3 (2002): 249–59.

6. Dwight Elliot, "NGLTF Responds to Flawed Spitzer Study on So-Called Reparative Therapy," National Gay and Lesbian Task Force press release, May 8, 2001, and Dwight Elliot, "Snake Oil versus Science: New Study by New York Researchers on Conversion Therapy Contradicts NARTH," National Gay and Lesbian Task Force press release, May 8, 2001.

7. Robert Spitzer, "Commentary: Psychiatry and Homosexuality," *Wall Street Journal,* May 23, 2001.

8. Ibid.

9. American Psychiatric Association position statement, May 2000.

10. See Richard Pillard, "The Search for a Genetic Influence on Sexual Orientation," in *Science and Homosexualities,* ed. Vernon Rosario (London: Routledge, 1997), 226–41.

11. Here again I refer to the study on the hypothalamus conducted by LeVay in which he argues that there are biological signs of sexual difference. He argues that there may be a difference in the size of the clusters of neurons called institial nuclei of the anterior hypothalamus (INAH) in men and women. See Simon LeVay, *The Sexual Brain* (Cambridge: MIT Press, 1993).

12. Hamer's study was designed to find a gay gene based on studies of inheritance and work on twins. See Dean Hamer and Peter Copeland, *The Science of Desire: The Search for the Gay Gene and the Biology of Behavior* (New York: Simon and Schuster, 1994).

13. Jennifer Terry, "The Seductive Power of Science in the Making of Deviant Subjectivity," in *Science and Homosexualities.*

14. Vernon Rosario, "Homosexual Bio-histories: Genetic Nostalgias and the Quest for Paternity," in *Science and Homosexualities,* 8.

15. Jennifer Terry, "The Seductive Power of Science," 265.

16. Garland E. Allen, "The Double-Edged Sword of Genetic Determinism: Social and Political Agendas in Genetic Studies of Homosexuality, 1940–1994," in *Science and Homosexualities.*

17. See Foucault, *The History of Sexuality*, vol. 1, *An Introduction*, and Jeffrey Weeks, *Sex, Politics and Society: The Regulation of Sexuality since 1800* (London: Longman, 1981). When I use the term "sexologists," I will be referring to the lawyers, researchers, doctors, psychiatrists, and psychoanalysts who sought to understand the origins of homosexuality through classification and research. Although I do not reproduce a complete history of sexology, I will be referring to some major historical figures such as Karl Heinrich Ulrichs, Magnus Hirschfield, Richard von Kraft-Ebbing, Havelock Ellis, Sigmund Freud, Alfred Kinsey, Irving Bieber, and Charles Socarides. In the present, I refer to the biological and genetic studies conducted by Simon LeVay, Richard Pillard, Dean Hamer, and Peter Copeland as well as psychological studies by Robert Spitzer and Ariel Shidlo.

18. See Jennifer Terry's work in *Deviant Bodies: Critical Perspectives on Difference in Science and Popular Culture* (Bloomington: Indiana University Press, 1995), and *An American Obsession: Science, Medicine and Homosexuality in Modern Society* (Chicago: University of Chicago Press, 1999).

19. See John D'Emilio, "Capitalism and Gay Identity," in *The Lesbian and Gay Studies Reader*, ed. Abelove, Barale, and Halperin, 467–76.

20. Vern Bullough, *Science in the Bedroom: A History of Sex Research* (New York: Basic Books, 1994).

21. See Hubert Kennedy, "Karl Heinrich Ulrichs, First Theorist of Homosexuality," 26–45, and James D. Streakley, "Per scientiam ad justitiam: Magnus Hirschfield and the Sexual Politics of Innate Homosexuality," in *Science and Homosexualities*, 133–55.

22. Janice Irvine, *Disorders of Desire: Sex and Gender in Modern American Society* (Philadelphia: Temple University Press, 1990), 73.

23. See Lisa Duggan's chapter "Doctors of Desires," in *Sapphic Slashers: Sex, Violence, and American Modernity* (Durham, NC: Duke University Press, 2000).

24. Ronald Bayer, *Homosexuality and American Psychiatry* (Princeton: Princeton University Press, 1987), 22.

25. Sigmund Freud, *Three Essays on the Theory of Sexuality* (1905; New York: Avon Books, 1962), 32.

26. As quoted in Bayer, *Homosexuality and American Psychiatry*, 26.

27. Henry Abelove, "Freud, Male Homosexuality and the Americans," in *The Lesbian and Gay Studies Reader*, 381–93.

28. Ibid., 387.

29. See Stephanie Kenen, "Who Counts When You're Counting Homosexuals? Hormones and Homosexuality in Mid-twentieth Century America," in *Science and Homosexualities*, 200.

30. Irvine, *Disorders of Desire*, 89.

31. See Martin Duberman, *Cures: A Gay Man's Odyssey* (New York: Dutton/ NAL: 1991).

32. See Robert Corber, *Homosexuality in Cold War America: Resistance and the Crisis of Masculinity* (Durham, NC: Duke University Press, 1997).

33. Irvine, *Disorders of Desire*, 109.

34. See Kenen, "Who Counts When You're Counting Homosexuals?" 209.

35. See John D'Emilio and Estelle Freedman, *Intimate Matters: A History of Sexuality in America*, 2nd ed. (Chicago: University of Chicago Press, 1997).

36. John D'Emilio, *Sexual Politics, Sexual Communities: The Making of a Homosexual Minority in the United States, 1940–1970* (Chicago: University of Chicago Press, 1983).

37. Irving Bieber, *Homosexuality: A Psychoanalytic Study of Male Homosexuals* (New York: Basic Books, 1962).

38. Ibid., 253.

39. Bayer, *Homosexuality and American Psychiatry*, 34.

40. Socarides's son, Richard Socarides, served the Clinton administration in various capacities, including liaison to the gay community. When asked by a reporter whether his own parenting caused his son to be gay, Socarides placed the blame on the fact that he divorced when his son was three and his wife was harsh to him afterward (Times Newspapers Limited, April 30, 1995).

41. Charles Socarides, "Psychoanalytic Therapy of a Male Homosexual," *Psychoanalytic Quarterly* 38 (April 1969): 173.

42. See Mel White, *Stranger at the Gate: To Be Gay and Christian in America* (New York: Penguin Books, 1995), 130–31. White talks about being given electroshock therapy by doctors while he looked at pictures of men and women in an attempt to cure his homosexuality.

43. Evelyn Hooker, "Male Homosexuals and Their Worlds," in *Sexual Inversion*, ed. Judd Marmor (New York: Basic Books, 1965), 92.

44. Judd Marmor, "Homosexuality: Mental Illness or Moral Dilemma," *International Journal of Psychiatry* 10 (March 1972): 114.

45. Richard Green, "Homosexuality as Mental Illness," *International Journal of Psychiatry* 10 (1972): 77.

46. Richard Green, *The Sissy Boy Syndrome and the Development of Homosexuality* (New Haven: Yale University Press, 1987).

47. As quoted in Bayer, *Homosexuality and American Psychiatry*, 95.

48. D'Emilio, *Sexual Politics, Sexual Communities*, 167.

49. As quoted in ibid., 163.

50. Ibid.

51. See Alice Echols, *Daring to Be Bad: Radical Feminism in America, 1967–1975* (Minneapolis: University of Minnesota Press, 1989).

52. See D'Emilio, *Sexual Politics, Sexual Communities*.

53. Bayer, *Homosexuality and American Psychiatry*, 112.

54. Ibid., 111.

55. Robert J. Stoller, Judd Marmor, Irving Bieber, Ronald Gold, Charles Socarides, Richard Green, and Robert Spitzer, "A Symposium: Should Homosexuality Be in the APA Nomenclature?" *American Journal of Psychiatry* 130 (November 11, 1973): 1207–16.

56. Ibid., 1211.

57. Ibid., 1208.

58. Ibid., 1215.

59. Bayer, *Homosexuality and American Psychiatry*, 170.

60. The APA, AMA, and other professional medical and scientific organizations do not endorse NARTH.

61. Joseph Nicolosi, "Taking a Stand," NARTH flyer.

62. NARTH statement of purpose, www.narth.com/menus/goals.html.

63. For example, "Retrospective Self-Reports of Changes in Homosexual Orientation: A Consumer Survey of Conversion Therapy Clients" is a study documenting treatment success for homosexuals by Joseph Nicolosi, A. Dean Byrd, and Richard W. Potts.

64. NARTH, "About NARTH," www.narth.com/menus/advisors.html.

65. Joseph Nicolosi, "I'm Dr. Joseph Nicolosi, President of NARTH," www.narth.com/docs/joe-why.html.

66. Joseph Nicolosi, *Reparative Therapy of Male Homosexuality: A New Clinical Approach* (Northvale, NJ: Jason Aronson, 1997), 186.

67. NARTH statement of purpose, www.narth.com/menus/goals.html.

68. NARTH publications, "NARTH and Gay Civil Rights," pamphlet, May 2001, p. 3.

69. Charles Socarides, Benjamin Kaufman, Joseph Nicolosi, Jeffrey Satinover, and Richard Fitzgibbons, "Don't Forsake Homosexuals Who Want Help," *Wall Street Journal,* January 9, 1997. See also Jeffrey Satinover, *Homosexuality and the Politics of Truth* (Grand Rapids, MI: Baker Books, 1996).

70. Nicolosi, *Reparative Therapy of Male Homosexuality,* 4.

71. Elizabeth Moberly, *Homosexuality: A New Christian Ethic* (Cambridge, England: James Clarke and Co., 1983), 42.

72. Ibid., 5.

73. Ibid., 15.

74. Ibid., 6.

75. Ibid., 18.

76. Ibid., 21.

77. Ibid., 26.

78. Ibid., 8.

79. Ibid., 9.

80. Starla Allen and Patricia Allan, "Understanding the Roots of Lesbianism: Common Factors in the Lives of Women with Same-Sex Struggles," Exodus resource booklet, "Prevention and Recovery," no. PR-05.

81. Ibid., 11.

82. Ibid.

83. Jeanette Howard, *Out of Egypt: Leaving Lesbianism Behind* (Kent, England: Bookprint Creative Services, 1991). Jeanette was the program leader for the women's residential program at New Hope from 1988 to 1990.

84. Starla Allen, public speech (Friends and Family Weekend, San Rafael, CA, August, 19, 1999).

85. Allen and Allan, "Understanding the Roots of Lesbianism," 5.

86. John Paulk and Anne Paulk, *Love Won Out: How God's Love Helped Two People Leave Homosexuality and Find Each Other* (Wheaton, IL: Tyndale House Publishers, 1999), 11–14.

87. Ibid., 16

88. Allen and Allan, "Understanding the Roots of Lesbianism," 14.

89. Irvine, *Disorders of Desire,* 70.

90. As quoted in ibid.

91. Anita Worthen, "When Passion Rules," New Hope Ministry newsletter, February 1999.

92. Anita Worthen, "Family Matters," New Hope Ministry newsletter, May 2000.

93. Ibid.

5. TESTIFYING TO SEXUAL HEALING

1. Worthen, "The Power of God to Change Lives," in "Steps Out," first quarter, meeting fifteen, 3.

2. Wendy Kaminer, *I'm Dysfunctional, You're Dysfunctional: The Recovery Movement and Other Self-Help Fashions* (Reading, MA: Addison-Wesley, 1992), 125.

3. Ellen Herman, *The Romance of American Psychology: Political Culture in the Age of Experts* (Berkeley: University of California Press, 1995).

4. Ibid., 262–63.

5. See Echols, *Daring to Be Bad*. Echols carefully examines the distinctions between radical, cultural, and liberal feminism, and points to the increasing focus on self-help ideas in lesbian feminism and women's communities in the 1970s.

6. Wendy Simonds, *Women and Self-Help Culture: Reading between the Lines* (New Brunswick, NJ: Rutgers University Press, 1992), 138.

7. Eva Moskowitz, *In Therapy We Trust: America's Obsession with Self-Fulfillment* (Baltimore: The Johns Hopkins University Press, 2001), 244.

8. For a wider discussion of the rise of the small group movement in the context of the therapeutic recovery model, see Robert Wuthnow, *Sharing the Journey: Support Groups and America's New Quest for Community* (New York: Free Press, 1994).

9. See Griffith, *God's Daughters,* 34. See also Robyn R. Warhol and Helena Michie, "Twelve-Step Teleology: Narratives of Recovery/Recovery as Narrative," in *Getting a Life: Everyday Uses of Autobiography,* ed. Sidonie Smith and Julia Watson (Minneapolis: University of Minnesota Press, 1996), 327–50.

10. Moskowitz, *In Therapy We Trust,* 247.

11. Ernest Kurtz, *AA: The Story* (New York: Harper and Row, 1988), 9.

12. Ibid., 23.

13. Ibid., 13.

14. These include Guy Charles of LIBERATION in Jesus Christ, Roger Grindstaff of Disciples Only, John Evans of Love in Action, Greg Reid of EAGLE, Colin Cook of Homosexuals Anonymous, and Rick Notch of Open Door.

15. Bob Davies, *History of Exodus International,* Resources Series: Homosexuality and Society (Seattle: Exodus International Publishing, 1988).

16. Ibid., 24.

17. *Alcoholics Anonymous* (New York: Alcoholics Anonymous World Services, 1955), 59.

18. Worthen, "Overview of the New Hope Program," in "Steps Out," first quarter, meeting three, 10.

19. Worthen, "Addictions," in "Steps Out," first quarter, meeting twenty-two, 3.

20. New Hope mission statement.

21. Worthen, "Addictions," in "Steps Out," first quarter, meeting twenty-two, 3.

22. Worthen, "Addictions Session 10," in "Steps Out," first quarter, meeting twenty-five, 3.

23. Frank Worthen, "A Review of Addictions," in "Steps Out," first quarter, meeting twenty-two, 2.

24. Worthen, "Addiction Session 2," in "Steps Out," first quarter, meeting twenty-two, 5.

25. Worthen, "Addiction Session 3," in "Steps Out," first quarter, meeting twenty-two, 6.

26. Desert Stream Ministries, "What Is Living Waters?" www.desertstream.org/programslivingwaters1.htm.

27. *Sexaholics Anonymous Handbook,* SA literature (Nashville: Sexaholics Anonymous, 1989), 4.

28. Christian Smith, *Christian America? What Evangelicals Really Want* (Berkeley: University of California Press, 2002), 137.

29. Mike Haley, Exodus International newsletter, March 2001.

30. Barbara Swallow, Exodus International newsletter, July 2000. Swallow published a book-length testimony of her personal story entitled *Free Indeed: One Woman's Victory over Lesbianism* (Seattle: Exodus International North America, 2000).

31. Andrew Comiskey, *Pursuing Sexual Wholeness: How Jesus Heals the Homosexual* (Lake Mary, FL: Creation House, 1989), 151.

32. Michel Foucault, *The History of Sexuality,* vol. 1, *An Introduction,* 59.

33. Ibid., 18.

34. Ibid., 62.

35. Ibid., 63.

36. David R. Renfroe, "How to Minister to the Homosexual," *Anita Bryant Ministries,* March 1979; Marilyn McGinnis and H. Norman Wright, "Ministering to the Homosexual," *Moody Monthly,* September 1974.

37. Chris Bernard, "A Gay Takes Anita's Cure," *Fort Lauderdale News and Sun Sentinel,* August 5, 1979, p. 1D.

38. International Healing Foundation, www.gaytostraight.org.

6. LOVE WON OUT?

1. A series of ads were placed in the national media beginning with an ad in the *New York Times* on July 13, 1998, followed by an ad on July 14, 1998, in the *Washington Post* and one in *USA Today* on July 15, 1998. The ad campaign continued with placements in the *Los Angeles Times* on July 27, the *Chicago Tribune* on July 28, the *Miami Herald* on July 29, and the *San Francisco Examiner* on August 16. The ads were sponsored and paid for by fifteen organizations: Alliance for Traditional Marriage–Hawaii, American Family Association, Americans for Truth about Homosexuality, Center for Reclaiming America,

Christian Family Network, Christian Coalition, Citizens for Community Values, Colorado for Family Values, Concerned Women for America, Coral Ridge Ministries, Family First, Family Research Council, Liberty Counsel, National Legal Foundation, and Kerusso Ministries.

2. I define the Christian Right as a loose coalition of politically active fundamentalist and evangelical conservative Christians who hold a view of America based on theological ideas that the government should be based on biblical values and morality.

See "Ex-Gay Ads Spark Media Firestorm: Millions Hear about Exodus through *Time, Newsweek,* 'Good Morning America' and a Host of Other Media," *Exodus North America Update,* August 1998.

3. John Leland and Mark Miller, "Can Gays Convert?" *Newsweek,* August 17, 1998.

4. John Paulk, "Sharing the Truth in Love," Focus on the Family pamphlet, 1999.

5. Ibid.

6. Alan Chambers, "A Dream Come True," Exodus International Web site, www.exodus.to/testimonials_left_homosexuality_chambers.shtml.

7. Jerry Falwell, telecast speech (National Coming Out of Homosexuality Day, San Francisco, October 11, 1999).

8. Gustav Niebuhr, "Falwell Finds an Accord with Gay Rights Backer," *New York Times,* October 23, 1999, p. A15.

9. James Morris, *The Preachers* (New York: St. Martin's Press, 1973), 260. According to Morris, Hargis was a pastor of a nondenominational Christian church in Sapulpa, Oklahoma, when he felt the calling to begin the anti-communist Christian Crusade in 1950. By 1962 the CC had a budget of over one million dollars as well as four hundred radio programs on a weekly basis in forty-six states. By then, Hargis was quite wealthy, owning a seven-hundred-acre farm and tour bus. In 1960 the CC built the Cathedral of the Christian Crusade, which was large enough to handle printing and shipping as well as seminars, conventions, and conferences for conservative Christians.

10. Ibid., 264.

11. Billy James Hargis, *Christian Crusade Membership Manual,* archive, Wilcox Collection.

12. Billy James Hargis, "A Message from Dr. Billy James Hargis," *Christian Crusader Weekly,* April 18, 1960, p. 1. Hargis published constantly. His books ranged from self-help titles like *How to Be Prosperous, Be Healthy, Be Happy; How to Get into God's Inner Circle; How to Cope with Your Problems; Communist America . . . Must It Be?; Why I Fight for Christian America;* and *The Federal Reserve Scandal.*

13. Billy James Hargis, *The Sex Revolution in the United States* (Tulsa: Christian Crusade, 1970), 14–15. Hargis was instrumental in opposing sex education programs in public schools in 1970. He specifically focused on the Sex Information and Education Council of the United States and managed to have schools suspend most sex education projects operating during that time.

14. Billy James Hargis, "Burn Baby Burn," *Christian Crusader Weekly,* May 20, 1968. Hargis writes that the riots in Detroit and Los Angeles were part of

an international communist conspiracy. He also writes in "Let's Face It! Plain Talk to American Negroes" that "granted that the Negroes were first brought here as slaves. You can't blame the whites of today for that. In fact, slavery may have been a blessing in disguise if it meant to introduce the feuding tribes of Africa to Western civilization."

15. Morris, *The Preachers*, 295.

16. Billy James Hargis, "The Fight against Sex Education," Christian Crusade letter, June 1970, archive, Wilcox Collection.

17. Billy James Hargis, "The Real 20th Century American Revolution," *Christian Crusader Weekly*, June 1968, p. 1, archive, Wilcox Collection.

18. Hargis, "Sex Replaces Prayer in Public Schools," *Christian Crusader Weekly*, February 1969, p. 1. This is part of the CC campaign against sex education campaigns by the Sex Information and Education Council of the United States.

19. American Christian College opened on September 14, 1970, and graduated its first class in 1974. Summit Ministries was established in 1962.

20. Billy James Hargis, Christian Crusade letter, 1970.

21. "Christian Crusade Anti-Communist Youth University," Summit Ministries pamphlet, 1965, p. 1. The brochure for Summit reads, "In six, two-week sessions, the Summit indoctrinates the young in the Conservative and Christian position on the issues of the day. It offers courses in Bible, American history, tactics of communism, creation and evolution, campus radicalism and the New Left in general."

22. Billy James Hargis, *Christian Crusader Weekly*, May 20, 1972, p. 1.

23. Billy James Hargis, fundraising letter, June 24, 1974.

24. "The Sins of Billy James," *Time* magazine, February 16, 1976, p. 52.

25. Billy James Hargis, "Satan Attempts to Destroy Christian Crusade," *Christian Crusader Weekly*, February 29, 1976, p. 1.

26. Noebel aimed his attacks at the communist conspiracy in music, especially the music of the Beatles and John Lennon. He quotes the song "Imagine" as being a paean to atheism in "The Marxist Minstrels, Christian Rock and Rock and Roll: A Pre-revolutionary Form of Cultural Subversion," *Summit Ministries* pamphlet, September 1981.

27. Billy James Hargis to M. Spencer, personal correspondence, October 22, 1975, archive, Wilcox Collection.

28. For a detailed discussion of the rise of the New Right, see Lisa McGirr, *Suburban Warriors*.

29. I define the New Right as a political and religious movement that includes the Religious Roundtable, the Free Congress Foundation, the Heritage Foundation, Christian Voice, the Conservative Caucus, the Moral Majority, Eagle Forum, and Concerned Women for America. Since the 1970s they have held frequent conferences and often publish in each others' journals and newsletters.

30. George Gallup Jr., *Religion in America: The Gallup Report* (Princeton: Princeton Religious Research Center, 1982), 31–32.

31. Ibid., 40.

32. Harding, *The Book of Jerry Falwell*, 20.

33. For a useful analysis of this strategy, see José Casanova, "Evangelical Protestantism: From Civil Religion to Fundamentalist Sect to New Christian Right," chap. 6 of *Public Religions in the Modern World* (Chicago: University of Chicago Press, 1994).

34. See Matthew Moen, *The Transformation of the Christian Right* (Tuscaloosa: University of Alabama Press, 1992); Robert C. Liebman, *The New Christian Right: Mobilization and Legitimation* (New York: Aldine Publishing Company, 1983); and Mark Shibley, *Resurgent Evangelicalism in the United States: Mapping Cultural Change since 1970* (Columbia: University of South Carolina Press, 1996).

35. The Family Protection Act, in *The Phyllis Schlafly Report,* vol. 13, no. 4, section 2, November 1979, p. 1. The pro-family movement began forming as an alliance of right-wing groups. With Connie Marshner, head of the Family Policy Division of Paul Weyrich's Free Congress Research and Education Foundation, members of the movement drafted the Family Protection Act as a smokescreen for a range of social and political goals. Senator Paul Laxalt (D-NV) introduced the bill in Congress.

36. Ibid.

37. In 2004 CWA claimed five hundred thousand members. The organization was incorporated in 1979 as a nonprofit and moved to Washington, D.C., in September 1983. Beverly LaHaye hired a lobbyist and a full-time attorney. CWA's organizing statement reads, "The specific purpose of CWA is to inform concerned women in America of the erosion of our historical Christian Judeo moral standards and to expose the dangerous and often insidious movements that are seeking to destroy the family." The CWA is organized on the local level with prayer and action chapters in each state that report back to the Washington, D.C., office.

38. David Noebel, "The ERA," *The Journal: A Summit Ministries Publication,* April 1981, p. 2.

39. See Betty DeBerg, *Ungodly Women: Gender and the First Wave of American Fundamentalism* (Minneapolis: University of Minnesota Press, 1990), and Margaret Bendroth, *Fundamentalism and Gender: 1875 to the Present* (New Haven: Yale University Press, 1996).

40. Beverly LaHaye, Concerned Women for America fundraising letter, May 1, 1980, archive, Wilcox Collection.

41. John Rees, "Christian Leader Beverly LaHaye: An Exclusive Interview," *The Review of the News,* May 8, 1985, p. 3.

42. Tim LaHaye is now better known as the coauthor with Jerry Jenkins of the twelve novels of the Left Behind series that chronicle the apocalypse, based on conservative Christian ideas of prophecy and the second coming of Christ. The Left Behind series has sold seventeen million copies and has been translated into twenty-one languages.

43. Rees, "Christian Leader Beverly LaHaye," 3.

44. Beverly LaHaye, quoted in "Concerned Women for America: Fighting for Judeo-Christian Values in the Public Arena," *The New American,* October 21, 1985.

45. Ibid.

46. Zondervan released an updated and expanded version in 1998, which has sold over two million copies.

47. Beverly LaHaye, "Ex-Feminists Are Finding Truth," Concerned Women for America newsletter, 1985, p. 4, archive, Sara Diamond Collection.

48. See Anita Bryant and Bob Green, *At Any Cost* (Old Tappan, NJ: Fleming H. Revell Company, 1978).

49. For more information on Anita Bryant, see Anita Bryant, *The Anita Bryant Story: The Survival of Our Nation's Families and the Threat of Militant Homosexuality* (Old Tappan, NJ: Fleming H. Revell Company, 1977).

50. Bryant experienced personal problems, including her divorce and the boycott mounted against Florida's orange industry, for which she was a spokesperson. Her organization was unable to expand its membership base through direct mail and fundraising. See Adon Taft, "Anita's Old Group Drops Gay Mission," *Miami Herald*, September 20, 1980, and Barry Bearak, "Turmoil within Ministry: Bryant Hears 'Anita . . . Please Repent,'" *Miami Herald*, June 8, 1980, p. 1A.

51. David Noebel, *The Homosexual Revolution* (Colorado Springs, CO: Summit Ministries, 1978).

52. Steve Schwalm, policy analyst for the Family Research Council, quoted in David Kyle Foster, "The Summer of Our Discontent: The Church Fights Back in the Culture Wars on Homosexuality," *Touchstone: A Journal of Mere Christianity*, November–December 1998, p. 2.

53. Jean Hardisty, "Constructing Homophobia: Colorado's Right-Wing Attack on Homosexuals," *The Public Eye*, March 1993, p. 4. She writes that the group Colorado for Family Values, which sponsored anti-gay legislation, was founded by Tony Marco and Will Perkins, a Colorado Springs car dealer. It promoted itself as a grassroots group but mainly had support from national organizations like Focus on the Family and Summit Ministries, both headquartered in Colorado, as well as CWA, Eagle Forum, and TVC.

54. Tim Kingston, "The Shape of Things to Come: Reverend Lou Sheldon's Paranoid Crusade," *Coming Up*, 1988, p. 5, archive, Sara Diamond Collection.

55. Jeremiah Films made the homophobic video *Gay Rights, Special Rights,* which claims gays and lesbians are degrading the civil rights movement. This video features Senator Trent Lott, Ed Meese (former attorney general), William Bennett (former secretary of education), and David Noebel of Summit Ministries. In the closing sequence, the film refers viewers to the Traditional Values Coalition.

56. William Dannemeyer, *Shadow in the Land: Homosexuality in America* (San Francisco: Ignatius Press, 1989), 13.

57. Ibid., 13.

58. Ibid., 19.

59. Lou Sheldon, TVC *Talking Points* 1, no. 2a, p. 1, archive, Sara Diamond Collection.

60. Sheldon, fundraising letter, Traditional Values Coalition, Anaheim, CA, June 16, 1994, p. 1, archive, Sara Diamond Collection.

61. According to Focus, Dobson's syndicated radio broadcast is heard on more than three thousand radio facilities in North America and in nine languages on approximately twenty-three hundred facilities in over ninety-eight other countries. By the mid-1990s Focus had an annual budget of over $100 million. See Sara Diamond, *Not by Politics Alone: The Enduring Influence of the Christian Right* (New York: Guilford Press, 1998), 30–36. For more information, see the Focus on the Family Web site at www.family.org.

62. Before Focus, Dobson was best known as an advocate of traditional discipline. His book, *Dare to Discipline*, advocated corporal punishment for children. In 1991 Focus relocated to an eighty-three-acre campus in Colorado Springs as a nonprofit organization. Previously connected to the Family Research Council headed by Gary Bauer, Focus separated officially in 1992 so the Family Research Council could pursue lobbying activities and not risk the tax-exempt status of the wider organization. In this way, Dobson has been able to pursue political change in Washington while running the culture industry of Focus.

63. James Dobson, "Created to Meet a Need," *Focus on the Family Citizen Magazine*, October 1989, p. 3.

64. James Dobson, "There Is Hope for the Homosexual: Ex-Gay Pastors and Christian Psychologists Agree That Homosexuals Can Change—but It's Not Easy," *Focus on the Family Citizen Magazine*, August 1988.

65. John Eldredge and Brad Hayton, "Homosexual Rights: What's Wrong?" *Focus on the Family Citizen Magazine*, March 1991, p. 6.

66. John Eldredge, "Gay Aggression," *Focus on the Family Citizen Magazine*, May 1989, p. 2.

67. Eldredge, "Homosexual Rights: What's Wrong?" p. 8.

68. James Dobson, "What Wives Wish Their Husbands Knew about Women," six cassette tapes, 1987.

69. James Dobson, "Dr. James Dobson Discusses America's Choice: Nine Key Issues That Will Shape Our Future," Focus on the Family booklet, 2000, p. 6.

70. Ibid., 6.

71. Amendment 2 was a 1992 Colorado ballot initiative that sought to amend the Colorado constitution in order to legally forbid the state, its municipalities, school districts, or agencies from guaranteeing nondiscrimination to those with "homosexual, lesbian, or bisexual orientation." The amendment passed in November 1992 but was subsequently overturned by the U.S. Supreme Court.

72. James Dobson, "Family News from Dr. James Dobson," Focus on the Family monthly newsletter, June 2002, p. 5.

73. Ibid.

74. John Eldredge, recorded speech (Colorado for Family Values–sponsored Glen Eyrie Conference, Colorado Springs, CO, May 16, 1994). Recorded by Cindy Beal of Peace and Justice Consulting, Northhampton, Massachusetts.

75. Headed by Reverend Don Wildmon and based in Tupelo, Mississippi, the AFA focuses on profanity, homosexuality, and popular culture. In 1989 the

AFA protested three television shows that it claimed promoted homosexuality and portrayed it in a positive light.

76. Quoted in Surina Khan from AFA press release, "National Coming Out Day Helps Homosexuals Leave Lifestyle," undated, included in Political Research Associates press packet, October 1997.

77. Michael Johnston was featured on the Christian Broadcasting Network's *NewsWatch Today* on May 15, 1996, where he said, "This is the brass ring of the homosexual movement. If they get same-sex marriage, they will get adoptions, they will get forced sex-education in the schools . . . because you can't call a homosexual couple a marriage and then deny them children."

78. Stephen Crampton, AFA press release, October 12, 1999.

79. Frederica Mathews-Green, "Chasing Amy: God Intervened in a NOW Activist's Unlikely Conversion," *Christianity Today*, January 10, 2000, 56–60.

80. James Dobson, "Family News from Dr. James Dobson," Focus on the Family monthly newsletter, June 1998, p. 1.

81. John Paulk, "Family News from Dr. James Dobson," Focus on the Family monthly newsletter, penned by John Paulk, July 2000, p. 4.

82. Frank Worthen, public speech (Friends and Family Weekend, San Rafael, CA, August 22, 1999).

83. Laurie Goodstein, "Woman behind Anti-gay Ads Sees Christians as Victims," *New York Times*, August 13, 1998, p. A10.

84. Ibid.

85. Mike Haley, Exodus workshop, "Why Is What They're Teaching So Dangerous?" (annual Exodus conference, Point Loma Nazarene University, San Diego, CA, July 27, 2000).

86. Project 10, founded by Dr. Virginia Uribe, is the nation's first public school program dedicated to providing on-site educational support services to gay, lesbian, bisexual, transgender, and questioning youth. Project 10 began in 1984 at Fairfax High School in the Los Angeles Unified School District. See www.project10.org/.

87. Jason Thompson, *The Map*, CD-ROM, Portland Fellowship, Exodus International Publications.

88. Frank Worthen, speech (annual Exodus conference, Point Loma Nazarene University, San Diego, CA, July 25, 2000).

89. James Dobson, "Why No Outrage This Time?" *Focus on the Family Citizen Magazine*, March 1990, p. 3.

90. Ibid., p. 6.

91. Michael Lumberger, speech (annual Exodus conference, Point Loma Nazarene University, San Diego, CA, July 28, 2000).

92. Joel Lawson, "Ex-Gay Leader Confronted in Gay Bar," *San Francisco Bay Times*, September 28, 2000, p. 3. Exodus also released a public statement regarding this incident. Bob Davies, "Statement by Exodus North America Regarding Chairman John Paulk," September 22, 2000.

93. John Paulk and Anne Paulk, "Reigniting the Hope for Homosexuals," interview with Dr. James Dobson, October 10, 2000, online at www.christianitytoday.com/ct/2000/141/53.0.html.

CONCLUSION

1. Frank Worthen, "Identity," in "Steps Out," second quarter, meeting thirty-six, 4.

2. Bob Davies, "Ex-Gay Sheds the Mocking Quotes: An Interview with Bob Davies," *Christianity Today*, January 7, 2002, p. 4.

3. As quoted in Barbara Dozetos, "UK Ex-Gay Leader Claims Conversion Therapy Futile," www.gay.com, accessed April 23, 2001.

4. Frank Worthen, "The Future of an Ex-Gay Person," New Hope publication, p. 10.

5. Ibid.

6. Ibid., p. 13.

7. Frank Worthen, "Identity," in "Steps Out," 6.

8. Ibid., 7.

Bibliography

ARCHIVAL SOURCES

Exodus International Archives, 1973–99. New Hope Ministry, San Rafael, CA.
Sara Diamond Collection on the Right. Bancroft Library, University of California, Berkeley.
Wilcox Collection of Contemporary Political Movements. Kenneth Spencer Research Library, University of Kansas, Lawrence.

BOOKS AND ARTICLES

Abelove, Henry. "Freud, Male Homosexuality and the Americans." In *Lesbian and Gay Studies Reader,* edited by Abelove, Barale, and Halperin, 381–93.
Abelove, Henry, Michele A. Barale, and David Halperin, eds. *The Lesbian and Gay Studies Reader.* New York: Routledge, 1993.
Alcoholics Anonymous. New York: Alcoholics Anonymous World Services, 1955.
Allen, Garland E. "The Double-Edged Sword of Genetic Determinism: Social and Political Agendas in Genetic Studies of Homosexuality, 1940–1994." In *Science and Homosexualities,* edited by Vernon A. Rosario, 242–70. New York: Routledge, 1997.
Allen, Starla. *The Roots of Lesbianism.* Video recording. Exodus International Foundational Issues series, no. 96-02, 1996.
Ammerman, Nancy Tatom. *Bible Believers: Fundamentalists in the Modern World.* New Brunswick, NJ: Rutgers University Press, 1987.
———. *Congregation and Community.* New Brunswick, NJ: Rutgers University Press, 1997.
Bailey, J. M., and R. C. Pillard. "A Genetic Study of Male Sexual Orientation." *Archives of General Psychiatry* 48 (1991): 1089–96.

Balmer, Randy. *Blessed Assurance: A History of Evangelicalism in America.* Boston: Beacon Press, 1999.

———. *Encyclopedia of Evangelicalism.* Louisville: Westminster John Knox Press, 2002.

———. *Mine Eyes Have Seen the Glory: A Journey into the Evangelical Subculture in America.* New York: Oxford University Press, 1993.

Bayer, Ronald. *Homosexuality and American Psychiatry.* Princeton: Princeton University Press, 1987.

Bederman, Gail. "'The Women Have Had Charge of the Church Work Long Enough': The Men and Religion Forward Movement of 1911–1912 and the Masculinization of Middle-Class Protestantism." *American Quarterly* 41 (September 1989): 432–65.

Bell, Daniel. *The Radical Right: The New American Right,* rev. and expanded. New York: Books for Libraries/Arno Press, 1977.

Bellah, Robert N., Richard Madsen, William M. Sullivan, Ann Swidler, and Steven M. Tipton. *Habits of the Heart: Individualism and Commitment in American Life.* Berkeley: University of California Press, 1985.

Bender, Courtney. *Heaven's Kitchen: Living Religion at God's Love We Deliver.* Chicago: University of Chicago Press, 2003.

Bendroth, Margaret. *Fundamentalism and Gender: 1875 to the Present.* New Haven: Yale University Press, 1993.

Bennett, David. *The Party of Fear: From Nativist Movements to the New Right in American History.* Rev. ed. New York: Vintage, 1995.

Berger, Peter. *The Sacred Canopy: Elements of a Sociological Theory of Religion.* New York: Anchor, 1967.

Berlant, Lauren. *The Queen of America Goes to Washington City: Essays on Sex and Citizenship.* Durham, NC: Duke University Press, 1997.

Besen, Wayne. *Anything but Straight: Unmasking the Scandals and Lies behind the Ex-Gay Myth.* Washington, D.C.: Harrington Park Press, 2003.

Bieber, Irving. *Homosexuality: A Psychoanalytic Study of Male Homosexuals.* New York: Basic Books, 1962.

Blee, Kathleen. "Evidence, Empathy and Ethics: Lessons from Oral Histories of the Klan." *Journal of American History* 80, no. 2 (September 1993): 596–606.

———. *Women of the Klan: Racism and Gender in the 1920s.* Berkeley: University of California Press, 1991.

Booth, Wayne C. "The Rhetoric of Fundamentalist Conversion Narratives." In *Fundamentalisms Comprehended,* edited by Martin E. Marty and R. Scott Appleby, 367–95. Chicago: University of Chicago Press, 1995.

Boswell, John. *Christianity, Social Tolerance and Homosexuality: Gay People in Western Europe from the Beginning of the Christian Era to the Fourteenth Century.* Chicago: University of Chicago Press, 1980.

Boyer, Paul. *When Time Shall Be No More: Prophecy Belief in Modern American Culture.* Cambridge: Harvard University Press, 1992.

Breedlove, Jamie. *Once Gay, Always Gay? One Woman's Walk Out of Homosexuality.* Baltimore: Regeneration Books, 1978.

Brettell, Carol B., ed. *When They Read What We Write: The Politics of Ethnography.* Westport, CT: Greenwood Publishing Group, 1993.

Brock, Raymond T. "When Gay Isn't Gay." *Pentecostal Evangel*, September 8, 1985.

Brown, Karen McCarthy. *Mama Lola: A Vodou Priestess in Brooklyn*. Updated ed. Berkeley: University of California Press, 2001.

Bruce, Steve. *The Rise and Fall of the New Christian Right: Protestant Politics in America, 1978–1988*. Oxford, England: Clarendon Press, 1988.

Bryant, Anita. *The Anita Bryant Story: The Survival of Our Nation's Families and the Threat of Militant Homosexuality*. Old Tappan, NJ: Fleming H. Revell Company, 1977.

Bryant, Anita, and Bob Green. *At Any Cost*. Old Tappan, NJ: Fleming H. Revell Company, 1978.

Bufe, Charles. *Alcoholics Anonymous: Cult or Cure?* San Francisco: Sharp Press, 1991.

Bullough, Vern. *Science in the Bedroom: A History of Sex Research*. New York: Basic Books, 1994.

Burlein, Meredith. *Lift High the Cross: Where White Supremacy and the Christian Right Converge*. Durham, NC: Duke University Press, 2002.

Butler, Judith. *The Psychic Life of Power: Theories in Subjection*. Stanford, CA: Stanford University Press, 1996.

Byne, W. "Science and Belief: Psychobiological Research on Sexual Orientation." *Journal of Homosexuality* 28, nos. 3–4 (1995): 303–44.

Capps, Walter. *The New Religious Right: Piety, Patriotism and Politics*. Columbia: University of South Carolina Press, 1990.

Carnes, Mark C. "Middle-Class Men and the Solace of Fraternal Ritual." In *Meanings for Manhood: Constructions of Masculinity in Victorian America*, edited by Mark C. Carnes and Clyde Griffen, 37–53. Chicago: Chicago University Press, 1990.

Carnes, Patrick. *Don't Call It Love: Recovery from Sexual Addiction*. New York: Bantam Books, 1991.

———. *Out of the Shadows: Understanding Sexual Addiction*. 3rd ed. Center City, MN: Hazelton, 2001.

Carpenter, Joel. *Revive Us Again: The Reawakening of American Fundamentalism*. New York: Oxford University Press, 1997.

Carroll, Jerry. "Changing a Sinful Life: Religious Wooing of Gays." *San Francisco Chronicle*, May 13, 1977.

Casanova, José. *Public Religions in the Modern World*. Chicago: University of Chicago Press, 1994.

Certeau, Michel de. *The Practice of Everyday Life*. Translated by Steven Rendell. Berkeley: University of California Press, 1988.

Chauncy, George. *Gay New York: Gender, Urban Culture and the Making of the Gay Male World, 1890–1940*. New York: Basic Books, 1995.

Chin, Justin. "Saved: Our Reporter Survives the Ex-Gay Ministries." *The Progressive*, December 1995, pp. 32–35.

Cohen. Richard. *Coming Out Straight: Understanding and Healing Homosexuality*. Winchester, VA: OakHill Press, 2001.

———. "Healing Homosexuality: A Four-Stage Model of Recovery." Collected papers from the 1999 NARTH conference, www.narth.com/menus/reso.html.

Coleman, Simon. "But Are They Really Christian? Contesting Knowledge and Identity in and out of the Field." In *Personal Knowledge and Beyond: Reshaping the Ethnography of Religion,* edited by Spickard, Landres, and McGuire, 75–87.

Comiskey, Andy. *Pursuing Sexual Wholeness: How Jesus Heals the Homosexual.* Lake Mary, FL: Creation House, 1989.

Cook, Colin. "I Found Freedom." *Christianity Today,* August 18, 1989, pp. 22–24.

Corber, Robert. *Homosexuality in Cold War America: Resistance and the Crisis of Masculinity.* Durham, NC: Duke University Press, 1997.

Crawford, Alan. *Thunder on the Right: The New Right and the Politics of Resentment.* New York: Pantheon, 1980.

Cross, Whitney. *The Burned-over District: The Social and Intellectual History of Enthusiastic Religion in Western New York, 1800–1850.* Ithaca, NY: Cornell University Press, 1950.

Dallas, Joe. *Desires in Conflict: Answering the Struggle for Sexual Identity.* Eugene, OR: Harvest House Publishers, 1990.

———. *A Strong Delusion: Confronting the "Gay Christian" Movement.* Eugene, OR: Harvest House Publishers, 1996.

———. *When Homosexuality Hits Home.* Eugene, OR: Harvest House Publishers, 2004.

Dallas, Joe, and Joseph Nicolosi. *Understanding Homosexuality and the Reality of Change.* Interviews with two men and two women on roots of homosexual orientation, 60 minutes, video, Impact Resources.

Dannemeyer, William. *Shadow in the Land: Homosexuality in America.* San Francisco: Ignatius Press, 1989.

Davies, Bob. "A Biblical Response to the Pro-Gay Movement." *Apologetics* (Exodus International flyer 1993), 1–4.

———. "Celebrating Twenty Years of Ministry!" *Exodus Standard* 13, no. 1, special issue (1996): 1–15.

Davies, Bob, and Lori Rentzel. *Coming Out of Homosexuality: New Freedom for Men and Women.* Los Angeles: Victor Books, 1990.

Davies, Bob, and Anita Worthen. *Someone I Love Is Gay.* Downers Grove, IL: InterVarsity Press, 1996.

Davison, Gerald C. "Not Can but Ought: The Treatment of Homosexuality." *Journal of Consulting and Clinical Psychology* 46, no.1 (1978): 170–72.

DeBerg, Betty. *Ungodly Women: Gender and the First Wave of American Fundamentalism.* Minneapolis: University of Minnesota Press, 1990.

D'Emilio, John. "Capitalism and Gay Identity." In *The Lesbian and Gay Studies Reader,* edited by Abelove, Barale, and Halperin, 467–76.

———. *Sexual Politics, Sexual Communities: The Making of a Homosexual Minority in the United States, 1940–1970.* Chicago: University of Chicago Press, 1983.

D'Emilio, John, and Estelle Freedman. *Intimate Matters: A History of Sexuality in America.* 2nd ed. Chicago: University of Chicago Press, 1997.

Diamond, Sara. *Not by Politics Alone: The Enduring Influence of the Christian Right.* New York: Guilford Press, 1998.

————. *Roads to Dominion: Right Wing Movements and Political Power.* New York: Guilford Press, 1995.

Duberman, Martin. *Cures: A Gay Man's Odyssey.* New York: Dutton/NAL: 1991.

Duggan, Lisa. "Making It Perfectly Queer" and "Queering the State." In *Sex Wars: Sexual Dissent and Political Culture,* edited by Lisa Duggan and Nan Hunter, 155–72, 179–93. New York: Routledge, 1995.

————. *Sapphic Slashers: Sex, Violence, and American Modernity.* Durham, NC: Duke University Press, 2000.

Echols, Alice. *Daring to Be Bad: Radical Feminism in America, 1967–1975.* Minneapolis: University of Minnesota Press, 1989.

Eiesland, Nancy, and Penny Edgell Becker. *Contemporary American Religion: An Ethnographic Reader.* Walnut Creek, CA: Sage Publications, 1997.

Ellison, Marvin. *Same-Sex Marriage? A Christian Ethical Analysis.* Cleveland: Pilgrim Press, 2004.

Elwell, Walter A., ed. *Evangelical Dictionary of Theology.* 2nd ed. Grand Rapids, MI: Baker Book House Company, 2001.

Emerson, Michael, and Christian Smith. *Divided by Faith: Evangelical Religion and the Problem of Race in America.* Chapel Hill: University of North Carolina Press, 2000.

Enroth, Ronald M., Edward E. Ericson Jr., and C. Breckinridge Peters. *The Jesus People: Old-Time Religion in the Age of Aquarius.* Grand Rapids, MI: Eerdmans, 1972.

Erling, Jorstad. *That New Time Religion: The Jesus Revival in America.* Minneapolis: Augsburg Publishing House, 1972.

Fernandez, Elizabeth. "This Ministry Works to Put Gays Straight." *San Francisco Chronicle,* February 4, 1990, pp. A1, 3.

"Finally Free: Personal Stories: How Love and Self-Acceptance Saved Us from Ex-Gay Ministries." *Human Rights Campaign Foundation,* July 2000.

Fine, Gary Alan. "Ten Lies of Ethnography: Moral Dilemmas of Field Research." *Journal of Contemporary Ethnography* 22 (1993): 267–94.

Finke, Roger, and Rodney Starke. *The Churching of America, 1776–1990: Winners and Losers in Our Religious Economy.* New Brunswick, NJ: Rutgers University Press, 1992.

Fitzgerald, Frances. *Cities on a Hill.* New York: Simon and Schuster Press, 1986.

Foucault, Michel. *The History of Sexuality.* Vol. 1, *An Introduction.* Translated by Robert Hurley. New York: Vintage Books, 1990.

————. *The History of Sexuality.* Vol. 2, *The Use of Pleasure.* Translated by Robert Hurley. New York: Vintage Books, 1990.

————. *The History of Sexuality.* Vol. 3, *The Care of the Self.* Translated by Robert Hurley. New York: Vintage Books, 1988.

Frame, Randy. "The Homosexual Lifestyle: Is There a Way Out?" *Christianity Today,* August 9, 1985, pp. 32–35.

Freud, Sigmund. *Three Essays on the Theory of Sexuality.* 1905. Reprint, New York: Avon Books, 1962.

Galst, Liz. "The Myth of the Ex-Gay Movement." *Boston Phoenix,* April 1, 1994, pp. 22–24.

Gangel, Kenneth. "The Gospel and the Gay." *Christian Life Magazine*, January 1978.

Garber, Marjorie, and Rebecca L. Walkowitz. *One Nation under God: Religion and American Culture.* New York: Routledge, 1999.

Gilmore, David. *Manhood in the Making: Cultural Concepts of Masculinity.* New Haven: Yale University Press, 1990.

Ginsburg, Faye. "The Case of Mistaken Identity: Problems in Representing Women on the Right." In *When They Read What We Write: The Politics of Ethnography,* edited by Caroline B. Brettell, 164–76. Westport, CT.: Greenwood Publishing Group, 1993.

———. *Contested Lives: The Abortion Debate in an American Community.* Berkeley: University of California Press, 1989.

Gonzalez, Nelson R. "Exploding Ex-Gay Myths: Pastoral Approaches to Homosexual Christians." *Regeneration Quarterly* (Summer 1995): 17–22.

Graham, Ronald W. "Homosexuality: A Look at the Scriptures." *The Disciple,* March 19, 1978.

Gray, Edward R., and Scott L. Thumma. *Gay Religion: Innovation and Tradition in Spiritual Practice.* Walnut Creek, CA: Altamira Press, 2005.

Green, Richard. "Homosexuality as Mental Illness." *International Journal of Psychiatry* 10 (1972): 77–98.

———. *The Sissy Boy Syndrome and the Development of Homosexuality.* New Haven: Yale University Press, 1987.

Griffen, Clyde. "Reconstructing Masculinity from the Evangelical Revival to the Waning of Progressivism: A Speculative Synthesis." In *Meanings for Manhood: Constructions of Masculinity in Victorian America Chicago,* edited by Mark C. Carnes and Clyde Griffen, 183–204. Chicago: University of Chicago Press, 1990.

Griffith, R. Marie. *Born Again Bodies: Flesh and Spirit in American Christianity.* Berkeley: University of California Press, 2004.

———. *God's Daughters: Evangelical Women and the Power of Submission.* Berkeley: University of California Press, 1997.

Grossberg, Lawrence. *We Gotta Get Out of This Place: Popular Conservatism and Postmodern Culture.* New York: Routledge, 1992.

Gulick, Luther. "The Alleged Effeminization of Our American Boys." *American Physical Education Review* 10 (September 1905): 61.

Haley, Mike. *101 Frequently Asked Questions about Homosexuality.* Eugene, OR: Harvest House, 2004.

Haldeman, Doug. "The Practice and Ethics of Sexual Orientation Conversion Therapy." *Journal of Consulting and Clinical Psychology* 62, no. 2 (1994): 221–27.

———. "Sexual Orientation Conversion Therapy for Gay Men and Lesbians: A Scientific Examination." In *Homosexuality: Research Implications for Public Policy,* edited by J. C. Gonsiorek and James D. Weinrich, 149–60. Newbury Park, CA: Sage Publications, 1991.

Halperin, David. "Is There a History of Sexuality?" In *The Lesbian and Gay Studies Reader,* edited by Abelove, Barale, and Halperin, 416–31.

Hamer, Dean, and Peter Copeland. *The Science of Desire: The Search for the Gay Gene and the Biology of Behavior.* New York: Simon and Schuster, 1994.

Hantover, Jeffrey P. "The Boy Scouts and the Validation of Masculinity." *Journal of Social Issues* 34, no. 1 (1978): 184–95.

Haraway, Donna. "Teddy Bear Patriarchy: Taxidermy in the Garden of Eden, New York City, 1908–1936." Chapter 3 of *Primate Visions: Gender, Race and Nature in the World of Modern Science.* New York: Routledge, 1990.

Harding, Susan. *The Book of Jerry Falwell: Fundamentalist Language and Politics.* Princeton: Princeton University Press, 2000.

———. "Representing Fundamentalism: The Problem of the Repugnant Cultural Other." *Social Research* 58, no. 2 (Summer 1991): 373–93.

Hatch, Nathan. *The Democratization of American Christianity.* New Haven: Yale University Press, 1989.

Hendershot, Heather. *Shaking the World for Jesus: Media and Conservative Evangelical Culture.* Chicago: University of Chicago Press, 2004.

Herman, Didi. *The Anti-Gay Agenda: Orthodox Vision and the Christian Right.* Chicago: University of Chicago Press, 1997.

Herman, Ellen. *The Romance of American Psychology: Political Culture in the Age of Experts.* Berkeley: University of California Press, 1995.

Herman, Judith Lewis. *Trauma and Recovery.* New York: Basic Books, 1992.

Heyrman, Christine. *Southern Cross: The Beginnings of the Bible Belt.* New York: Alfred A. Knopf, 1997.

Himmelstein, Jerome L. *To the Right: The Transformation of American Conservatism.* Berkeley: University of California Press, 1990.

Hooker, Evelyn. "Male Homosexuals and Their Worlds." In *Sexual Inversion: The Multiple Roots of Homosexuality,* edited by Judd Marmor, 83–107. New York: Basic Books, 1965.

Howard, Jeanette. *Out of Egypt: Leaving Lesbianism Behind.* Kent, England: Monarch Publications Ltd., 1993.

Hughes, Thomas. *The Manliness of Christ.* Boston: Houghton Mifflin, 1879.

Hull, Anne. "A Slow Journey from Isolation." *Washington Post,* September 27, 2004, p. A01.

Hunter, James Davidson. *American Evangelicalism: Conservative Religion and the Quandary of Modernity.* New Brunswick, NJ: Rutgers University, 1983.

Hurst, Ed. *The Struggle with Life Dominating Sin.* Baltimore: Regeneration Books, 1979.

Irvine, Janice. *Disorders of Desire: Sex and Gender in Modern American Society.* Philadelphia: Temple University Press, 1990.

Johnson, Barbara. *Where Does a Mother Go to Resign?* Minneapolis: Bethany House Publishers, 1994.

Johnston, Robert. "Curing Homosexuals: Impossible and Inappropriate?" *Radix Magazine,* July–August 1982.

Jones, Stanton L. "Homosexuality According to Science." *Christianity Today,* August 18, 1989, pp. 26–29.

Kaminer, Wendy. *I'm Dysfunctional, You're Dysfunctional: The Recovery Movement and Other Self-Help Fashions.* Reading, MA: Addison-Wesley, 1992.

Kaplan, Lawrence. *Fundamentalism in Comparative Perspective.* Amherst: University of Massachusetts Press, 1992.

Katz, Jonathon Ned. *The Invention of Heterosexuality.* New York: Plume Books, 1996.

Kenen, Stephanie. "Who Counts When You're Counting Homosexuals? Hormones and Homosexuality in Mid-twentieth Century America." In *Science and Homosexualities,* edited by Rosario, 197–218.

Kennedy, Hubert. "Karl Heinrich Ulrichs, First Theorist of Homosexuality." In *Science and Homosexualities,* edited by Rosario, 26–45.

Khan, Surina. "Calculated Compassion: How the Ex-Gay Movement Serves the Right's Attack on Democracy." *A Report from Political Research Associates, the Policy Institute of the National Gay and Lesbian Task Force, and Equal Partners in Faith,* October 1998.

———. "Inside Exodus: A Report from the Anti-gay Ministry's 21st National Conference." *Gay Community News,* Fall 1996, pp. 10–11.

Kimmel, Michael. "Men's Responses to Feminism at the Turn of the Century." *Gender and Society* 1, no. 3 (September 1987): 261–83.

Kintz, Linda. *Between Jesus and the Market: The Emotions That Matter in Right Wing America.* Durham, NC: Duke University Press, 1997.

Kintz, Linda, and Julia Lesage, eds. *Media, Culture and the Religious Right.* Minneapolis: University of Minnesota Press, 1998.

Klatch, Rebecca. *A Generation Divided: The New Left, the New Right and the 1960s.* Berkeley: University of California Press, 1999.

———. *Women of the New Right.* Philadelphia: Temple University Press, 1987.

Konrad, Jeff. *You Don't Have to Be Gay: Hope and Freedom for Males Struggling with Homosexuality or for Those Who Know of Someone Who Is.* Baltimore: Regeneration Books, 1987.

Kurtz, Ernest. *AA: The Story.* San Francisco: Harper/Hazelden, 1988.

LaHaye, Tim. *The Unhappy Gays: What Everyone Should Know about Homosexuality.* Carol Stream, IL: Tyndale House, 1978.

LaHaye, Tim, and Beverly LaHaye. *The Act of Marriage: The Beauty of Sexual Love.* 1974. Rev. and updated ed. Grand Rapids, MI: Zondervan, 1998.

Larson, Edward J. *Summer for the Gods: The Scopes Trial and America's Continuing Debate over Science and Religion.* New York: Basic Books, 1997.

Lawrence, Bruce. *Defenders of God: The Fundamentalist Revolt against the Modern Age.* New York: Harper and Row, 1989.

Lawson, Merritt E. "Homosexuality, Psychiatry and the Church." *Christian News,* July 26, 1982.

Leland, John, Mark Miller. "Can Gays 'Convert'?" *Newsweek,* August 17, 1998, pp. 46–53.

LeVay, Simon. *The Sexual Brain.* Cambridge: MIT Press, 1993.

Liebman, Robert C. *The New Christian Right: Mobilization and Legitimation.* New York: Aldine Publishing Company, 1983.

Lienesch, Michael. *Redeeming America: Piety and Politics in the New Christian Right*. Chapel Hill: University of North Carolina Press, 1993.

Lipset, Seymour Martin. *The Politics of Unreason: Right Wing Movements in Political Perspective*. New York: Harper & Row, 1970.

Maddoux, Marlin, and Christopher Corbett. *Answers to the Gay Deception*. Downers Grove, IL: InterVarsity Press, 1994.

Mangan, J. A., and James Walvin, eds. *Manliness and Morality: Middle-Class Masculinity in Britain and America, 1800–1940*. New York: St. Martin's Press, 1987.

Marsden, George. *Fundamentalism and American Culture: The Shaping of Twentieth-Century Evangelicalism, 1870–1925*. New York: Oxford University Press, 1980.

Mayerson, Peter, and Harold I. Lief. "Psychotherapy of Homosexuals: A Follow-Up Study of Nineteen Cases." In *Sexual Inversion: The Multiple Roots of Homosexuality*, edited by Judd Marmor, 302–43. New York: Basic Books, 1965.

McAlister, Melani. *Epic Encounters: Culture, Media, and U.S. Interests in the Middle East, 1945–2000*. Berkeley: University of California Press, 2001.

McGirr, Lisa. *Suburban Warriors: The Origins of the New American Right*. Princeton: Princeton University Press, 2001.

Medinger, Alan. *Growth into Manhood: Resuming the Journey*. Colorado Springs: Shaw WaterBrook Press, 2000.

———. *Starting an Exodus Ministry Manual*. Baltimore: Regeneration Books, 1983.

Miller, Donald. *Reinventing American Protestantism: Christianity in the New Millennium*. Berkeley: University of California Press, 1997.

Mills, Kim I. "Mission Impossible: Why Reparative Therapy and Ex-Gay Ministries Fail." *Report from the Human Rights Campaign*, February 1999.

Minkowitz, Donna. *Ferocious Romance: What My Encounters with the Right Taught Me about Sex, God and Fury*. New York: Free Press, 1998.

Minton, Henry L. *Departing from Deviance: A History of Homosexual Rights and Emancipatory Science in America*. Chicago: University of Chicago Press, 2001.

Moberly, Elizabeth. *Homosexuality: A New Christian Ethic*. Cambridge, England: James Clarke and Co., 1983.

———. *Psychogenesis: The Early Development of Gender Identity*. London: Routledge and Kegan Paul Ltd., 1983.

Moen, Matthew. *The Transformation of the Christian Right*. Tuscaloosa: University of Alabama Press, 1992.

Moon, Dawne. *God, Sex and Politics: Homosexuality and Everyday Theologies*. Chicago, University of Chicago Press, 2004.

Moore, R. Laurence. *Selling God: American Religion in the Marketplace of Culture*. New York: Oxford University Press, 1994.

Morris, James. *The Preachers*. New York: St. Martin's Press, 1973.

Morton, Ferenc Szasz. *The Divided Mind of Protestant America, 1880–1930*. Tuscaloosa: University of Alabama Press, 1982.

Morud, Jim. "Hope for the Homosexual: Special Outreaches Minister to Gays Who Want Christ to Change Their Lives." *Worldwide Challenge*, September 1980.

Moskowitz, Eva. *In Therapy We Trust: America's Obsession with Self-Fulfillment*. Baltimore: The Johns Hopkins University Press, 2001.

Murphy, T. "Redirecting Sexual Orientation: Techniques and Justifications." *Journal of Sex Research* 29, no. 4 (1992): 501–23.

NARTH. "Remembering Irving Bieber." *NARTH Bulletin* 2, no. 3 (December 1994): 1, 6–7.

Nicolosi, Joseph. *Healing Homosexuality: Case Stories of Reparative Therapy*. Northvale, NJ: Jason Aronson, 1993.

———. *Reparative Therapy of Male Homosexuality: A New Clinical Approach*. Northvale, NJ: Jason Aronson, 1997.

———. "Treatment of Male Homosexuality: A Developmental Model." Collected papers from the 2000 NARTH conference, www.narth.com/menus/reso.html.

———. "Why NARTH?" *Narth Bulletin* 4, no. 2 (August 1996): 2.

Nicolosi, Joseph, and Linda Ames Nicolosi. *A Parent's Guide to Preventing Homosexuality*. Downers Grove, IL: InterVarsity Press, 2002.

Noebel, David. *The Homosexual Revolution*. Colorado Springs, CO: Summit Ministries, 1978.

Oliver, Kay, and Wayne Christianson. "Unhappily Gay: From the Closet to the Front Page." *Moody Bible Institute*, January 1978.

Orsi, Robert. *Between Heaven and Earth: The Religious Worlds People Make and the Scholars Who Study Them*. Princeton: Princeton University Press, 2004.

———. "'Have You Ever Prayed to St. Jude?' Reflections on Fieldwork in Catholic Chicago." In *Reimagining Denominationalism: Interpretive Essays*, edited by Robert Bruce Mullin and Russell E. Richey, 134–61. New York: Oxford University Press, 1994.

Pattison, Mansell, and Myrna Loy Pattison. "Ex-Gays: Religiously Mediated Change in Homosexuals." *American Journal of Psychiatry* 137, no. 12 (December 1980): 1553–62.

Paulk, Anne. *Restoring Sexual Identity: Hope for Women Who Struggle with Same-Sex Attraction*. Eugene, OR: Harvest House, 2003.

Paulk, John. *Not Afraid to Change: The Remarkable Story of How One Man Overcame Homosexuality*. Enumclaw, WA: WinePress, 1997.

Paulk, John, and Anne Paulk. *Love Won Out: How God's Love Helped Two People Leave Homosexuality and Find Each Other*. Wheaton, IL: Tyndale House Publishers, 1999

Payne, Leanne. *Crisis in Masculinity*. Grand Rapids, MI: Hamewith Books, 1995.

Peele, Stanton. *Diseasing of America: Addiction Treatment Out of Control*. Lexington, MA: Lexington Books, 1989.

Peters, Robert, and Jesse Lee. "The Tragedy of San Francisco: Don't Let It Happen to Your City." *Faith and Citizenship Team*, April 1983.

Philpott, Kent. *The Gay Theology*. San Rafael, CA: Rydell Publishers, 1979.

———. *The Third Sex? Six Homosexuals Tell Their Stories.* Plainfield, NJ: Logos Publishers, 1975.

Pillard, Richard. "The Search for a Genetic Influence on Sexual Orientation." In *Science and Homosexualities,* edited by Rosario, 226–41.

Prothero, Stephen. *American Jesus: How the Son of God Became a National Icon.* New York: Farrar, Straus and Giroux, 2003.

Quebedeaux, Richard. *The New Charismatics: The Origins, Development, and Significance of Neo-Pentecostalism.* Garden City, NJ: Doubleday and Co., 1976.

Rabey, Steve. "Gay for Life?" *Gazette Telegraph,* May 21, 1994, pp. E1–3.

Reality: A Monthly Newsletter for People with Transgender Issues. Cross Over Ministries newsletter, Lexington, KY, 1989–99.

Ribuffo, Leo. *The Old Christian Right: The Protestant Far Right from the Great Depression to the Cold War.* Philadelphia: Temple University Press, 1983.

Rice, Marie S. *Michelle Danielle Is Dead.* Baltimore: Regeneration Books, 1994.

Richardson, James T., Mary W. Stewart, and Robert B. Simmonds. *Organized Miracles.* New Brunswick, NJ: Transaction, 1979.

Richardson, Valerie. "Can Therapy Turn Gays Straight?" *Washington Times,* April 22, 1993, pp. A1, B4.

Rivera, Geraldo. "Can Gays and Lesbians Go Straight?" *Geraldo* transcript no. 974, Investigative News Group, June 11, 1991.

Robertson, Nan. *Getting Better: Inside Alcoholics Anonymous.* New York: William Morrow and Company, 1987.

Rogers, Sinclair. *Questions I'm Most Asked about Homosexuality.* Baltimore: Regeneration Books, 1996.

Rogers, Sinclair, and Alan Medinger. "Homosexuality and the Truth." *Apologetics* (Exodus International flyer 1990), 1–4.

Rosario, Vernon, ed., *Science and Homosexualities.* New York: Routledge, 1997.

Rotundo, Anthony. *American Manhood: Transformations in Masculinity from the Revolution to the Modern Era.* New York: Basic Books, 1993.

Rudy, Kathy. *Sex and the Church: Gender, Homosexuality and the Transformation of Christian Ethics.* Boston: Beacon Press, 1997.

Saia, Michael R. *Counseling the Homosexual.* Eugene, OR: Bethany House, 1993.

Sandeen, Ernest R. *The Roots of Fundamentalism: British and American Millenarianism, 1800–1930.* Chicago: University of Chicago Press, 1970.

Sands, Alicia Marie. "Controversial Ministry Discusses Alternate Lifestyle." *Michigan Chronicle,* November 4, 1992, pp. A3.

Satinover, Jeffrey. *Homosexuality and the Politics of Truth.* Grand Rapids, MI: Hamewith Books, 1996.

Sayres, Sohnya, and Stanley Aronowitz, eds. *The Sixties without Apology.* Minneapolis: University of Minnesota Press, 1984.

Scroggs, Robin. *New Testament and Homosexuality.* New York: Fortress Press, 1984.

Sedgwick, Eve Kosofsky. *Between Men: English Literature and Male Homosocial Desire.* New York: Columbia University Press, 1985.

Sexaholics Anonymous Handbook. SA literature. Nashville: Sexaholics Anonymous, 1989.

Shibley, Mark A. *Resurgent Evangelicalism in the United States: Mapping Cultural Change since 1970.* Columbia: University of South Carolina Press, 1996.

Shidlo, Ariel, and Michael Schroeder. "Changing Sexual Orientation: A Consumers' Report." *Professional Psychology: Research and Practice* 33, no. 3 (2002): 249–59.

Shumate, Richard. "Divine Intervention: Undercover in an Ex-Gay Ministry." *Out,* November 1995, pp. 108–11, 152–58.

Siegel, Elaine V. *Female Homosexuality: Choice without Volition.* Hillsdale, NJ: Analytic Press, 1988.

Silverstein, C. "Psychological and Medical Treatments of Homosexuality." In *Homosexuality: Research Implications for Public Policy,* edited by J. C. Gonsiorek and James D. Weinrich, 101–14. Newbury Park, CA: Sage Publications, 1991.

Simonds, Wendy. *Women and Self-Help Culture: Reading between the Lines.* New Brunswick, NJ: Rutgers University Press, 1992.

Sims, Bennett J. "Sex and Homosexuality: A Pastoral Statement." *Christianity Today,* February 24, 1978, pp. 23–30.

Smith, Andrea. "Devil's in the Details." *Colorlines Magazine,* Spring 2002.

Smith, Anna Marie. *New Right Discourse on Race and Sexuality: Britain, 1968–1990.* Oxford: Oxford University Press, 1994.

Smith, Christian. *American Evangelicalism: Embattled and Thriving.* Chicago: University of Chicago Press, 1998.

———. *Christian America? What Evangelicals Really Want.* Berkeley: University of California Press, 2000.

Socarides, Charles. *Homosexuality.* New York: J. Aronson, 1978.

———. "Sexual Politics and Scientific Logic: The Issue of Homosexuality." *Journal of Psychohistory* 19, no. 3 (Winter 1992): 307–29.

Spickard, James V., R. Shawn Landres, and Meredith B. McGuire, eds. *Personal Knowledge and Beyond: Reshaping the Ethnography of Religion.* New York: New York University Press, 2002.

Spitzer, Robert L. "Can Some Gay Men and Lesbians Change Their Sexual Orientation? 200 Participants Reporting a Change from Homosexual to Heterosexual Orientation." Presentation at the American Psychiatric Association annual convention, New Orleans, May 9, 2001. Subsequently published in *Archives of Sexual Behavior* 32, no. 5 (October 2003): 403–17.

Spring, Beth. "These Christians Are Helping Gays Escape from Homosexual Lifestyles." *Christianity Today,* September 21, 1984, pp. 56–60.

Stacy, Judith. *Brave New Families: Stories of Domestic Upheaval in Late Twentieth Century America.* New York: Basic Books, 1991.

Stafford, Tim. "Coming Out." *Christianity Today,* August 18, 1989, pp. 16–21.

Stern, Mark. "Results of the APA Meeting: A Personal Report." *NARTH Bulletin* 3, no. 2 (September 1995): 1–5.

Stock, Catherine McNicol. *Rural Radicals: From Bacon's Rebellion to the Oklahoma City Bombing.* New York: Penguin, 1997.

Streakley, James D. "Per scientiam ad justitiam: Magnus Hirschfield and the Sexual Politics of Innate Homosexuality." In *Science and Homosexualities,* edited by Rosario, 133–54.

Sullivan, Andrew. *Virtually Normal: An Argument about Homosexuality.* New York: Vintage Books, 1996.

Terry, Jennifer. *An American Obsession: Science, Medicine and Homosexuality in Modern Society.* Chicago: University of Chicago Press, 1999.

———. *Deviant Bodies: Critical Perspectives on Difference in Science and Popular Culture.* Bloomington: Indiana University Press, 1995.

———. "The Seductive Power of Science in the Making of Deviant Subjectivity." In *Science and Homosexualities,* edited by Rosario, 271–96.

"Testimonies of Former Transvestites, Female Impersonators, and Transsexuals." Love in Action, Memphis, TN, no. 901-542-0250.

Van Zandt, David E. *Living in the Children of God.* Princeton: Princeton University Press, 1991.

Wacker, Grant. *Heaven Below: Early Pentecostals and American Culture.* Cambridge: Harvard University Press, 2001.

Warhol, Robyn R., and Helena Michie. "Twelve-Step Teleology: Narratives of Recovery/Recovery as Narrative." In *Getting a Life: Everyday Uses of Autobiography,* edited by Sidonie Smith and Julia Watson, 327–50. Minneapolis: University of Minnesota Press, 1996.

Warner, Michael, ed. *Fear of a Queer Planet: Queer Politics and Social Theory.* Minneapolis: University of Minnesota Press, 1993.

Warner, Stephen. "The Place of the Congregation in the American Religious Configuration." In *American Congregations,* vol. 2, edited by J. P. Wind and J. W. Lewis. Chicago: University of Chicago Press, 1994.

Watt, David Harrington. *Bible-Carrying Christians: Conservative Protestants and Social Power.* Oxford: Oxford University Press, 2002.

———. *A Transforming Faith: Explorations of Twentieth-Century American Evangelicalism.* New Brunswick, NJ: Rutgers University Press, 1991.

Weeks, Jeffrey. *Sex, Politics and Society: The Regulation of Sexuality since 1800.* London: Longman, 1981.

Weinrich, James. "Therapy Terminable and Interminable: 'Non-gay Homosexuals' Come Out of the Closet." *Journal of Sex Research* 30, no. 3 (August 1993): 291–94.

Whisman, Vera. *Queer by Choice: Lesbians, Gay Men, and the Politics of Identity.* New York: Routledge Press, 1996.

White, Mel. *Stranger at the Gate: To Be Gay and Christian in America.* New York: Penguin Books, 1995.

Wilcox, Clyde. *God's Warriors: The Christian Right in Twentieth-Century America.* Baltimore: The Johns Hopkins University Press, 1992.

Wilcox, Melissa. *Coming Out in Christianity: Religion, Identity and Community.* Bloomington: Indiana University Press, 2003.

Willingham, Russell. *Breaking Free: Understanding Sexual Addiction and the Healing Power of Jesus.* Downers Grove, IL: InterVarsity Press, 1999.

Worthen, Frank. *Helping People Step Out of Homosexuality*. San Rafael, CA: Love in Action, 1980.

Wray, Robert. "The New Conversion: EXIT, Giving up Gay for God." *Newswest,* May 12–26, 1977.

Wuthnow, Robert. *The Restructuring of American Religion*. Princeton: Princeton University Press, 1988.

———. *Sharing the Journey: Support Groups and America's New Quest for Community*. New York: Free Press, 1994.

Yamamoto, Isamu J. *The Crisis of Homosexuality*. Los Angeles: Victor Books, 1990.

Ybarra, Michael. "Going Straight: Christian Groups Press Gay People to Take a Heterosexual Path." *Wall Street Journal,* April 21, 1993, pp. 1–2, 6.

Young, Allen. Introduction to *Lavender Culture,* edited by Karla Jay and Allen Young. New York: New York University Press, 1978.

Index

therapy *(continued)*
179–82; recovery groups for, 162–65, 166; self-help model of, 162, 250n5; testimonies as, 11–13, 173–75; touch, 181, 182; twelve-step programs for, 162–65. *See also* reparative therapy
Third Sex?, The (Philpott), 27–28, 29, 31
Thomas (pseudonym), 68–69
Thomas, Randy, 43, 44
Thompson, Jason, 210
Three Essays on the Theory of Sexuality (Freud), 135
Thumma, Scott, 79
Tim (pseudonym), 84, 93, 217
touch therapy, 181, 182
Tracey (pseudonym), 47
Tracy, Amy, 206–7
Traditional Values Coalition (TVC), 199–200, 202, 255n55
Trembling before God (movie), 49
twelve-step programs, 162–65, 167–68

Ulrichs, Karl, 134, 135
United Church of Christ, 242n41; Coalition for LGBT Concerns, 78
United Methodists for LGBT Concerns, 78
Uribe, Virginia, 257n86
urning, 134–35

Viguerie, Richard, 193
Vineyard Fellowship, 25, 27
Vratny, Jim, 153
Vratny, Terry, 153

Westar media group, 43
Weyrich, Paul, 193
White, Mel, 185, 248n42
Wildmon, Don, 205, 256n75
Wilkerson, Ralph, 31
Will and Grace, 94–95
women: ex-gays' lack of sexual attraction to, 117–19; in marriages or relationships with ex-gays, 120–21; New Hope's program for, 30, 151, 152; residential ex-gay programs for, 30. *See also* Concerned Women for America (CWA); lesbians
Worthen, Anita, 8, 129; advice from, on marriage, 116–17, 118–19; author's initial encounter with, 5–6, 7; on crises and traumatic personal experiences, 70, 160; on Curtis's hairdressing activities, 101; on death of Paul,

124; on Exodus chairman Paulk scandal, 213–15; gay son of, 115, 156–58; marriage of, 4, 115–16; ministry by, to parents of gays, 4, 155–56, 157–58; as missionary in Philippines, 37–38; negative view of, by New Hope participants, 158–59; at New Hope graduation ceremony, 216, 217; on relationship with Jesus, 72, 73, 74; television avoided by, 93; on women's program at New Hope, 152
Worthen, Frank, 8, 10; on accepting gay identity, 77–78; at APA conference, 126; behaviors required by, of New Hope participants, 93, 94, 95; on Bible's statements about homosexuality, 62; on Catholics and Jews, 48; on change experienced by ex-gays, 52, 53, 218, 219, 220, 221; Christian Right ad campaign and, 188, 189; on churches and ex-gay movement, 40–41; on civil rights approach to gay rights, 211–12; concepts introduced to ex-gay movement by, 163–64; conversion experience of, 22–23; early ministry to ex-gays by, 4, 23–24; on envying characteristics of heterosexual men, 107; on ex-gays as embattled, 208; EXIT and, 31, 32; Exodus and, 33, 34, 35–36, 49; on "gay lifestyle," 111, 121; on homosexuality as addiction, 165–66; inquiry about author's family background, 160; Lord's Land retreat direction by, 66, 67, 70, 71; Love in Action (LIA) program and, 27, 28–29, 37, 162; marriage and family of, 115–16, 156; on masculinity, 104–5; ministry to ex-gays abroad by, 37–38, 50, 228; Moberly's ideas accepted by, 147, 148; New Hope formed by, 3–4; at New Hope graduation ceremony, 216, 217–18, 221–22; on relationship with Jesus/God, 71, 72–73, 75, 164, 165, 220, 221; testimonies and confessions encouraged by, 99, 175, 178; touch therapy viewed negatively by, 181; women and, 30, 118, 121, 152, 157. *See also* "Steps Out" program manual; "Steps Out" workbook
Wylie, Philip, 156

Text: 10/13 Sabon
Display: Sabon
Compositor: International Typesetting and Composition
Printer and binder: Maple-Vail Manufacturing Group
Indexer: Jean Mann